Ruby on Rails for PHP and Java Developers

Deepak Vohra

Ruby on Rails for PHP and Java Developers

With 202 Figures and 32 Tables

 Springer

Deepak Vohra

dvohra09@yahoo.com

Library of Congress Control Number: 2007929957

ISBN 978-3-540-73144-3 Springer Berlin Heidelberg New York

Springer is a part of Springer Science+Business Media

springer.com

© Springer-Verlag Berlin Heidelberg 2007

Typesetting: by the Author
Production: LE-TEX Jelonek, Schmidt & Vöckler GbR, Leipzig
Cover design: KünkelLopka Werbeagentur, Heidelberg

Printed on acid-free paper   45/3180/YL - 5 4 3 2 1 0

Preface

Ruby[1] is an open source programming language that was released in 1995. Ruby is ranked 10th in the TIOBE Programming Community index[2]. Ruby on Rails[3] is an open source web framework that was released in 2004. Ruby on Rails is being widely adopted because of its simplicity, maintainability and development speed. Computerworld[4] lists Ruby on Rails as the one of the top 5 technologies for 2007.

Motivation for this Book

Ruby is often compared with PHP, which is the most commonly used scripting language, and with Java, which is the most commonly used programming language. In the trends graph of TIOBE index you might notice that since the middle of 2006 Ruby shows an increase in usage while PHP and Java show a decrease in usage. OReilly Radar[5] has noted the trend towards an increased usage of Ruby on Rails. Statistics aside, Ruby on Rails has some advantages over PHP, which are discussed below.

1. Ruby on Rails is more object-oriented than PHP, thus providing all the inherent advantages of an object-oriented language such as simplicity, modularity, modifiability, extensibility, maintainability and re-usability.
2. Ruby on Rails is web framework whereas PHP is only a scripting language.

---

[1] Ruby-http://www.ruby-lang.org/en/
[2] TIOBE Index-http://www.tiobe.com/tpci.htm
[3] Ruby on Rails-http://www.rubyonrails.org/
[4] ComputerWorld-
http://computerworld.com/action/article.do?command=viewArticleBasic
&articleId=9011969
[5] OReilly Radar-
http://radar.oreilly.com/archives/2006/08/programming_language_trends_1.html

3. Ruby on Rails includes a web server for development, whereas a web server has to be installed for PHP.
4. Ruby on Rails implements the Model-View-Controller (MVC) architecture, whereas the MVC architecture has to be implemented externally in PHP.
5. Ruby on Rails framework provides the Create-Read-Update-Delete (CRUD) functionality, PHP doesn't.

While Java has advantages over Ruby on Rails in scalability, security, transaction management and availability of development tools, Ruby on Rails has advantages over Java in simplicity, development speed, and maintainability. Ruby on Rails provides a tightly coupled web framework consisting of a persistence framework, a web application framework, and a Web Services framework. The J2EE application framework is not as seamless as Ruby on Rails and requires much more configuration. Ruby on Rails also has the advantage of being dynamically typed, while Java is statically typed.

While a number of books have been published on Ruby on Rails, none of the books compare Ruby on Rails with PHP and very few compare Ruby on Rails with Java.

Who Should Read this Book?

A comparison with PHP and Java is included in most chapters where relevant. But, you don't have to be a PHP or Java developer to read the book. You may be using another scripting language or Ruby on Rails may be the first scripting language based web framework you are learning about. If you have used Ajax you would be familiar with the requirement for a server-side tier, which may be PHP-based, Java-based , or .NET-based. Ruby on Rails supports Ajax and according to an Ajaxian.com survey[6] 14% of Ajax developers use Rails as the Ajax platform. If you have been using PHP or Java class libraries to develop PDF and Excel reports, Ruby on Rails provides Ruby gems for generating PDF and Excel reports. If you are a web developer and often use PHP or Java to create/read/update/delete database entries, Ruby on Rails provides a built-in support for CRUD. If you have been using Java Naming and Directory Interface (JNDI) or a PHP class library to implement directory services

---

[6] Ajaxian.com Survey- http://ajaxian.com/archives/ajaxiancom-2006-survey-results

Ruby on Rails provides an alternative for creating lightweight directory access protocol (LDAP) directory services.

It is not a goal to instruct the reader about PHP or Java. Most chapters include a brief comparison with PHP and Java. The reader shall notice the similarity between PHP, Java and Ruby, all being object oriented languages. If a reader is not familiar with PHP or Java, he/she may skip the comparison sections.

Outline to the Book Structure

In Chap. 1 we introduce the Ruby programming language. We install Ruby and use the IRB (Interactive Ruby shell) to discuss the syntax of the Ruby language. The chapter concludes with a comparison of Ruby with PHP and Java.

Chap. 2 introduces the Rails framework. We install the Rails framework and discuss the different components of the Rails framework. We discuss how Rails requests are routed and how helpers, layouts and stylesheets may be used. We configure the Rails framework with the MySQL database. The chapter concludes with a comparison with PHP and Java.

Chap. 3 discusses the CRUD functionality provided by Ruby on Rails. We create a database table in the MySQL database and also discuss configuring Rails with Oracle and SQL Server databases. We create a CRUD application to create, read, update and delete catalog entries.

Chap. 4 introduces Ajax and discusses Ajax support in the Rails framework. We create a database search application to list catalog entries for a specified section.

Chap. 5 discusses the procedure to create PDF and Excel spreadsheet reports with Ruby on Rails. A comparison is made with the PHP and Java class libraries for generating reports.

Chap. 6 discusses the Ruby gems for processing XML. We create an XML document with the RubyGem builder-2.0.0.gem. We create an XML document from an Oracle database table. Parsing an XML document with REXML, an XML processor in Ruby, is also discussed.

In Chap. 7 we discuss PHP on Trax, a PHP web application and persistence framework for Ruby on Rails. We create a CRUD application similar to the one in Chap. 3, but without using any Ruby.

In Chap. 8 we discuss creating a directory service with Ruby on Rails. We also discuss the procedure to install the commonly used directory servers.

Chap. 9 discusses the Web Services support in Ruby on Rails. We discuss the different dispatching modes and protocol clients. A comparison with creating Web Services with PHP and Java is made.

Chap. 10 discusses the Eclipse plugins for Ruby on Rails. We explain the procedure to install and use the Ruby Development Tools (RDT) and RadRails plugins.

Chap. 11 discusses Rails testing. The development phase is not complete without testing. We discuss unit testing for Rails models and functional testing for Rails controllers. We also discuss fixtures, sample data for testing.

Chap. 12 discusses the production aspect of Ruby on Rails. We deploy a Rails application to Apache2 and FastCGI. We discuss Ruby on Rails best practices that may improve performance. We also host a Rails application on a web host.

Prerequisite Skills

Familiarity with PHP and/or Java is assumed to be able to compare Ruby on Rails with PHP and/or Java. Familiarity with object-oriented concepts such as classes, methods and inheritance is required. An introduction is included in all chapters, but a familiarity with Ajax and the concepts of directory service and Web Service is a pre-requisite.

Acknowledgements

The author would like to thank Hermann Engesser, Executive Editor Computer Science, Springer. Thanks are also due to Gabriele Fischer, the project manager at Springer, and to Michael Reinfarth, Production Editor, LE-TeX Jelonek.

About the Author

Deepak Vohra is a Sun Certified Java Programmer and Sun Certified Web Component Developer. He has a Master of Science degree in mechanical engineering from Southern Illinois University, Carbondale. Deepak is an Oracle Certified Associate. Moreover, he is a Manning Publications

Technical editor and edited the Prototype and Scriptaculous in Action book.

Contents

1 Ruby

1.1 Introduction

Ruby is an interpreted scripting language for object-oriented programming. Interpretive implies that a ruby application is run without first compiling the application. Variables in Ruby do not have a type; a Ruby variable may contain data of any type. Variables in Ruby may be used without any variable declarations. Ruby being an object oriented language has features such as classes, inheritance and methods. Everything in Ruby is an object including methods, strings, floats and integers. A ruby script is stored in a file with the .rb extension and run with the ruby command. First, we need to install Ruby.

1.2 Installing Ruby

In this section we shall install Ruby, and RubyGems. RubyGems is the standard Ruby package manager used with Ruby applications and libraries. To install Ruby, and RubyGems the procedure is as follows. Download the Ruby Windows Installer[1] application. Double-click on *ruby184-19.exe* application. Ruby Setup Wizard gets started. Click on Next.

---

[1] Ruby Window Installer- http://rubyforge.org/frs/?group_id=167

Fig. 1.1 Ruby Setup Wizard

Accept the license agreement and click on Next. Select the default components to install, which include the RubyGems package manager, and SciTE, a Scintilla based Text Editor, and click on Next.

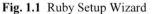

Fig. 1.2 Selecting Components to install

Specify a directory to install Ruby (default is *c:/ruby*) and click on Next.

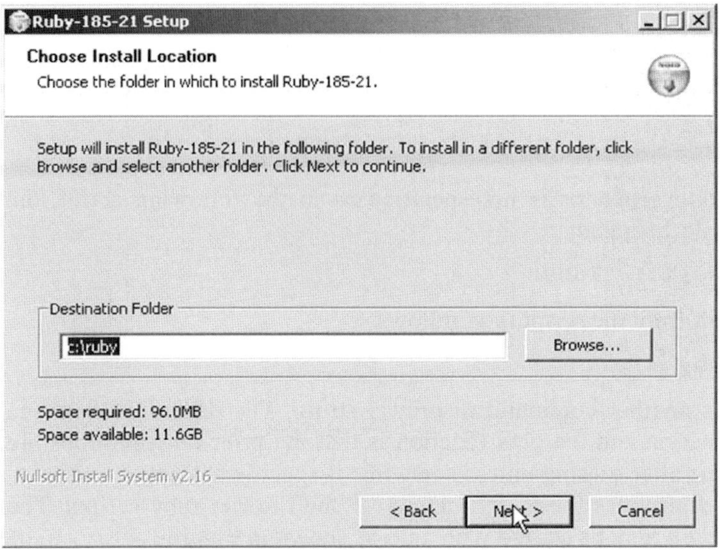

Fig. 1.3 Specifying Installation Folder

Specify a start folder and click on Install. Ruby and RubyGems gets installed. Click on Finish to close the Ruby Setup wizard. Ruby gets installed. Directory path *c:/ruby/bin* gets added to System environment variable PATH. System environment variable RUBYOPT with value – rubygems gets added.

1.3 Creating a Ruby Application

Next, we shall create a Ruby application. For example, create a Ruby script *helloruby.rb* with the following Ruby code.

```
puts "Hello Ruby"
```

Run the Ruby script with the following command.

```
C:/>ruby helloruby.rb
```

The output from the Ruby script is as follows.

```
Hello Ruby
```

The `puts` function is used to print text. The puts function adds a newline after each text string. For example, modify the Ruby script to the following script, which includes a string separator.

```ruby
puts "Hello", "Ruby"
```

The output from the Ruby script is as follows.

```
Hello
Ruby
```

If the string separator is not specified as in the following script, the strings are concatenated.

```ruby
puts "Hello" "Ruby"
```

The output from the script is as follows.

```
HelloRuby
```

`Print` is another command to print a string. The difference between the print function and the puts function is that the print function does not add a newline after a string unless a newline is specified.

Ruby also provides the Ruby interactive shell to run ruby scripts. The interactive shell may be started with `irb` as shown in Figure 1.4.

Fig. 1.4 Ruby Interactive Shell

The example Ruby scripts in this chapter are run in irb. A ruby script may be run from the interactive shell as shown below.

```
irb(main):001:0> puts "Hello Ruby"
```

The output is as the same as for running a .rb script as shown in Figure 1.5.

Fig. 1.5 Running a Ruby Script in irb

Ruby also provides the `gets` function to get a string input by a user. In the Ruby interactive shell specify gets and press Enter.

```
irb(main):001:0>gets
```

Input a string, "Hello Ruby" for example, and press Enter. The string specified gets output.

Fig. 1.6 The gets Function

1.4 Identifiers and Comments

Identifiers are names used to identify variables, methods and classes in a Ruby script. A Ruby identifier begins with a letter [a-zA-Z] or a '_' and consists of alphanumeric characters and underscores. A class name is required to begin with an uppercase letter. An identifier may not be a reserved word. Reserved words are listed below.

```
=begin    =end      alias     and       begin     BEGIN
break     case      class     def       defined?  do
else      elsif     END       end       ensure    false
for       if        in        module    next      nil
not       or        redo      rescue    retry     return
self      super     then      true      undef     unless
until     when      while     yield
```

A comment begins with a # and a comment is defined upto the end of the line.

```
# Example of a comment
```

Documentation may be embedded in a script with `=begin` `=end`. The following listing defines documentation.

```
=begin
Example Of
Embedded Documentation
=end
```

1.5 Strings

A string may be specified using single quotes or double quotes. In single quotes a single quote may be escaped using \' and a backslash may be escaped using \\. In double quotes a double quote is escaped using \" and a backslash is escaped using \\. In double quotes, other characters may also be escaped such as backspace (\b), carriage return (\r), newline (\n), space (\s) and tab (\t). Double quotes also has the provision to evaluate embedded expressions using interpolation with #{}. For example, run the following ruby script.

```
puts "#{"Hello"+"Ruby"}"
```

The output is as follows.

```
HelloRuby
```

Variables referenced in #{} are required to be pre-defined. In the previous example the + operator is used to concatenate strings. The * may be used to repeat strings as in the following script.

```
puts "Hello Ruby" *3
```

The output from the script is as follows.

```
Hello RubyHello RubyHello Ruby
```

Characters are integers in Ruby. Characters may be extracted from strings as shown in the following script.

```
hello= "Hello Ruby"
puts hello[8]
```

The character index is 0 based. The output from the script is the ASCII code for character 'b', 98.

Substrings may also be extracted by specifying a start index and an end index as in the following script.

```
hello= "Hello Ruby"
puts hello[6,10]
```

The output from the script is shown below.

```
Ruby
```

Character index offsets may be specified from the end of the string with −ve indices. Offsets from the end of the string are 1 based and the second parameter represents the number of characters in the substring, as in the following script.

```
hello= "Hello Ruby"
puts hello[-4,4]
```

The output from the script is as follows.

```
Ruby
```

If more number of characters are specified than available in the string, the substring is created including upto the end of the string. Strings may be compared using the == operator as in the following script.

```
puts "Hello Ruby"=="Hello Ruby"
```

The output from the script is as follows.

```
true
```

Regular expressions may be used in a string. A regular expression is specified using character patterns. Some of the character patterns are discussed in Table 1.1.

Table 1.1 Character Patterns

Pattern	Description
[]	Specifies a range. For example, [a-c] specifies a character in the range of a-c.
\w	Specifies a letter or a digit.
\W	Specifies that neither a letter nor digit should be specified.
\s	Specifies a space character.
\S	Specifies a non-space character.
\d	Specifies a digit character.
\D	Specifies a non digit character.
\b	Specifies a backspace if in a range specification. Also specifies a word boundary if not in a range specification.
\f	Form feed
\t	Horizontal tab
\v	Vertical tab
\B	Specifies a non-word boundary.

Table 1.1 (continued)

Pattern	Description
*	Specifies 0 or more repetitions of the preceding.
+	Specifies 1 or more repetitions of the preceding.
{m,n}	Specifies at least m and at most n repetitions of the preceding.
?	Specifies at most 1 repetition of the preceding.
|	Specifies that either the preceding or the next expression may match.
()	Specifies a grouping.

The % notation may be used to create string variables. The % notation is used with delimiting characters to create a string. For example, all of the following create the string "Hello Ruby".

```
%[Hello Ruby]
%{Hello Ruby}
%(Hello Ruby)
%!Hello Ruby!
%@Hello Ruby@
```

The % notation is useful if a string contains quotes; with the % notation quotes may not be escaped. For example the following strings are equivalent.

```
"Hello \"Ruby\""
%[Hello "Ruby"]
```

1.6 Arrays Hashes and Ranges

Arrays are created in Ruby by listing items in [] and separating the items with a ','.

```
hello =["Hello", "Ruby"]
```

Arrays may be concatenated. For example, create an array, *hello_array*, by concatenating another array. Run the following script in irb.

```
hello =["Hello", "Ruby"]
hello_array=hello+["ruby", "RUBY"]
```

The output is the following array.

```
=>["Hello", "Ruby", "ruby", "RUBY"]
```

An array may be referenced using indices, which are 0 based. For example the following array reference produces output "RUBY".

```
hello_array[3]
```

An array may be created from another array by specifying the start index and the number of items in the array as in the following script.

```
hello_array[0,2]
```

The output from the script in irb is as follows.

```
=>["Hello","Ruby"]
```

An array may be created from another array by specifying a range of indices. For example, create an array from hello_array, which consists of items at indices 0, 1, and 2.

```
hello_array[0..2]
```

The output is the array shown below.

```
=>["Hello","Ruby", "ruby"]
```

Negative indices indicate offsets from the end of the array and are 1 based. For example, create an array from the hello_array with the last two elements.

```
hello_array[-2, 2]
```

The following array gets produced.

```
=>["ruby","RUBY"]
```

An array may be converted to a string using the `join` function. For example, create a string by joining the members of the hello_array using a ','.

```
hello_array.join(",")
```

The following string gets output.

```
"Hello Ruby,ruby,RUBY"
```

A string may be converted to an array using `split()`. The following script produces the array ["Hello", "Ruby","ruby","RUBY"].

```
"Hello Ruby,ruby,RUBY".split(",")
```

A Hash is an associative array consisting of key-value pairs in {} brackets.

```
hello={1=>"hello", 2=>"Ruby", 3=>"ruby", 4=>"RUBY"}
```

A hash item is accessed using a key. For example, access the value of the hash entry with key 3.

```
hello[3]
```

A hash entry may be added to a hash. For example, add a hash entry with key 5.

```
hello[5]="RUby"
hello
```

The resulting hash has the new entry appended in the beginning of the hash.

```
{5=>"RUby",1=>"hello",       2=>"Ruby",       3=>"ruby",
4=>"RUBY"}
```

A hash entry may be deleted using `delete`. The following command in irb deletes the hash entry with key 5.

```
hello.delete 5
```

Each key may occur only once in a hash. Commonly symbols are used as hash keys. The following hash is declared without using symbols.

```
hello={"a"=>"hello",       "b"=>"Ruby",       "c"=>"ruby",
"d"=>"RUBY"}
```

If symbols are used, the hash is declared as follows.

```
hello={:a=>"hello",       :b=>"Ruby",       :c=>"ruby",
:d=>"RUBY"}
```

A range represents a range of values. A range is specified with a start value and an end value and with 2 or three '.' between. Two '.' specify that the end value is included in the range. Three '.' specify that the end value is not included in the range. For example, create a range of integers between 0 and 10, excluding 10.

```
0...10
```

As another example, define a range of characters between 'a' and d' including 'd'.

```
'a'..'d'
```

Ranges represent increasing sequences. The following range would create an empty sequence.

```
'd'..'a'
```

To determine if a value is within a range use the $===$ method. For example, create a range between 'a' and 'd' and determine if 'c' is in the range and if 'e' is in the range.

```
r = 'a'..'d'
puts r === 'c'
puts r === 'e'
```

The output is true for 'c' and false for 'e'.

1.7 Variables Constants and Operators

Variables in Ruby are dynamically typed, therefore, variable declarations are not used. Ruby provides four types of variables.

1. Local Variables
2. Instance Variables
3. Global Variables
4. Class Variables

The prefix of an identifier specifies the type of the variable Different variable types are discussed in Table 1.2.

Table 1.2 Variable Types

Variable Type	Notation	Example
Local Variable	First character [a-z] or _	var
Instance Variable	First character @	@var
Global Variable	First character $	$var
Class Variables	Prefix @@	@@var

Instance and global variables have the value nil before being initialized. Local variables are required to be initialized before being used. Class variables are available since Ruby 1.5.3 and also required to be initialized before being used. Ruby also provides some psuedo variables: self, nil, true and false. Self is a global variable and refers to the current object. Nil is a constant and is the value assigned to uninitialized global and instance variables. The scope of a local variable is the loop, method, class, procedure object, or module in which it is defined. If the local variable is not defined in any of these constructs, the scope is the complete script. The defined? operator is used to check if a variable is defined as in the following script.

```
hello="Hello Ruby"
puts defined?(hello)
```

The output from the script is "local-variable". Local variables defined in a method are not available in another method. For example, in the following script local variable *hello* is defined in the *helloRuby* method, but not in the *hello_Ruby* method.

```
class HelloRuby
  def helloRuby

    hello= "Hello Ruby"
    return defined?(hello)
  end

  def hello_Ruby
    return defined?(hello)
  end
end
helloRubyInstance=HelloRuby.new
helloRubyInstance.helloRuby
helloRubyInstance.hello_Ruby
```

The output is local-variable for the helloRuby method and nil for the hello_Ruby method.

Instance variables are defined in the scope of an object and have the initial value nil if uninitialized. For example define a class and define a method in the class. Define an instance variable *@hello* in the method.

```
class HelloRuby
  def hello(name)
    @hello=name
    return "Hello" + @hello
  end

end
```

The instance variable @hello is only available to instances of the HelloRuby class. For example, create a class instance and invoke the *hello* method.

```
helloRuby=HelloRuby.new
helloRuby.hello("Ruby")
```

Create another class instance and invoke the hello method with a different value.

```
hello_Ruby=HelloRuby.new
hello_Ruby.hello("ruby")
```

Run the following script in irb.

```
irb(main):001:0>class HelloRuby
  def hello(name)
  @hello=name

  return "Hello" + @hello
  end

end
helloRuby=HelloRuby.new
helloRuby.hello("Ruby")

hello_Ruby=HelloRuby.new
hello_Ruby.hello("ruby")
```

The output is "HelloRuby" for the first class instance method invocation and "Helloruby" for the second class instance. The instance variable has the value "Ruby" for the first class instance method invocation and "ruby" for the second class instance method invocation.

Global variables are available throughout a ruby script. For example, declare a global variable *$hello* and output its value by invoking a method. Modify the variable's value in another method and output the variable's value as shown in the following script.

```
$hello="Ruby"
class HelloRuby
  def hello
    $hello= "Hello" +$hello
  end

  def varValue
    return $hello
  end
end
```

```
helloRuby=HelloRuby.new
helloRuby.varValue
helloRuby.hello
helloRuby.varValue
```

The $hello variable's value   is "Ruby"   before being modified by invoking the hello method and "HelloRuby" after being modified.

Class variables are associated with a class and all instances of a class have the same class variable copy. The difference between class variables and global variables is that class variables are required to be initialized before being used and do not have the default value nil. As an example, create a class variable *@@hello* and modify the value of the variable by invoking a method of the class. The value of the variable changes for all instances of the class. The following script returns the @@hello variable value for class instance hello_Ruby as "HelloRuby", because another class instance has modified the variable value.

```
@@hello="Ruby"
class HelloRuby
  def hello
    @@hello= "Hello" + @@hello
  end

  def varValue
    return @@hello
  end
end
helloRuby=HelloRuby.new
helloRuby.varValue
helloRuby.hello

hello_Ruby=HelloRuby.new
hello_Ruby.varValue
```

Some pre-defined system variables are defined that consist of $ as the first character and these may not be defined as global variables. Some of these system variables are discussed in Table 1.3.

Table 1.3 System Variables

System Variable	Description
$!	Specifies latest error message.
$@	Specifies error location.
$_	Specifies string last read by gets

Table 1.3 (continued)

System Variable	Description
$.	Specifies line number last read by interpreter.
$/	Specifies input record separator.
$\	Specifies output record separator.
$0	Specifies name of ruby script file.
$*	Specifies the command line arguments.
$.	Specifies line number last read by interpreter.

A constant is an identifier with a constant value and starts with an uppercase letter. Constants may be defined within classes and modules and are accessible outside the class or module. For example, define a constant *Hello* in a class and access the constant outside the class. Run the following ruby script in irb.

```
irb(main):001:0>class HelloRuby
   Hello="Hello Ruby"
end

HelloRuby::Hello
```

The output is as follows.

```
=>"Hello Ruby"
```

Constants may be reassigned value, but a warning gets generated that the constant has already been initialized.

Ruby handles all operators by converting them to methods. The method name is the same as the operator name. The '=' operator is used for assignment in following Ruby. example.

```
var=1
strvar="String Variable"
hello=Hello.new
```

Ruby supports the +=, -=, *=, /=, **= operators. Ruby also supports multiple assignments as shown below.

```
x,y,z='Hello', 'Ruby', 'ruby'
```

```
puts x
puts y
puts z
```

The output is as follows.

```
Hello
Ruby
Ruby
```

Arrays may be created using %w() or %{}. For example, the following script outputs "Ruby".

```
array=%w(Hello Ruby ruby)
puts array[1]
```

The ||= operator is used for conditional assignment. If a variable value is nil the value specified with ||= is assigned to the variable. For example, the following script outputs "default value".

```
var=nil
var||="default value"
puts var
```

Ruby also provides symbols. A symbol is a variable prefixed with a colon (:), which is stored with a unique id, for example :var1. Symbols are like constants and are used for comparison in Rails as they require less processing than strings.

1.8 Classes

Ruby is an object oriented language and a class represents the template from which objects may be created. An object is an instance of a class. A class consists of variables and methods. A class definition starts with class and ends with end. A class name is required to begin with a capital letter. The following script defines a class *Hello*, which consists of a method *hello*.

```
class Hello

  def hello
   return "Hello Ruby"
  end
end
```

A class is instantiated with the new method. For example, create an instance of the class Hello.

```
hello=Hello.new
```

Using the class object invoke the method hello.

```
hello.hello
```

The output from the method invocation is "Hello Ruby". Classes in Ruby support inheritance. For example create another class *Msg*, which extends class Hello. Extending a class is denoted with '<'. Define a method *msg* in class Msg that return a string. Create an instance of class Msg and invoke the msg method. As the Msg class extends the Hello class, an instance of class Msg is also an instance of class Hello. Invoke the hello method of class Hello with an instance of class Msg. Run the following script .

```
class Hello

  def hello
   return "Hello Ruby"
   end
end

class Msg <Hello
   def msg
   return "Hello ruby"
   end
end

msg=Msg.new
msg.msg
msg.hello
```

The output from invoking the msg method is "Hello ruby" and the output from invoking the hello method is "Hello Ruby". Ruby does not support multiple inheritance, therefore, a class may extend only one other class.

A `initialize` function may be defined to initialize a class. The initialize function is invoked after a class instance is created. For example, define a class with the initialize function. Initialize an instance variable @hello in the initialize function. Output the value of the instance variable by invoking another method of a class instance.

```
class Hello
  @hello
```

```
def initialize(hello)
 @hello=hello

end

def hello
 return @hello
 end
end

hello=Hello.new("Hello Ruby")
hello.hello
```

The output from the Ruby script is "Hello Ruby".

1.9 Methods

Methods in Ruby begin with def and end with end.   The following
method takes a name parameter and returns a string.

```
class Hello

 def hello(name)
  return "Hello" +name
  end

end
```

A method is invoked with an instance of the class in which the method
is defined. The hello method of class Hello may be invoked as follows.

```
helloObj=Hello.new
helloObj.hello("Deepak")
```

The output from the method invocation is "HelloDeepak". Method
names in Ruby should begin with a lowercase letter. By default, methods
return the last statement in the method. Therefore, the following method,
which does not have a return statement, would also return a "Hello …"
string.

```
def hello(name)
    "Hello" +name
    end
```

Method parameters may be assigned default values. For example, in the
following method definition parameter name is assigned a default value.

```
def hello(name="John")
    return "Hello" +name
    end
```

If the method is invoked without an argument, the default value is used. The following script outputs "HelloRuby".

```
class Hello

    def hello(name="Ruby")
     return "Hello" +name
     end

end

helloObj=Hello.new
helloObj.hello
```

Ruby has the provision to define methods with a variable number of arguments by preceding the last parameter of a method with an asterisk (*). For example, define method *hello* to take a variable number of arguments. The following script outputs "Hello Ruby,ruby, RUBY".

```
class Hello

    def hello(*name)
     return "Hello " +name.join(',')
     end

end

helloObj=Hello.new
helloObj.hello("Ruby", "ruby", "RUBY")
```

The asterisk operator may also precede an Array argument in a method invocation. In the following script the hello method is invoked with an array using the * operator.

```
class Hello

    def hello(name1,name2,name3)
     return "Hello " +name1+", "+name2+", "+name3
     end

end
helloObj=Hello.new
array=["Ruby", "ruby", "RUBY"]
helloObj.hello(*array)
```

The output from the script is "Hello Ruby, ruby, RUBY". The parentheses in method invocation may be omitted. The hello method may be invoked with arguments as follows.

```
helloObj.hello "Ruby", "ruby", "RUBY"
```

Parentheses are required if another method is to be invoked on the method invocation result. For example if a method returns an array and the order of the elements in the array is to be reversed, parentheses are required as shown below.

```
array= helloObj.hello("Ruby", "ruby", "RUBY").reverse
```

A hash may be used as an argument to a method. For example, define a method hello and invoke the method with a hash as shown below.

```
class Hello

   def hello(name)
    return "Hello " +name[:c]
    end

end

helloObj=Hello.new
helloObj.hello :a=>"Ruby", :b=>"ruby", :c=>"RUBY"
```

The output from the method invocation is "Hello RUBY".Methods in Ruby are public, by default. The access may be restricted by `public`, `private` and `protected` methods, Public, private, and protected are not keywords, but methods that operate on a class.

For example, in the following class/method definition hello is declared as a private method.

```
class Hello
  def hello(name)
    return "Hello " +name
  end
  private :hello
end
```

If private is invoked without arguments, all methods following private are set to private, as in the following example.

```
class Hello

   private
   def methodA
   end
```

```
      def methodB
      end
  end
```

Methods *methodA* and *methodB* are set to private. A method may also be set to private with the method `private_class_method`.

```
  private_class_method :hello
```

Private methods may only be accessed within the class they are declared or a subclass of the class. . For example, if class *Hello* defines a private method *hello*, and *helloObj1* is an instance of class Hello, helloObj1 may only access non-private methods of class Hello eventhough helloObj1 is an instance of class Hello. In the following script, method hello is private to class Hello, and may only be invoked within the class.

```
  class Hello

      def hello(name)
       return "Hello " +name
       end
  private :hello

      def helloRuby
      hello "Ruby"
       end
  end

  helloObj1=Hello.new
  helloObj1.helloRuby
  helloObj1.hello "Ruby"
```

The output from the script is the string "Hello Ruby" for the helloRuby method invocation, which invokes private method hello. When the hello method is invoked directly by an instance of class Hello an error gets output: "NoMethodError: private method 'hello' called…".

Protected methods also may be accessed within the defining class and subclasses of the class. The difference between private methods and protected methods is that a protected method may be invoked with an explicit receiver while a private method may be invoked with only `self` as the receiver, which implies that a protected method may be invoked by an instance of the defining class and by an instance of a subclass of the defining class while a private method may only be invoked within the context of the defining class or a subclass of the defining class. In the preceding example, method hello may be invoked with an instance of class

Hello, as shown below, or an instance of a sub-class of Hello, if method
hello is protected.

```
class Hello

   def hello(name)
    return "Hello " +name
    end
protected :hello
helloObj1=Hello.new

helloObj1.hello "Ruby"

end
```

Ruby provides accessor methods for instance variables. Without the
accessor methods getter/setter methods would have to be used. For
example, getter/setter methods are used in the following listing to access
an instance variable.

```
class Catalog

  def initialize(catalogid)
    @catalogid=catalogid
    end

    def getCatalogid
     @catalogid
     end

    def setCatalogid(catalogid)
     @catalogid=catalogid
     end

end
catalog=Catalog.new("catalog1")
catalog.getCatalogid
catalog.setCatalogid("catalog2")
catalog.getCatalogid
```

The output from the Ruby script is as follows.

```
"catalog1"
"catalog2"
"catalog2"
```

The `attr_accessor` function provides the getter/setter functionality. In the following script, the attr_accessor method is used on the *catalogid* instance variable.

```ruby
class Catalog

  def initialize(catalogid)
    @catalogid=catalogid
    end
attr_accessor :catalogid

end

catalog=Catalog.new("catalog1")
catalog.catalogid
catalog.catalogid="catalog2"
catalog.catalogid
```

More than one instance variables may be specified in an attr_accessor function.

```ruby
attr_accessor :var1, :var2
```

If only getter functionality is required use function `attr_reader`, and if only setter functionality is required use the `attr_writer` function.

Ruby provides Singleton methods, which are defined only for an object of a class. For example, define a class Hello with a method hello. Create an instance of the class and define a singleton method for the instance of the class.

```ruby
class Hello

  def hello
  return "Hello Ruby"
  end

end


helloObj=Hello.new
helloObj.hello

def helloObj.hello(name)
"Hello"+ name
end
helloObj.hello("ruby")
```

The script returns "Hello Ruby" for the invocation of the hello method and "Helloruby" for the invocation of the singleton method hello(name), which is defined for the helloObj object.

1.10 Procs and Blocks

Proc objects are blocks of code bound to a set of local variables. A block:

```
{ |x| ... }
```

is equivalent to:

```
do |x| .
```

A Proc object is created using the `Proc.new` method. Create a proc that outputs a Hello message.

```
hello=Proc.new{|name| puts "Hello "+name}
hello.call("Ruby")
```

The output from the script in irb is "Hello Ruby".

If a local variable specified in a Proc object is previously specified, and the Proc object is invoked with a variable value, the previously specified variable value gets changed. In the following script variable *x* value gets changed to 10 after invoking the Proc object.

```
x=1
proc = Proc.new {|x| puts x }
proc.call(10)
puts x
```

The parameters of a Proc object are specified in the || in the beginning of the block. The code following the parameters is run when the Proc is invoked. A Proc is invoked with the `call` method, which takes the arguments to the Proc object and returns the last expression evaluated in the block. More than one parameters may be specified in a Proc object. The following script, which invokes a Proc object with 3 parameters, outputs the message "Hello Ruby, ruby, RUBY".

```
hello=Proc.new{|name1,  name2,  name3| puts  "Hello
"+name1+",  "+name2+",  "+name3}
  hello.call("Ruby",  "ruby",  "RUBY")
```

The parameters may be omitted from a Proc object as in the following script, which outputs "Hello Ruby".

```
hello=Proc.new{ puts "Hello Ruby"}
hello.call()
```

A method may be invoked with a Proc object argument. For example, create a class Hello and a method helloMthd, which takes 2 parameters. Create a Proc object, create an instance of the class and invoke the method with the Proc object as shown in following listing.

```
class Hello
def helloMthd(param1, param2)
 return param1.call(param2)
end

end
```

```
helloProc=Proc.new{|name| puts "Hello "+name}
helloObj=Hello.new
helloObj.helloMthd(helloProc, "Ruby")
```

The output from invoking the helloMthd method with a Proc object is "Hello Ruby". If a Proc.new object in a method contains a return statement, invoking the Proc object returns from the enclosing method. In the following script, a method creates a Proc object with Proc.new. In the Proc object a return statement is specified. The Proc object is invoked in the method. When the method is invoked, the Proc object gets invoked, and the method invocation returns.

```
class Hello
def hello()
 helloProc=Proc.new{return "Return from Proc"}
 helloProc.call()
 puts "Hello Ruby"
end

end


helloObj=Hello.new
helloObj.hello()
```

The output from the script is "Return from Proc". The "Hello Ruby" string is not output. The Kernel module provides a method called proc or lambda, which is equivalent to Proc.new, but which does not return from the enclosing method. If the preceding script is run with the proc method, instead of Proc.new, the output is "Hello Ruby". Another difference between Proc.new and the proc method is that the proc method checks for the number of arguments, while Proc.new doesn't. For example, a Proc.new block, which defines 2 parameters, may be invoked with 3 arguments as in the following script.

```
hello=Proc.new{|name1, name2| puts "Hello "+name1}
hello.call("Ruby",  "ruby","RUBY")
```

The output is "Hello Ruby".

In contrast, if the proc method is used to create a Proc object and the Proc object is invoked with a different number of arguments than specified, an error gets generated. For example, the following script creates a Proc object with the proc method that defines 2 parameters, and when the Proc object is invoked with 3 arguments an error gets generated: "ArgumentError: wrong number of arguments (3 for 2)".

```
hello=proc{|name1, name2| puts "Hello "+name1}
hello.call("Ruby",  "ruby","RUBY")
```

The Proc.new method may be used without a block, if invoked in a method and the method has an attached block, as in the following script.

```
def hello
  Proc.new
end
helloProc = hello { "hello ruby" }
helloProc.call
```

A block of code may be used with a method without using Proc.new to create a Proc object. When a block is appended to a method call, Ruby converts the block of code to a Proc object without a name. The Proc object may be invoked in the method using the yield method, which is equivalent to an explicit call to an explicit Proc object. In the following listing method hello is invoked with a block. Ruby converts the block to a Proc object, which may be called using the yield method.

```
def hello
    yield
```

```
      yield
  end

hello {puts "Hello Ruby"}
```

The output from the script is as follows.

```
Hello Ruby
Hello Ruby
```

The ampersand operator (&) may be used to explicitly convert between a block and a Proc object. If an & is prepended to the last parameter of a method and a block attached with the method, the block gets converted to a Proc object and gets assigned to the last argument. In the following example, the last argument of the hello method is prepended with an &. When the method invocation is attached with a block, the block gets converted to a Proc object and gets assigned to the last argument of the method. The call method may be invoked on the Proc object 'name' in the method definition. The yield method may still be used to invoke the Proc object.

```
def hello(msg,&name)

    name.call(msg)
    yield(msg)
  end

hello ("Ruby") {|name| puts "Hello " +name}
```

The output from the Ruby script is as follows.

```
Hello Ruby
Hello Ruby
```

The argument prepended with & isn't really an argument, but meant to convert a block of code to a Proc object. A method may not be invoked with a Proc object where a block is expected. For example, if the hello method in the preceding script is invoked with a Proc object instead of a block, as in the following listing, an ArgumentError gets generated.

```
def hello(msg,&name)
name.call(msg)
  yield(msg)
 end

hello ("Ruby", proc {|name| puts "Hello " +name})
```

But, a Proc object may be converted to a block and a method that expects a block invoked with the converted block. A Proc object is converted to a block by prepending the Proc object with an &. In the following script, the procObj Proc object is prepended with a & in the hello method invocation.

```
def hello(msg,&name)

     name.call(msg)
     yield(msg)
 end

procObj=proc {|name| puts "Hello " +name}
hello ("Ruby", &procObj)
```

The output is the same as invoking the method with a block.

1.11 Control Structures and Iterators

Ruby provides control structures to run code conditionally. A conditional branch evaluates a test expression and evaluates code in a block depending on whether the expression evaluates to true or false. The if control structure is used evaluate a block of code if the expression following if evaluates to true as shown in the following example.

```
var1=nil
if var1==nil
 var1="Nil Variable"
end
```

The output is "Nil Variable". The test expression and code block may be put on the same line using then.

```
var1=nil
if var1==nil then var1="Nil Variable" end
```

The if expression may also be used as follows.

```
var1=nil
var1="Nil Variable" if var1==nil
```

The `unless` expression evaluates a block of code if an expression evaluates to false.

```
var1=nil
unless var1!=nil
"Variable is Nil"
end
```

The output is "Nil Variable". The if-elsif-else expression evaluates a series of expressions. For example, the following if-elsif-else script outputs "Var1 is nil".

```
var1=nil
if var1==1
  "Var1 is 1"
elsif var1==2
  "Var1 is 2"
elsif var1==5
"Var1 is 5"
else
"Var1 is nil"
end
```

The short-if statement is used to evaluate one expression if a Boolean expression is true and another expression if the Boolean expression is false.

```
var1=5
(var1==nil)? nil : "Var1 is not nil"
```

The preceding Ruby script outputs "Var1 is not nil". The `case` statement is used to test a sequence of conditions. The following script tests name with different strings and outputs "Ruby".

```
name="Ruby"
case name
  when "RUBY"
    puts "RUBY"
  when "ruby"
    puts "ruby"
  when "Ruby"
    puts "Ruby"
end
```

The `while` statement runs a block of code while a specified condition is true. The following script outputs an integer and increments the integer while the integer is not 10.

```
var=1
while var!=10
  puts var
  var +=1
end
```

The `until` statement is a negated while. The following script outputs an integer and increments an integer until the integer is 10.

```
var=1
until var==10
  puts var
  var +=1
end
```

Ruby provides four methods to exit a while/until loop: `break`, `next`, `redo`, and `return`. The break exits the loop. In the following script, integers are output only upto 7.

```
var=1
while var!=10
  if var==8
  break
  end
  puts var
  var +=1
end
```

The `next` statement invokes the next iteration of a loop. In the following script, which has a next statement, integers 2 to 10 are output except integer 8, because the next iteration is invoked if var value is 8.

```
var=1
while var!=10
  var +=1
  if var==8
  next
  end
  puts var

end
```

The `redo` statement restarts the current iteration again. The following script restarts current iteration if var value is 8. The output is integers 1 to 9.

```
var=1
while var!=10
   puts var
   var +=1
   if var==8
   redo
   end

end
```

A `return` statement in a loop exits the loop and also the method that contains the loop. The following script iterates the while loop twice.

```
class Hello

def hello
var=1
while var!=10
puts "Hello Ruby"
var+=1
if var==3
return "Hello Ruby"
end
end
end

end
hello=Hello.new
hello.hello
```

The `for` statement iterates over a collection without using indices. The collection may be a hash, an array, a range or any other collection. The following script iterates over an array and outputs a Hello message for each element in the collection.

```
array =["Ruby", "ruby", "RUBY"]

for name in array
puts "Hello"+ name
end
```

The output is as follows.

"Hello Ruby"
"Hello ruby"
Hello RUBY"

A collection may also be iterated using the each method. The following script also produces the same output as the preceding script.

```
array =["Ruby", "ruby", "RUBY"]

array.each do |name|
puts "Hello "+ name
end
```

A string type provides a method each_byte, which iterates over each character in the string. The following snippet outputs ASCII character codes for the characters in the "RUBY" string.

```
str="RUBY"

str.each_byte do |c|
puts c
end
```

Ruby provides another iterator for string type, each_line, which iterates over each line in a string.

```
str="RUBY\nRuby\nruby"

str.each_line do |l|
puts l
end
```

The output from the code snippet is as follows.

```
RUBY
Ruby
Ruby
```

The each method for a string type is the same as the each_line method. The retry statement restarts the iteration from the beginning. The following script, outputs "Hello Ruby" twice.

```
array =["Ruby", "ruby", "RUBY"]
c=0
array.each do |name|
if name=="ruby" and c==1
retry
end
puts "Hello "+ name
```

```
c +=1
end
```

The `redo` statement is used to restart the current iteration. The following script does not output a string if c is 1.

```
array =["Ruby", "ruby", "RUBY"]
c=0
array.each do |name|
if c==1
c +=1
redo
end
puts c
puts "Hello "+ name
c +=1
end
```

Ruby provides the `n.times` do iterator for n iterations. For example, the following iteration outputs 0, 1, 2, 3.

```
4.times do |num|
    puts num
end
```

1.12 Exception Handling

Exceptions are conditions in the running of code that prevent the code from running. An Exception is an instance of class `Exception` or a sub-class of Exception. In the section on methods, we discussed that if a private method of a class is invoked with an instance of the class, a NoMethodError gets generated. NoMethodError is a sub-class of NameError class, which is a sub-class of StandardError class, which is a sub-class of the Exception class. Ruby provides exception handling mechanism with `begin/end` block. If an exception is raised in a begin/end block Ruby provides the `rescue` clause to handle the exception. Multiple rescue clauses may be specified in a begin/end block to handle different error conditions. An `ensure` clause may also be specified that consists of statements that are run whether an exception occurs or not. The format of a begin/end block is as follows.

```
begin

rescue Exception1
   Statements  to  run  when  an  exception  of  type
   Exception1 occurs
rescue Exception2
   Statements   to   run   when   exception   of   type
   Exception2 occurs.
ensure
   Statements  to  run  whether  an  exception  occurs  or
   not.

end
```

A reference to the exception object associated with the latest exception is available in the global variable $!.   In the following script, a NoMethodError gets generated when a private method a class is invoked. An error message is output in the rescue statement.

```
class Hello

   def hello(name)
    return "Hello " +name
    end

private :hello

end

begin
helloObj1=Hello.new
helloObj1.hello "Ruby"
rescue NoMethodError
$stderr.print "The NoMethodError has been generated:
" + $!
end
```

The output from the script is as follows.

```
The NoMethodError has been generated: private method
hello called for #<Hello:>
```

If no exception class is specified in the rescue clause, the StandardError exception is the default. Multiple exception classes may be specified in a rescue class, and a local variable may be specified to receive the matched exception. For example, in the following script multiple exception classes have been assigned to a rescue clause and also a local variable has been assigned to the rescue class.

```
class Hello

    def hello(name)
      return "Hello " +name
    end
private :hello

end

begin
helloObj1=Hello.new
helloObj1.hello "Ruby"
rescue NoMethodError, SyntaxError =>error
$stderr.print error
end
```

The output from the script is as follows.

```
private method hello called for #<Hello:>
```

Parameters to the rescue clause may be expressions that return an Exception class. Exceptions may also be raised explicitly using the raise method. The raise method has one of the following syntaxes.

```
raise
raise( aString )
raise( anException [, aString [ anArray ] ] )
```

With no arguments, raise raises the exception in !$ or raises a RuntimeError if !$ is nil. With a single argument, raise raises a RuntimeError with the string message. With the third syntax, the first parameter is the Exception class or a sub-class of the Exception class. The optional second parameter is string message associated with the exception. The optional third parameter is an array of callback information. In the following script, an exception of type Exception is raised in the hello method and the rescue clause outputs the error message.

```
class Hello

    def hello(name)
      raise Exception, "An exception has been generated
in the hello method"
      return "Hello " +name
    end

end
```

```
begin
helloObj1=Hello.new
helloObj1.hello "Ruby"
rescue NoMethodError, Exception =>error
$stderr.print error
end
```

The output from the script is as follows.

"An exception has been generated in the hello
method".

The raise method is available in the kernel module.

1.13 Modules

A module is a collection of classes, methods, variables, and constants. A module is defined with the following syntax.

```
module

end
```

A module is similar to a class in that it is a collection of methods, variables, and constants. But, a module is different from a class, because a module may not be instantiated or sub-classed. Members of a module are referenced with the :: notation. For example, if class Class1 is in module Module1, the class is referenced as Module1::Class1. Modules provide multiple inheritance with mixins. A module may be included in a class, thus, the members of the module become the members of the class. A module is included in a class with the include statement. If the module is another file, first import the module with a require statement.

```
require Module1
include Module1
```


1.14 Comparing Ruby with PHP

Both PHP and Ruby are interpreted scripting languages. Both PHP and Ruby are object-oriented and provide classes, methods, and class inheritance. Ruby is more object-oriented than PHP; in Ruby everything is an object. In both Ruby and PHP, a class may extend one other class; single inheritance. In both Ruby and PHP access to classes and methods may be public, protected or private. The PHP script runs on the web server and output may be viewed in a web browser. For server-side-scripting three components are required; PHP Installation, Web Server, and a Web Browser. PHP is dynamically typed; variables are not declared, just as in Ruby. Ruby provides the constant nil corresponding to PHP type NULL. Both Ruby and PHP provide the constants TRUE and FALSE. Both Ruby and PHP support expression interpolation for double-quoted strings using #{}; expressions enclosed in #{} in a double quoted string are evaluated and replaced with the result. Both Ruby and PHP support exception handling. Both Ruby and PHP may be embedded in HTML, the syntax though is different. PHP code is embedded using <? ?> and Ruby code is embedded using <% %>, or <%= %> to output to a browser. Ruby and PHP are different in some other aspects too. Ruby is a strongly typed language, which means that explicit conversions have to be performed between data types, unlike PHP, which performs the type conversions automatically. Strings, numbers, arrays, and hashes are objects in Ruby unlike in PHP. Integers in Ruby may contain underscores as markers, which are not evaluated by the parser. Ruby provides symbols, which PHP doesn't. In Ruby parentheses are optional in method invocation, unlike in PHP. Ruby provides control structures if, else and elsif corresponding to PHP's control structures if, else and elseif. Corresponding to PHP's while, do-while, for and foreach, Ruby provides n.times do, while, begin-end-until, for and .each do. Ruby does not support abstract classes or interfaces, which PHP does. Almost everything in Ruby gets converted to a method call.

1.15 Comparing Ruby with Java

Ruby is similar to Java in that both are object-oriented languages and are strongly typed. But, Ruby is dynamically typed, whereas Java is statically typed; in Ruby type declarations are not used while in Java type declarations are required. Both Java and Ruby provide inheritance and have public, private and protected methods. Ruby is simpler than Java and faster than Java too. Ruby is different from Java in a number of features. The differences between Java and Ruby are discussed in Table 1.4.

Table 1.4 Comparing Ruby with Java

Feature	Ruby	Java
Interpreted/Compiled	Ruby is an interpreted scripting language and is run directly.	Java applications are required to be compiled before running.
Defining Blocks	Ruby defines a class/method block using the end keyword.	Java uses braces to define a class/method block.
Importing packages/modules	The require statement is used to import a class or a module.	The import statement is used to import a package or a class.
Multiple Inheritance.	Uses mixins for multiple inheritance.	Uses interfaces for multiple inheritance.
Typed Variables	Variables do not have an explicit type associated.	Variables have an explicit type.
Constructor	Constructor is the initialize method.	Constructor is the name of the class.
Class Instantiation.	A class Class1 is instantiated as follows: class1=Class1.new	A class Class1 is instantiated as follows: class1=new Class1()
Configuration file	YAML files are used.	XML files
Null value	nil	null
Casting	No casting.	Casting is used.
Type declarations.	No type declarations. Variables are dynamically typed.	Variables are statically typed.

Table 1.4 (continued)

Feature	Ruby	Java
Objects	Everything is an object including numbers.	Objects
Parentheses in method invocation.	Parentheses in method invocation are optional.	Parentheses in method invocation.
Member variables.	All member variables are private.	Member variables.

1.16 Summary

In this chapter we installed Ruby. We discussed the Ruby syntax. We compared Ruby with PHP another commonly used scripting language. We also compared Ruby with Java.

2 Rails Framework

2.1 Introduction

A J2EE web application requires a lot of different components such as JSPs/HTMLs, EJBs, Servlets and also requires some configuration files. Ruby on Rails requires lesser code in comparison to a J2EE MVC application and does not require any configuration files (except a database configuration file). Ruby is an interpretive object oriented scripting language. Rails is a Ruby based framework for developing web applications with a database component using the Model-View-Controller pattern. To develop a Ruby on Rails application a web server and a database are required. Rails includes a built-in web server, WEBrick. Rails also supports other web servers such as Apache HTTP server. Rails is configured with the MySQL database by default. Rails also supports other databases such as PostgreSQL, SQL Server, IBM's DB2 UDB, Oracle and SyabaseASA. Rails supports most operating systems. We shall be using the Windows operating system.

2.2 Overview of Rails

Rails is a web application and persistence framework to develop database-based web applications according to the Model-View-Controller pattern. Views are the user interfaces of a web application. A view is rendered using RHTML or RXML. RHTML is Ruby embedded HTML, and RXML is Ruby-generated XML. The controller sets instance variables required by a view and renders a view. A view contains links to methods (actions) defined in the controller with which controller actions are invoked. Models model business objects in a MVC application. In Rails, models are typically based on Active Record design pattern, which provides an object-relational mapping (ORM) between business objects and a database. With

Active record pattern a database table is represented by a class, and an object instance represents a row in the database table. The database table columns are represented by the attributes of the class, and the class provides accessors for each column in the database table. The controller is a class that extends the `ApplicationController` class and consists of actions (methods). A controller integrates the model with the view using public methods (actions). The model provides the data, the controller provides business logic to process the data, and the view presents the data. A request is initiated from a view template in a browser. The web server forwards the request to a dispatcher. The dispatcher loads the controller. The controller provides the business logic and interacts with the Active Record persistence layer to return a response to the view template, which gets displayed in the browser.

Rails is a combination of the following sub-projects:

1. Model: Active Record is an object relational mapping package built on the Active Record pattern.
2. Control: Action Controller (Action Pack package).
3. View: Action View (Action Pack package).

The Rails Model-View-Controller framework is shown in Figure 2.1.

Rails Model-View-Controller Framework

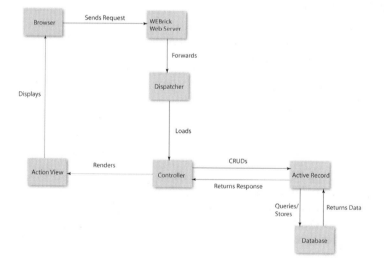

Fig. 2.1. Rails Model-View-Controller Framework

2.3 Active Record

Active Record objects extend the `ActiveRecord::Base` class. Active Record integrates business objects and database tables to create a persistable domain model. An Active Record object is linked with a database table. An Active Record does not specify its attributes directly, but the attributes have a 1-1 mapping to the database table columns it is linked to. Adding, removing and modification of attributes is performed directly in the database table. An Active Record object may be initialized using a hash or a block with the `new()` method. An Active Record object created with the new() method is not saved in the database table. To create an Active Record object that is saved in the database table use the `create()` method. An example of creating an Active Record object for model class Catalog with attributes journal, edition, title, author is as follows.

```
Catalog=Catalog.new(:journal=>"Oracle      Magazine",
:edition=>"Jan-Feb 2007",  :title=>"Modeling Tables and
Components",  :author=>"Steve Muench")
```

Only attributes that have matching column names in the associated database table may be specified. Using block initialization a Catalog class Active Record object is created using accessors on the Active Record object as follows.

```
catalog= Catalog.new do |c|
    c.journal="Oracle Magazine"
    c.edition="Jan-Feb 2007"
    c.title="Modeling Tables and Components"
    c.author="Steve Muench"
end
```

Active Record object initialization may also be performed by creating an Active Record object and subsequently settings its attributes using accessors.

```
catalog= Catalog.new
catalog.journal="Oracle Magazine"
catalog.edition="Jan-Feb 2007"
catalog.title="Modeling Tables and Components"
catalog.author="Steve Muench"
```

Active record does not require any configuration files. Active Record uses transactions for database operations. By default the Rails framework uses the connection settings in the *config/database.yml* file for connecting to the database. The `establish_connection()` method of the Active:Record:Base class may be used to create a class specific connection with the database. By default the Rails framework uses pluralization to obtain the database table name with the Inflector module. If the model class name is Catalog the database table name is "catalogs". The database table name may also be set with the `set_table_name` method of the ActiveRecord:Base class. ActiveRecord:Base class methods are used to create a database record, find a database record, update a record and delete a record. Some of the methods in the ActiveRecord:Base class are discussed in Table 2.1.

Table 2.1 ActiveRecord::Base Class Methods

Method	Description
attribute_names()	Returns an array of attributes names for an Active Record object.
attributes()	Returns a hash of attributes.
columns()	Returns an array of columns for the database table associated with the Active Record.
establish_connection()	Establishes a connection to the database.
remove_connection()	Removes a connection associated with an ActiveRecord object.
connection()	Returns a connection associated with an Active Record object.
set_table_name()	Sets the table name.
set_primary_key()	Sets the primary key.
create()	Creates an object and saves it as a record.

Table 2.1 (continued)

Method	Description
find(*)	The find() method may be used with one of the following retrieval methods: Find by id: Finds a record for a specified id or a list/array of ids. Find first: Retrieves the first record that matches the specified options. Find all: Retrieves all the record that match the specified options. Some of the options that may be specified are: :conditions: An SQL fragment such as "catalogId=catalog1". :limit: An integer specifying a limit on the number of records returned. :offset: An integer specifying the row offset to retrieve rows. For example, if :offset is 5, the first 4 rows are skipped. :select: Specifies a SELECT statement to retrieve rows. By default SELECT * FROM is used.
find_by_sql(sql)	Retrieves a result set for the specifies SELECT statement.
id()	Returns the primary key for an Active Record object.
save()	Creates a new record. If the record already exists, the record is updated.

Table 2.1 (continued)

Method	Description
update(id, attributes)	Updates a record.
update_all()	Updates all records.
update_attribute(name, value)	Updates a single attribute and saves the record.
delete(id)	Deletes a record.

Next, we shall discuss each of theses methods with an example. An example to create a connection with the Oracle database with establish_connection method, which takes a hash as input, is as follows.

```
ActiveRecord::Base.establish_connection(
    :adapter  => "oci",
    :host     => "",
    :username => "oe",
    :password => "oracle"
    :database => "ORCL"
)
```

The :adapter key specifies a database adapter in lower-case. Table name and primary key may be set in a model class Catalog, which extends the ActiveRecord:Base class as in following listing.

```
class Catalog < ActiveRecord::Base
set_table_name "catalogs"
set_primary_key "id"
end
```

The default primary key is "id". As an example, the "catalogs" table has columns id, journal, publisher, edition, section, title and author. The create method is used to create a record. For example add a record with values specified for column1, column2 and column3 with Catalog as the model class.

```
Catalog.create        :column1   =>   "column1value",
:column2 => "column2value",  :column3 => "column3value"
```

Active Record may be used to save any object such as a hash or an array in a text column with the serialize method. The following example creates and saves a journal hash.

```
class Catalog < ActiveRecord::Base
    serialize :journal
    end
    catalog = Catalog.create(:journal => { "title" =>
  "Oracle Magazine", "edition" => "January-February
  2007" })
```

The find method is used to find a record. For example, find the first record that matches the SQL section.

```
find(:first, :conditions => "section = 'SQL'")
```

The find_by_sql method finds a result set for a specified SQL statement. An example of find_by_sql is as follows in which a result set is created for SQL section.

```
@resultset=Catalog.find_by_sql("SELECT    *    from
catalogs WHERE SECTION='SQL'")
```

The update method updates a record for the specified id. For example, the following listing updates journal and title columns of a row with id 1.

```
Catalog.update  (1,  {:journal=>'Oracle  Magazine',
title=>'Introduction to Ruby on Rails'} )
```

The update_all method updates all the records. For example, update all records to set journal to "Oracle Magazine" and publisher to "Oracle Publishing".

```
Catalog.update_all    "journal="'Oracle    Magazine'
publisher='Oracle Publishing'"
```

The delete method deletes a record. For example, delete a record with id 10.

```
Catalog.delete(10)
```

2.4 Action Controller

An Action Controller extends the ActionController::Base class. An Action controller is made up of one or more actions (methods) that perform a business logic and then either render a template, partial, file, or text, or redirect to an action, url, file or back to the page that issued the request. An action is defined as a public method that is made available to the web server through Rails routes. A request is handled by the Action Controller framework by extracting the value of the `:action` key and invoking the action (method) specified in the :action key. An action assumes that you want to render a template matching the name of the action in the *app/views/controllername* directory when the method code has run, controllername being the variable controller name. You may also redirect to an action or a page with `redirect_to`. A controller action should conclude with a single render or redirect. Multiple renders/redirects result in DoubleRenderError error. Example in following listing redirects to a controller action.

```
redirect_to :action=>"index"
```

An action may be redirected to another page as in the following listing.

```
redirect_to "http://www.rubyonrails.org"
```

An action may be redirected to an image file.

```
redirect_to "logo.jpg"
```

`Redirect_to:back` redirects back to the page that issued the request. A request is sent to a Action Controller from a view template with the :action key. The :action key specifies name of an action in the Action Controller as shown in following listing.

```
:action=>:index
```

The request parameters are made available to the controller action and the action code is run. The request parameters are available to a controller action with the `params` method, which returns a hash. For example, :section param may be retrieved in a controller action with params hash as shown below.

```
@section=params[:section]
```

Each controller action results in a response that is constructed using renders and redirects. By default a controller action renders a view template with matching name. For example, an *index* action would render the *index* template. If no action is specified the default controller action, index, gets rendered. The instance variables set in a controller action are available to the template rendered. A controller action may render a template other than the default template. For example, render an *edit* template using the `render` method as shown below.

```
render :template=>"catalog/edit"
```

Template rendering takes a path relative to the template root. The current layout is applied in template rendering. A controller action may invoke a template for another action instead of the default template. The HTTP status code may be specified using the `:status` option. The default status code for the render method is "200 OK". By default, templates associated with actions are rendered using the current layout (Layouts are discussed in a later section). If the current layout is not to be used specify `:layout=>false` in the render method invocation. A layout for the template may be specified using the `:layout` option. For example, a controller action may invoke controller action index's template as shown in following listing.

```
render :action=>"index",    :status=>"200",    :layout
=>"index"
```

The :action, :status, and :layout options may be specified in any order. A file may also be rendered from a controller action. For example, render a file index.rhtml as shown below.

```
render                                          :file=>"
C:/ruby/railsapp/app/views/catalog/index.rhtml",
:layout => true, :status => 404
```

File rendering takes absolute file path by default and the current layout is not applied. Text may be rendered in a browser with `render:text` as shown below.

```
render:text =>"Example of render text"
```

The current layout is not applied in text rendering. In an Ajax request (Ajax is discussed in Chap. 3) the text rendered is returned as Ajax response to the view template in the browser that invoked the controller action. An inline template may also be rendered. The inline template is interpreted using ERb or Builder. By default ERb is used for rendering and the current layout is not applied. For example, in the following listing an inline template is rendered.

```
render :inline => "<%= 'hello ' + name %>", :locals
=> { :name => "Deepak" }
```

The :locals option specifies local variables. The render method may also be used to render JavaScriptGenerator (JavaScriptGenerator is discussed in the next section) page updates. For example, insert HTML in a catalog list.

```
render update_page do |page|
      page.insert_html        :bottom,        'catalog',
  "<li>#{@catalog.name}</li>"

    end
```

Nothing may be rendered as in the following example.

```
render :nothing => true
```

2.5 Action View

The Action View consists of templates that provide a user interface. The ActionView::Base class defines 3 types of Action View templates.

1. Templates with .rhtml extension.
2. Templates with .rxml extension.
3. Templates with .rjs extension.

A .rhtml extension template consists of a mixture of ERb (embedded Ruby) and HTML. ERb is used with embeddings tags, for example, <% %> and <%= %>. The <%= %> tag set is used for output. The <% %> tag set is used to embed Ruby code.

A .rxml template is used to generate XML output using the Builder::XmlMarkup library. An XmlMarkup object, @xml, is made available to an .rxml template by default. The Builder:XmlMarkup library is used in Chap. 6 to generate an XML document.

An .rjs extension template is a JavaScriptGenerator template and generates JavaScript instructions for updating an already rendered page. RJS templates are used in combination with Ajax to modify multiple elements on a page. A JavaScriptGenerator object, page, is made available to an .rjs template. The Ajax scaffolding example in Chap. 3 uses .rjs templates. A JavaScriptGenerator object is created using the PrototypeHelper#update_page method and subsequent invocations of JavaScriptGenerator methods are used to update the content of the current page. In the following example the catalog name is added at the bottom of the catalog list and journals div is replaced by rendering a partial.

```
update_page do |page|
    page.insert_html :bottom, 'catalog',
"<li>#{@catalog.name}</li>"
page.replace_html 'journals', :partial =>
'journal', :collection => @journals
  end
```

Some of the JavaScriptGenerator methods are discussed in Table 2.2.

Table 2.2 JavaScriptGenerator Method

Method	Description
alert(message)	Displays an alert dialog with the given message.
assign(variable, value)	Assigns a JavaScript variable a value.
insert_html(position,id, *options_for_render)	Inserts HTML at the specified position relative to the specified DOM ID. Position is one of the following: :top, :bottom,:before,:after. options_for_render may be either an HTML string or a hash of options with which the ActionView::Base#render method is invoked.
remove(*ids)	Removes the DOM elements with the specified ids.
replace(id, *options_for_render)	Replaces the outer HTML of an element. options_for_render may be either an HTML string or a hash of options with which the ActionView::Base#render method is invoked.
replace_html(id, *options_for_render)	Replaces the inner HTML.

2.5.1 Sub-Templates

A template may include content from a sub-template by including the result of rendering a sub-template with an output embedding. For example, output from a header template and a footer template may be included in a template as follows.

```
<%= render "header" %>
  Table
<%= render "footer" %>
```

Instance variables defined in a template are available in a sub-template. For example, define an instance variable @title and include the output of a header sub-template as follows.

```
<% @title = "Page Title" %>
<%= render "header" %>
```

In the header sub-template the @title instance variable may be used as follows.

```
<title><%= @title %></title>
```

Local variables may be passed to a sub-template using a hash of variable names and values in the render method. The following example renders the header sub-template and passes local variables title and edition.

```
<%= render "header", { :title => "Page Title",
:edition => "2nd" } %>
```

In the header sub-template the title and edition local variables may be accessed as follows.

```
Page Title: <%= title %>
Edition: <%= edition %>
```

2.6 Ruby on Rails Commands

A MVC Rails application consists of the following Ruby, RHTML and configuration files.

1. View templates(.rhtml files) in the app/views directory.
2. Model classes in the app/models directory.
3. Controller classes in the app/controllers directory.
4. Database Configuration file (database.yml) in the config directory.

Ruby on Rails provides some commands with which model and controller scripts may be generated. Some of the commonly used Ruby on Rails commands are discussed in Table 2.3.

Table 2.3 Ruby on Rails Commands

Command	Description
rails *application*	Creates a Rails application.
ruby script/server	Starts Ruby Rails web server WEBrick at http://localhost:3000
ruby script/generate model *modelname*	Generates a model class of specified model name.
ruby script/generate controller *controllername* *controlleraction* *controlleraction*	Generates a controller class of specified name. Also generates the controller actions if specified.
ruby script/generate scaffold *modelname* *controllername*	Generates a scaffolding for a database table, the model class and a controller class. *controllername* is optional in the scaffold generator command and is the same as the model name by default.
ruby script/generate migration *migrationname*	Generates an ActiveRecord migration.

2.7 Installing Rails

In the previous chapter we installed Ruby. In this section we shall install the Rails framework. Cd (change directory) to the *c:/ruby* directory, the directory in which Ruby is installed, in a command line window, and run the following command to install Rails and dependencies including activerecord and actionpack; activerecord implements the model layer of a Rails MVC application and actionpack implements the view and controller.

```
c:/ruby>gem install rails --include-dependencies
```

The rails framework including dependencies gets installed as shown in Figure 2.2.

Fig. 2.2. Installing Rails

2.8 Developing a Rails Application

Create a Rails application, *railsapp*, with the following command.

```
c:/ruby>rails railsapp
```

A Rails application directory structure gets generated. The root directory of the Rails application is railsapp, as shown in Figure. 2.3.

Fig. 2.3. Rails Application Directory Structure

The railsapp directory contains the sub-directories of the Rails application. The *app* sub-directory consists of sub-directories *models*, *views*, *controllers* and *helpers*. The models directory is for model Ruby scripts, the views directory is for view templates and layouts. The controllers directory is for controller scripts. The *config* directory contains a *database.yml* configuration file in which a database configuration is defined. The config directory also contains a *routes.rb* file in which Rails framework routes are defined. The *public* directory contains the index.html file, which is displayed when the railsapp Rails application is accessed in a browser with the URL http://localhost:3000. The public directory also contains the *images* directory, the *javascripts* directory for JavaScript files, and the *stylesheets* directory for the css stylesheets.

2.9 Rails Routes

Rails Routes are used to map matching URLs to controllers and actions and are configured in the *config/routes.rb* file. An example route is defined below.

```
map.connect 'catalog/:id', :controller => 'catalog',
:action => 'view'
```

If the URL http://localhost:3000/catalog/1 is specified in the browser, the *view* action of the *catalog* controller gets invoked and the first entry in the catalog is displayed. Routes are generated in the order in which they are specified in the routes.rb file. The default route has the lowest priority and is specified as shown below.

```
map.connect ':controller/:action/:id'
```

The default route implies that a controller action may be invoked with the url http://localhost:3000/controllername/actionname. Controllername and actionname are variables. The :id specifies the id of the view. A default controller may be associated with the default route.

```
map.connect ':controller/:action/:id', :controller
=> 'catalog'
```

Delete the *public/index.html* file to use the default controller. The URL http://localhost:3000/ would invoke the index.rhtml view of the catalog controller. The root of the a site may be routed as shown below.

```
map.connect '', :controller => "catalog", :action
=> 'listCatalogs'
```

Delete the public/index.html file to use the empty path route. The URL http://localhost:3000 would invoke the listCatalogs action of the catalog controller. Named routes may also be created. For example, a named route for catalog controller may be created as shown below.

```
map.catalog '', :controller => 'catalog', :action =>
'list'
```

The named route creates a method called catalog_url. Using the named route the following redirect may be specified as redirect_to catalog_url.

```
redirect_to :controller => 'catalog', :action =>
'list'
```

2.10 Stylesheets

Stylesheets represent the formatting information such as fonts, colors and layouts of a web page and separate the formatting from the content. Using stylesheets makes the formatting and the content easier to maintain. Stylesheets in the public/stylesheets directory are used with view templates and may be included in a template with HTML.

```
<link rel="Stylesheet"
href="/stylesheets/catalog.css" type="text/css"
media="screen" />
```

Stylesheets may also be included using Ruby code. The .css suffix is not required to be added to the stylesheet.

```
<%= stylesheet_link_tag "catalog" %>
```

2.11 Helpers

Helpers are modules that are available to the associated view templates and are located in the app/helpers directory. For example, if a controller catalog and an associated view index are generated, a `CatalogHelper` module also gets generated.

```
module CatalogHelper

end
```

The methods in the CatalogHelper module are available to the index view and to other views associated with the catalog controller. By default, only one helper module is available to views associated with a controller. Additional helper modules may be added by specifying the helpers in the controller using the `helper` method of the ActionController::Helpers::ClassMethods module. For example, a helper module catalog2_helper may be added to the catalog controller.

```
class CatalogController < ApplicationController
  helper :catalog2_helper
  def index
  end
end
```

A controller method may be declared a helper method using the `helper_method` method of the ActionController::Helpers::ClassMethods module. For example, in the following example the helperMethod method is declared as a helper method.

```
helper_method :helperMethod
def helperMethod
 end
```

2.12 Layouts

Layouts in the views/layouts directory are used to add presentation to the views. Layouts are also used to define common content, headers and footers for example, which may be used by different content pages. Variables defined in the layout are available in the views and variables defined in the views are available in the layout. Layouts are .rxml or .rhtml templates. If a layout with the same name as the controller is available in the views/layouts directory, the template becomes the default layout for the controller. For example, if the controller class is CatalogController, a catalog.rhtml or catalog.rxml template in the views/layouts directory becomes the default layout. If a layout layout by the same name is not available, an application.rhtml or application.rxml template may be created in the layouts directory and the template becomes the default layout for the views associated with the controller. A layout may also be assigned in the controller class with the `layout` method. For example a layout "catalog" is set in the catalog controller.

```
    class CatalogController < ApplicationController
        layout "catalog"
        def index
        end
    end
```

As a directory is not specified the *catalog* template should be in the app/views/layouts/ directory. The layout specified in the controller class overrides the default layout. Layouts may be applied to specific controller actions or may exclude some actions. If the catalog layout in the preceding example is to be applied to *index* action only specify the following.

```
    layout "catalog" , :only=> :index
```

If a layout is to be specified to all actions except the index action specify the layout method as follows.

```
layout "catalog" :except=> :index
```

More than one actions may be specified using :only and :except. The following example applies the catalog template to all actions except the index and list actions.

```
layout "catalog" :except=> [:index, :list]
```

A method reference may be specified in the layout method instead of a layout template to select a layout based on a condition such as whether a user is logged in or not.

```
class CatalogController < ActionController::Base
    layout :select_layout

    def index
    end
    private
      def select_layout
        logged_in? ? "layout_template1" :
"layout_template2"
    end
```

In a layout template, you may specify variables for adding stylesheets to a view template. For example, in the layout specify:

```
<%=@content_for_page_stylesheets%>
  <style>
  <%=@content_for_page_styles%>
  </style>
```

In the view template specify the stylesheets.

```
<% content_for :page_stylesheets do %>
<%=stylesheet_link_tag 'stylesheet1'%>
<%=stylesheet_link_tag 'stylesheet2'%>
<% end %>
```

A layout may be specified in the action rendering.

```
render :action => "index", :layout => "index"
```

2.13 Partials

Partials ("partial views") are used in views to update one or more elements on a web page. A partial is an .rhtml or .rxml view template that is evaluated and the result inserted into the view. The same partial may be used by different views. By default partials do not use the current layout. Partials are represented by the ActionView::Partials module. Partials are invoked with `render` `:partial`. The syntax of using a partial is as follows.

```
<%= render :partial=> 'partialname',  :locals => {}
%>
```

The first parameter to the `render` method is the name of the partial. The second parameter specifies a hash of local variables. The rails framework invokes a file _partialname.rhtml, which is required to be in the same directory as the view, and adds the result to the view in which the partial is specified. For example the following code snippet renders a partial _form.rhtml.

```
<%= render :partial=> 'form' %>
```

A partial from a different controller may be rendered by specifying the controller views sub-directory. For example, render a 'form' partial in the views sub-directory app/views/catalog.

```
<%= render :partial=> 'catalog/form' %>
```

A partial may be rendered for each of the elements in an array collection by specifying a collection with `:collection`. Without :collection a collection is rendered by iterating over the collection and rendering a partial for each of elements in the collection. In the following example, a collection represented with the @catalogs instance variable is iterated and the _catalog.rhtml partial is rendered for each of the elements in the collection. Local variable catalog is passed to the partial as local variable catalog.

```
<% for catalog in @catalogs %>
    <%= render :partial => "catalog", :locals => {
:catalog => catalog } %>
   <% end %>
```

Partials provide a method for rendering a partial by the same name as the elements in an array collection for each of the elements in the array collection. The preceding example may also be represented as shown below.

```
<%= render :partial => "catalog", :collection =>
@catalogs %>
```

The catalog.rhtml template gets rendered for each of the elements in the @catalogs array and a local variable catalog, representing an element in the collection, is passed to the partial. Iteration counter catalog_counter is made available to the partial template. An iteration counter has the name partialname_counter, partialname being the name of the partial. When rendering partials with a collection, a spacer partial may be specified that is rendered between rendering of the partial for the different elements of the collection. The spacer partial is specified with :spacer_template as shown below.

```
<%= render :partial => "catalog", :collection =>
@catalogs, :spacer_template => "spacer" %>
```

Local variables may be made available to partials using the :locals option. In the following listing a partial is rendered using a local variable catalog whose value is the Ruby local variable catalog. Local variable var2 is passed as local variable var2.

```
<%= render :partial=> 'form', :locals
=>{:catalog=>catalog, :var2=>var2}%>
```

With :locals, symbols are used for variable names. Instance variables that are defined in a view are also available in the partials. Partials are commonly used with Ajax to update an element without reloading the page. The Ajax scaffolding example in Chap. 2 uses partials to update sections of a page.The advantage of using partials is that views may be refactored with sub-templates. Another advantage is that sub-views may be reused by different views.

2.14 Rails Framework Examples

Next, we shall discuss the integration of the view templates with the controller framework. As an example, create a controller class *catalog*, with an *index* action, and an index.rhtml view template.

```
C:/ruby/railsapp>ruby     script/generate     controller
catalog index
```

A controller script catalog_controller.rb gets generated in the app/controllers directory. The controller class has an action *index* and extends the ApplicationController class. The Application Controller class extends the ActionController::Base class, which we discussed earlier.

```
class CatalogController < ApplicationController

  def index
  end
end
```

A view template index.rhtml gets generated in the app/views/catalog directory.

```
<h1>Catalog#index</h1>
<p>Find me in app/views/catalog/index.rhtml</p>
```

Start the WEBrick server with the following command.

```
C:/ruby/railsapp>ruby script/server
```

Invoke the index controller action with the url http://localhost:3000/catalog/index. The controller action index gets invoked, which renders the index.rhtml view template as shown in Figure 2.4.

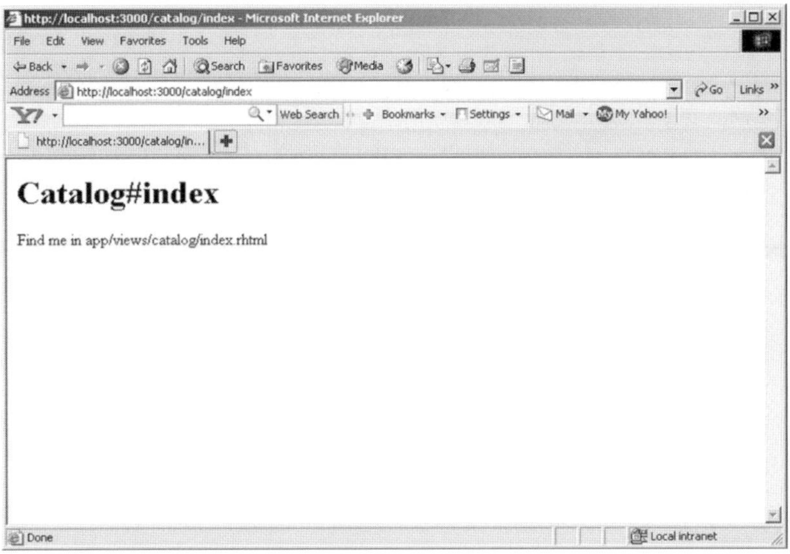

Fig. 2.4. Invoking a Controller Action

To demonstrate generating an output from the controller, modify the controller class to render text.

```
class CatalogController < ApplicationController

  def index
    render:text =>"Introduction to Ruby on Rails"
  end
end
```

Invoke the following url.

```
http://localhost:3000/catalog/index
```

The index action gets invoked and the text gets rendered as shown in Figure 2.5.

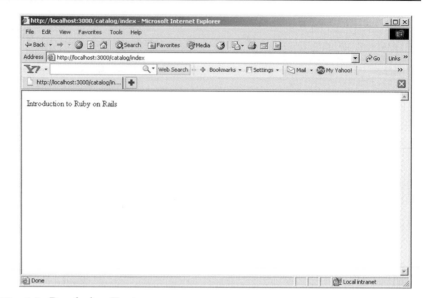

Fig. 2.5. Rendering Text

As an example of integration between the controller class and the view template, modify the controller class, catalog_controller.rb, to specify an instance variable, which is subsequently accessed in the view template.

```
class CatalogController < ApplicationController

  def index
   @msg="Message  to  View  Template  from  Controller
   Class"
  end
end
```

Modify the index.rhtml view template to output the @msg variable using ERb.

```
<%=@msg   %>
```

Invoke   the   controller   action   *index*   with   url http://localhost:3000/catalog/index. The *index* action in *catalog* controller gets invoked. The @msg variable is set in the index action. The index.rhtml template is rendered. The @msg variable is output in the view template as shown in Figure 2.6.

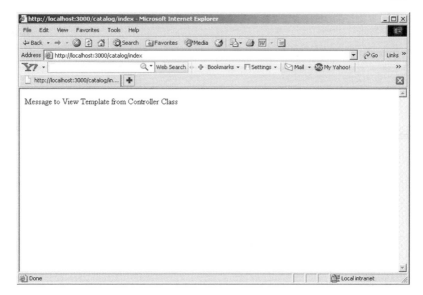

Fig. 2.6. Accessing Controller Instance Variable in View

Next, we shall create an example with Helpers. Modify the app/helpers/catalog_helper.rb script associated with the catalog controller. Add a method, getMsg, to the CatalogHelper class as shown below.

```
module CatalogHelper
def getMsg
  return "Message from Helper"
  end
end
```

The Helper method becomes available to views associated with the catalog controller. Modify the views/catalog/index.rhtml view to invoke the getMsg method.

```
<%=getMsg  %>
```

Invoke the controller action index with the URL http://localhost:3000/index. The index.rhtml view template gets rendered and the getMsg method gets invoked as shown in Figure 2.7.

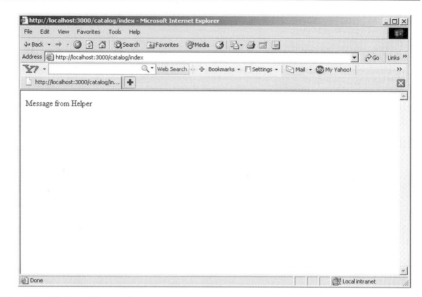

Fig. 2.7. Helper Example

Next, we shall create an example using Layouts. Define a layout, catalog.rhtml, for the catalog controller in the views/layouts directory. The layout defines a @page_title variable, a header and a footer. The yield variable specifies the region for the view template content.

```
<html>
    <head>
        <title><%= @page_title %></title>
    </head>
    <body>
        <div>The header part of this layout</div>
        <div><%= yield%></div>
        <div>The footer part of this layout</div>
    </body>
</html>
```

Modify the index.rhtml view template to specify a value for the @page_title variable and add some page content.

```
<% @page_title = "Layouts" %>
Example with Layouts
```

Invoke the index action with following URL.

```
http://localhost:3000/catalog/index.
```

The layout gets applied to the index view as shown in Figure 2.8.

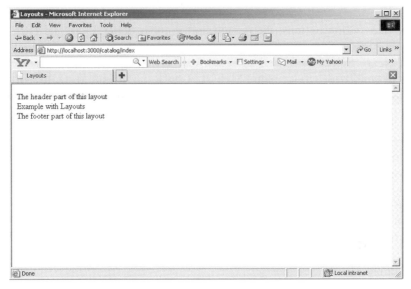

Fig. 2.8. Layouts Example

2.15 Configuring Rails with the MySQL Database

By default the MySQL database is configured with a Ruby on Rails application. Next, we shall install the MySQL database. Download the MySQL 5.0[1] and extract the zip file mysql-5.0.27-win32.zip to a directory. Double-click on the Setup.exe application. The MySQL Server 5.0 Setup Wizard gets started. Click on Next. Select the Typical (the default) Setup Type and click on Next. The installation folder is specified as C:\Program Files\MySQL\MySQL Server 5.0. Click on Install to install the MySQL database. In the Sign-up frame, select Skip Sign-Up and click on Next. Click on Finish. The MySQL Server Instance Configuration Wizard gets started. Click on Next. Select the Detailed Configuration configuration type, the default, and click on Next. Select the default server type, Developer Machine, and click on Next. Select the default database usage, Multifunctional Database, and click on Next. Select the default settings

---

[1] MySQL 5.0 -http://dev.mysql.com/downloads/mysql/5.0.html

for the InnoDB Tablespace settings and click on Next. Select Decision Support (DSS)/OLAP for the approximate number of concurrent connections to the server and click on Next. Select the default settings in the networking options, the default port number being 3306, and click on Next. Select Standard Character Set as the default character set and click on Next. Select the Install as Windows Service option, which is selected by default, with service name MySQL. Check the Include Bin Directory in Windows PATH checkbox and click on Next. In the security options frame check the Modify Security Settings checkbox and specify a password for the root user. To create an anonymous account, check the Create an Anonymous Account checkbox and uncheck the Modify Security Settings checkbox. By default the user root does not require a password. It is recommended to specify a password for the root user. Click on Next. Click on Execute. A MySQL database instance gets created and the service associated with the database instance gets started. Click on Finish. To set a password for the root user if a password was not specified during installation run the following command.

```
SET PASSWORD FOR 'root'@'localhost' =
PASSWORD('rootpw');
```

The database.yml configuration file provides three modes of connection: development environment (default), production environment and test environment. The WEBrick server starts in development mode by default. The WEBrick server may be started in another mode using the –e option. For example the following command starts the WEBrick server in production environment.

```
ruby script/server  -e production
```

Rails environment may be set to production mode by uncommenting the following line in the config/environment.rb file.

```
ENV['RAILS_ENV'] ||= 'production'
```

As the default environment is development, modify the development environment settings in database.yml file to as shown below.

```
development:
adapter: mysql
database: test
username: root
password: rootpw
host: localhost
```

Add a space between the ':' and the configuration values. For example, specify adapter: mysql instead of adapter:mysql.

2.16 Comparing Rails with PHP

PHP is a scripting language while Ruby on Rails is a web framework. PHP may be used to develop a web application and is one of the most commonly used scripting language used for developing web applications. Ruby on Rails provides a Model-View-Controller (MVC) architecture, which minimizes external configuration using naming conventions for mapping database tables to model objects, routing URLs, and rendering view templates. PHP provides a view-centric architecture and a MVC architecture has to implemented externally. Ruby on Rails provides a scaffolding, classes and .rhtml files, for CRUD functionality, while CRUD has to be implemented in a PHP based web application.

2.17 Comparing Rails with Java

Java Platform, Enterprise Edition (Java EE) is the application framework for developing MVC Java applications. Java EE consists of many different components such as JSPs, EJBs, Servlets, Java API for XML Processing (JAXP) and Java Database Connectivity (JDBC) API, and Java Naming and Directory Interface (JNDI) API. In comparison Ruby on Rails web framework consists of only the model, the controller and the view. Ruby on Rails requires fewer configuration files than JEE and is easier to maintain and faster to develop. The Ruby on Rails framework is seamlessly integrated in comparison to the JEE framework.

2.18 Summary

In this chapter we discussed the rails framework. Rails comprises of the Active Record, Action Controller and Action View sub-projects. We created a rails application and configured the application with MySQL database. We compared Rails with PHP and Java.

3 CRUD on Rails

3.1 Introduction

CRUD is an acronym for Create-Read- Update-Delete. Rails is a web application and database persistence framework to develop web applications according to the Model-View-Controller (MVC) pattern. The Rails framework may be used to develop a CRUD application using a relational database. Rails is configured with MySQL database by default. Models model objects in a Rails application and are based on Active Record. An Active Record model class extends the ActiveRecord::Base class. Models provide object-relational mapping (ORM) between business objects and a database. Action View provides the .rhtml view templates as user interfaces for a CRUD application. From a view template a user may invoke actions on a controller class. The controller class uses the model class to establish a connection with the database table and retrieve data from the data. A controller integrates the model with the view. The model models data objects, the controller defines business logic to process the data, and the view presents the data.

3.2 Scaffolding

Scaffolding provides an interface to data in the database. The rails framework has the provision to generate scaffolding, Ruby classes and .rhtml files, for a CRUD application. Scaffolding consists of controller and model Ruby classes and view templates for creating retrieving, updating and deleting table rows. Rails provides two types of scaffoldings, dynamic scaffolding and scaffolding created with the *ScaffoldGenerator*. Dynamic scaffolding is created by adding the following scaffold method invocation to the controller class.

```
scaffold :modelname
```

The `scaffold` method generates controller logic and view templates dynamically using model class obtained with naming conventions. The first letter of the model name is uppercased to obtain the model class. For example, if the model name specified in the scaffold method is *catalog*, the *Catalog* model class is used in the scaffolding. Instance variables `@catalog/@catalogs` are used in the controller class; controller instance variables are also available in the view templates. Controller actions `index`, `list`, `show`, `new`, `create`, `edit`, `update`, `destroy` and corresponding view templates are generated with dynamic scaffolding.

More than one scaffoldings may be generated in a controller class by specifying multiple scaffold method invocations and by setting the `:suffix` option to true. For example, the following scaffold method invocations generate two scaffoldings dynamically.

```
scaffold :catalog,  :suffix=>true
scaffold :journal,  :suffix=>true
```

If multiple scaffoldings are specified using the :suffix option the controller actions for the different scaffoldings are distinguished with the _model name suffix. The preceding example would generate controller actions list_catalog, show_catalog, new_catalog, create_catalog, edit_catalog, update_catalog, destroy_catalog and list_journal, show_journal, new_journal, create_journal, edit_journal, update_journal, destroy_journal. If suffix is used the `index` action is not created.

Scaffolding generated with the ScaffoldGenerator is similar to the one generated with the scaffold method, except that the controller logic and view templates are generated explicitly. We shall discuss the ScaffoldGenerator in a later section.

Rails provides another type of scaffolding, Ajax scaffolding, which is similar to the non-Ajax scaffolding except that the table entries are created, retrieved, updated and deleted using Ajax. Ajax scaffolding is created using the *AjaxScaffold* generator, which we shall discuss in a later section. The AjaxScaffold generator also generates CSS stylesheets for the view templates.

3.3 CRUD with PHP

PHP does not provide any built-in functionality for creating a CRUD application as Ruby on Rails does. A CRUD application may be created by using a form to input field/column values and connecting with a database using one of the PHP class libraries for databases. PHP supports form processing with the `$_GET`, `$_POST`, `$_REQUEST` variables. The `$_GET` variable is an associative array of variables sent to a PHP script with the HTTP GET method. The $_POST variable is an associative array of variables sent to a PHP script with the HTTP POST method. The $_REQUEST variable consists of the contents of $_GET, $_POST, and $_COOKIE. For example, a form, addEntry.html, to create a catalog entry would be as shown below.

```html
<html>
 <head>
  <title>Add Entry</title>
 </head>
 <body>

<form action="addEntry.php" method="get">
     <p>Catalog        ID:        <input        type="text"
     name="catalogID" /></p>
   <p>Journal: <input type="text" name="journal" /></p>
      <p>Publisher:          <input          type="text"
      name="publisher" /></p>
   <p>Edition: <input type="text" name="edition" /></p>
   <p>Title: <input type="text" name="title" /></p>
   <p>Author: <input type="text" name="author" /></p>
   <p><input type="submit" /></p>
 </form>

 </body>
 </html>
```

To create a CRUD application with PHP we would create a PHP script, addEntry.php, in the *C:/Apache/htdocs* directory. As the HTTP method is GET, retrieve the form fields with the $_GET variable in the PHP script.

```php
$catalogid= $_GET['catalogID'];
$journal=$_GET['journal'];
$publisher= $_GET['publisher'];
$edition=$_GET['edition'];
$title= $_GET['title'];
$author=$_GET['author'];
```

We would connect with a database using PHP class library for database such as MySQL. Create a database entry using the PHP class library for MySQL. In the PHP script specify variables for username and password and connect with the MySQL database using the mysql_connect() function. The username "root" does not require a password by default. Specify the server parameter of the mysql_connect() method as localhost:3306.

```
$username='root';
$password='';
$connection    =    mysql_connect('localhost:3306',
$username, $password);
```

If a connection does not get established output the error message using the `mysql_error()` function.

```
if (!$connection) {
  $e = mysql_error($connection);
  echo "Error in connecting to MySQL Database.".$e;
}
```

We would need to select the database in which a table is to be created. Select the MySQL database instance "test" using the `mysql_select_db()` function.

```
$selectdb=mysql_select_db('test');
```

Create a SQL statement to add data to MySQL database. Database table Catalog consists of columns CatalogId, Journal, Publisher, Edition, Title, Author.

```
$sql   =   "INSERT   INTO   Catalog   VALUES($catalogid,
$journal,  $publisher, $edition, $title, $author)";
```

Run the SQL statement using the `mysql_query()` function.

```
$addrow=mysql_query ($sql, $connection );
```

Similary database table entries may be retrieved, updated and deleted.

3.4 CRUD with Java

A CRUD application with Java is developed using the JDBC API. JSPs may be used as the views for user input and struts/scrvlets may be used to connect with the database and create, retrieve, update, and delete database entries. First, we would need to create a datasource JNDI in an application server such as JBoss or WebLogic. Create a DataSource object using JNDI lookup.

```
javax.naming.InitialContext    ic      =    new
javax.naming.InitialContext();
 javax.sql.DataSource dataSource =
 (javax.sql.DataSource)ic.lookup("jdbc/MySQLDS");
```

We would need to obtain a connection with the database from the DataSource object.

```
java.sql.Connection        connection            =
dataSource.getConnection();
```

To create, read, update or delete a table row we would need to create a `Statement` object.

```
Statement stmt = connection.createStatement();
```

Next, we would require to specify the SQL statement to run. For example to add a row to a table *catalog* specify the following SQL statement.

```
String sql="INSERT INTO CATALOG VALUES ('Oracle
Magazine', 'Oracle Publishing', 'Jan-Feb 2007',
'Modeling Tables and Components', 'Steve Muench')";
```

We would run the SQL statement.

```
stmt.execute(sql);
```

Similarly, to retrieve data from database table we would need to run a SELECT sql statement, to update data run a UPDATE statement, and to delete data, run a DELETE statement.

3.5 Creating a Rails Application

In this section we shall create a Ruby on Rails application. The application that we shall create represents a journal catalog. The `rails` Ruby command is used to create a Ruby on Rails application. On the command line run the `rails` command to create an application.

```
C:\ruby>rails catalog
```

A rails application gets created in the *catalog* directory in the *rails_apps* directory. The *app* directory contains sub-directories *controllers*, *models* and *views* for the controller classes, model classes and view templates respectively. The *config* directory contains the *database.yml* file in which the database configuration is specified. A rails application may be run in development, test, or production mode. We shall run the rails application in development mode. Modify the development mode settings in *database.yml* file to specify the database as `mysql`. The development mode settings for MySQL database are shown below.

```
development:
adapter: mysql
database: test
username: root
password: password
host: localhost
```

The *db* directory is used for migration scripts, which we shall discuss in the next section.

3.6 Creating a Database Table

In this section we shall create an ActiveRecord migration script to create a database table. Migrations perform transformations on a database schema. Migrations support the MySQL, PostgreSQL, SQLite, SQL Server, Sybase and Oracle databases; the DB2 database is not supported. A migration class extends the `ActiveRecord::Migration` class and is run with the `rake` command. The `rake` command is similar to Ant's build tool for creating J2EE applications. A migration class may be created with the migration generator as follows.

```
C:/ruby/catalog>ruby script/generate migration
migrationname
```

A migration script gets created in the *db/migrate* directory. A migration script name has the format *nnn_migrationname*; nnn being the migration number, which is incremented for each additional migration in a rails application. A migration script gets created when a model class script is created. Create a model script with the following command in the Ruby Console Window.

```
C:\ruby\catalog>ruby script/generate model catalog
```

A model class `catalog.rb` gets created in the *app/models* directory. A migration script, based on migrations naming conventions, `001_create_catalogs.rb` gets created in the *db/migrate* directory. The migration script class, `CreateCatalogs`, extends the `ActiveRecord::Migration` class as shown in listing below.

```
class CreateCatalogs < ActiveRecord::Migration
  def self.up
    create_table :catalogs do |t|
       # t.column :name, :string
    end
  end
  def self.down
     drop_table :catalogs
  end
end
```

3.7 Migrations

All migration scripts consist of methods self.up and self.down, which contain the transformations required to implement (migrate) or remove (revert) the migration. Migrations are run with the following rake command.

```
>rake db:migrate VERSION=version number
```

The `rake db:migrate` command migrates the database through scripts in the *db/migrate* directory. The first time the rake db:migrate command is run on a database a `schema_info` table gets created, which has a version column specifying the current version of the migration applied to the database. VERSION is optional and if specified is required to be specified in uppercase. If VERSION is not specified rake migrates the database to the most recent version. The version number corresponds to the migration number of the migration scripts. The rake command runs all migrations with migration number up to version number. If the version number specified is higher than the current version the self.up method of migrations up to version number, including the migration with migration number the same as the version number specified, gets invoked starting with the current version. For example, if no migrations have yet been applied the following command implements migrations up to migration number 003 including the 003 migration.

```
>rake db:migrate VERSION=3
```

In the preceding example the self.up method of the migrations 001, and 002, and 003 gets invoked in order. If the current version number is higher than the version number specified the self.down method of all migrations up to version number, excluding the migration with migration number as the version number, get run starting with the current migration.

For example, if the current version is 4, the following command runs the self.down method of migrations 004, 003, and 002.

```
>rake db:migrate VERSION=1
```

Migrations are implemented (migrated) by specifying the version number to be higher than the current version and migrations are removed(reverted) by specifying the version number to be lower than the current version. The `self.up` method is usually invoked to create a database table and add columns, but the transformations in the self.up method may remove columns, and the transformations in the self.down method may add columns.

Next, we shall discuss migrations with an example. Create 4 migrations, *migration1*, *migration2*, *migration3*, and *migration4* in the Rails application catalog as shown in Figure 3.1.

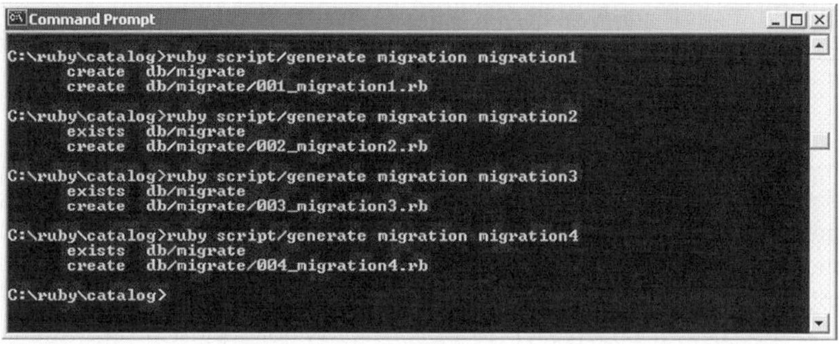

Fig. 3.1 Generating Migrations

A schema_info table also gets created for the selected database. Run a SELECT query on the schema_info table as shown in Figure 3.2. The version column specifies the current version as 0.

Fig. 3.2 Obtaining Migration Version

Run the rake db:migrate command. All the migrations get implemented in order as shown in Figure 3.3. The self.up methods of migrations migration1, migration2, migration3 and migration4 get invoked.

Fig. 3.3 Implementing Migrations

The version gets set to 4 corresponding to migration 004 as shown in Figure 3.4.

```
Command Prompt - mysql -u root                                    _ □ ×
mysql> SELECT * FROM schema_info;
+---------+
| version |
+---------+
|       4 |
+---------+
1 row in set (0.00 sec)

mysql>
```

Fig. 3.4 Migration Version Increased

Next, revert the migrations up to version 1 with the following command.

```
>rake db:migrate VERSION=1
```

Migrations migration4, migration3, and migration2 get reverted as shown in Figure 3.5. The self.down methods of migrations migration4, migration3, and migration2 get invoked.

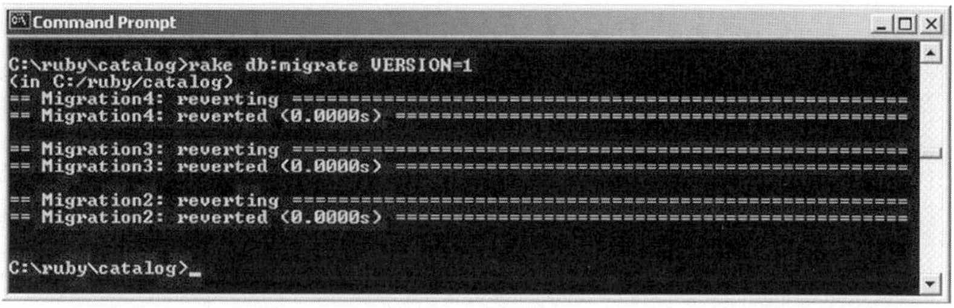

Fig. 3.5 Reverting Migrations

The current version gets set to 1 as shown in Figure 3.6.

Fig. 3.6 Migration Version Decreased

To revert migration migration1 run the rake db:migrate command with VERSION=0 as shown in Figure 3.7.

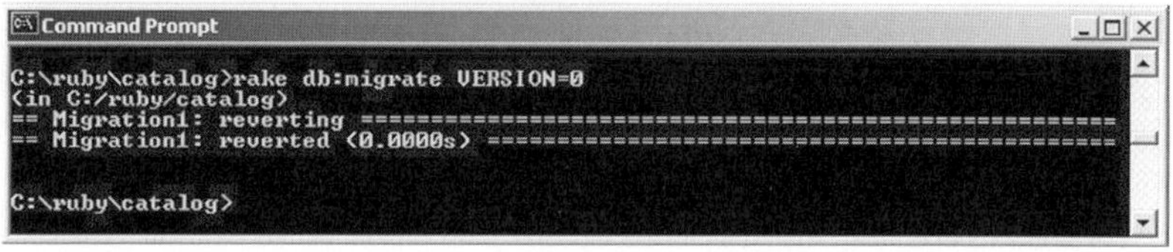

Fig. 3.7 Reverting migration1

When migrations are implemented by specifying version higher than the current version self.up methods of all the migrations, including the migration with migration number the same as the version number specified, gets invoked as shown in Figure 3.8.

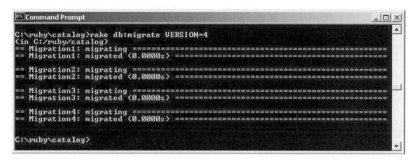

Fig. 3.8 Migrating to a Higher Migration Version

The self.up and self.down methods may also be used to run SQL with the execute statement. For example, in the following self.up method an ALTER statement is run.

```
def self.up
   execute "ALTER TABLE ..."
 end
```

The `create_table` transformation of class `ActiveRecord::Migration` is used to create a database table. ActiveRecord uses pluralization to map a model class to a database table. The model class is singular and upper case and the database table is plural and lower case. In the example Ruby on Rails application, the model class is `Catalog` and the database table is `catalogs`.

The `ActiveRecord::Migration` class provides various transformations for a database. Some of the transformations are discussed in Table 3.1.

Table 3.1 Migration Transformations

Transformation	Description
create_table(name, options)	Creates a table and makes the table available to a block to add columns. The options hash consists of fragments such as "DEFAULT CHARSET=UTF-8" and is used in the create table definition.
drop_table(name)	Drops a table
rename_table(old_name, new_name)	Renames a table.

Table 3.1 (continued)

Transformation	Description
add_column(table_name, column_name, type, options)	Adds a column. Options that may be specified are :default, :limit, and :null.
rename_column(table_name, column_name, new_column_name)	Renames a column
change_column(table_name, column_name, type, options)	Changes a column type
remove_column(table_name, column_name)	Removes a column

3.8 Creating catalogs Table with Migrations

Modify the migration script `001_create_catalogs.rb` to create a database table and add data to the table. In the `create_table` transformation create a table `catalogs` with columns journal, publisher, edition, title, author as shown in following listing.

```
create_table :catalogs do |t|
    t.column :journal, :string, :limit => 255
    t.column :publisher, :string, :limit => 255
    t.column :edition, :string, :limit => 255
    t.column :title, :string, :limit => 255
    t.column :author, :string, :limit => 255
end
```

Valid column types are integer, float, datetime, date, timestamp, time, text, string binary, and boolean. Valid column options are `limit`, `default` and `null`. Next, add data to the table with the `ActiveRecord::Base` class method `create`. The following listing adds a table row.

```
Catalog.create :journal => "developerWorks",
:publisher => "IBM", :edition => "September 2006",
:title=> "A PHP V5 migration guide", :author=>"Jack
D. Herrington"
```

The complete migration script, 001_create_catalogs.rb, is listed below.

```ruby
class CreateCatalogs < ActiveRecord::Migration
  def self.up
    create_table :catalogs do |t|
    t.column :journal, :string, :limit => 255
    t.column :publisher, :string, :limit => 255
    t.column :edition, :string, :limit => 255
     t.column :title, :string, :limit => 255
    t.column :author, :string, :limit => 255

end

Catalog.create :journal => "developerWorks",
:publisher => "IBM", :edition =>
"September 2006", :title=> "A PHP V5 migration
guide",:author=>"Jack D. Herrington"
Catalog.create :journal => "developerWorks",
:publisher => "IBM", :edition =>
"September 2006", :title=> "Make Ruby on Rails easy
with RadRails and Eclipse",:author=>"Pat Eyler"

  end

  def self.down
    drop_table :catalogs
  end
end
```

Run the migration with rake. Rails has a target called `migrate` to run migrations.

```
C:\ruby\catalog>rake db:migrate
```

A database table `catalogs` gets created in the MySQL database `test`. The catalogs table has a primary key field of type int(11) and has the `auto_increment` attribute. The auto_increment attribute generates a unique identity for new rows. For Oracle database, which does not support the auto_increment attribute, a sequence `catalogs_seq` also gets created.

3.9 Configuring with Oracle Database

In the previous section we configured Ruby on Rails with the MySQL database and created a table in the MySQL database. Ruby on Rails may also be configured with the Oracle database by modifying the connection parameters in the `database.yml` configuration file. First, we need to install the Oracle database. Download the Oracle 10g database[1] zip file.

Extract the *10201_database_win32.zip* file to an installation directory. Double-click on the *database/install/oui* application. The Oracle Universal Installer gets started. Click on the Next button. In the Select Installation Type frame select an installation type, Enterprise Edition for example. Click on the Next button. Specify an installation directory in the Specify Home Details frame and click on Next. In the Select Configuration Option frame select Create a Database, which creates a database instance, and click on Next. In the Select Database Configuration frame select General Purpose and click on Next. In the Specify Dataabse Configuration Options frame specify a Global Database Name and SID, or select the default 'orcl'. To create the sample schemas in the database instance select the Create Database with sample schemas checkbox. Click on Next. In the Select Database Management Option frame select Use Database Control for Database Management and click on Next. In the Specify Database Storage Option frame select File System (the default), or another storage option and click on Next. In the Specify Backup and Recovery Options frame select Enable Automated Backups to automate backups or select Do not Enable Automated backups. Click on Next. In the Specify Database Schema Passwords frame specify schema passwords or use the same password for the different schemas. Click on Next. In the Summary page click on Install. The database and the configuration assistants get installed.

We also need to install Ruby oci8 driver, which is required to connect to Oracle database from a Ruby on Rails application. Download the ruby-oci8-0.1.15-mswin32.rb[2] file. Cd to the c:/ruby directory and run the Ruby application ruby-oci8-0.1.15-mswin32.rb.

```
c:/ruby>ruby ruby-oci8-0.1.15-mswin32.rb
```

Modify the development environment settings in database.yml file to as shown below.

---

[1]Oracle   database   10g   -
http://www.oracle.com/technology/software/products/database/oracle10g/index.html

[2] Ruby OCI8 Driver- http://rubyforge.org/frs/?group_id=256

```
development:
 adapter: oci
  database: ORCL
  username: OE
  password: password
  host:
```

ORCL is the Oracle database instance. OE is the schema name. The host value should be kept empty.

3.10 Configuring with SQL Server 2005 Database

Ruby on Rails provides an adapter for the SQL Server database that may be used with an ADO driver. Install SQL Server 2005. First, install the .NET Framework 2.0[3]. Download Microsoft SQL Server 2005 Express Edition SP1[4]. Double-click on *SQLEXPR.EXE* application. SQL Server files get extracted and Microsoft SQL Server 2005 Setup wizard gets started. Accept the licensing terms and click on Next. In the Installing Prerequisites frame, click on Install button to install Microsoft SQL Native Client and Microsoft SQL Server 2005 Setup Support Files. Click on Next button. SQL Server Installation Wizard gets started. Click on Next. A System Configuration Check gets run. Click on Next button. In the Registration Information frame, specify registration information and click on button Next. In the Feature Selection frame, select Database Services node and click on Next. Install the SQL Server 2005 Express edition in Mixed Mode Authentication. In the Authentication Mode frame select Mixed Mode and specify a sa login password. Click on Next. In the Error and Usage Report Settings frame, select the checkboxes if error and features are to be reported automatically, and click on Next. In the Ready To Install frame click on Install button. The SQL Server components get configured. Click on Next. SQL Server installation gets completed. Click on Finish.

Next, enable TCP/IP protocol. Select Microsoft SQL Server 2005>Configuration Tools>SQL Server Configuration Manager. In the SQL Server Configuration Manager select the node SQL Server 2005 Network Configuration>Protocols for SQLEXPRESS. Right-click on the

---

[3].NET Framework 2.0- http://msdn2.microsoft.com/en-us/netframework/aa731542.aspx

[4]Microsoft SQL Server 2005 Express Edition SP1- http://msdn.microsoft.com/vstudio/express/sql/download/

TCP/IP node and select Enable. Restart the SQL Server (SQLEXPRESS) service. In Adminstrative Tools>Services, right-click on the SQL Server (SQLEXPRESS) service and select Restart.

Next, configure the Rails framework with the SQL Server database for the Windows operating system. The Rails installation includes a SQL Server adapter. The ADO driver is required to use the SQL Server adapter. Install the ADO driver. The ADO driver is included in the Ruby-DBI distribution. Obtain the Ruby-DBI distribution[5]. Extract the dbi-0.1.1.tar.gz file to a directory. Create an *ADO* directory in the *C:\ruby\lib\ruby\site_ruby\1.8\DBD* directory   and copy the *\ruby-dbi\lib\dbd\ADO.rb* file to the *ADO* directory.

Modify the database.yml configuration file in the *config* directory of the   Rails application   with the SQL Server database connection parameters as shown below.

```
development:
  adapter: sqlserver
  database: tempdb
  username: sqlserver
  password: sqlserver
  host: localhost, portnumber
  mode: DBI:ADO
```

Variable portnumber is obtained from the SQL Server configuration Manager. When the SQL Server 2005 SQLEXPRESS is restarted the port number changes. To obtain the portnumber in the SQL Server Configuration Manager, select the node SQL Server 2005 Network Configuration>Protocols for SQLEXPRESS. Right-click on TCP/IP node and select Properties. Select the IP Addresses tab. In IP ALL, the TCP Dynamic Ports specifies the portnumber value.

3.11 Developing a CRUD Application

In this section we shall develop a Ruby on Rails application. A Ruby on Rails application consists of the following Ruby scripts/view templates.

1. Model class in the app/models directory.
2. Controller class in the app/controllers directory.
3. View templates (RHTML files) in the views directory.
4. Database Configuration file (database.yml) in the config directory.

---

[5] Ruby-DBI Distribution- http://rubyforge.org/projects/ruby-dbi/

A MVC Ruby on Rails CRUD application may be developed either by creating the model and controller classes separately and adding scaffolding dynamically with the `scaffold` method in the controller class, or by creating the scaffolding classes and view templates with the Scaffold generator.   We shall discuss both the methods, and create scaffolding for a rails application with the scaffold generator.

3.11.1 Creating Dynamic Scaffolding

Dynamic scaffolding consists of creating model and controller separately and adding scaffolding using the scaffold method in the controller class. A model class is created with the following ruby command.

```
>ruby script/generate model catalog
```

This generates a ruby script `catalog.rb` in the *models* directory of the Rails application's *app* directory. The model class extends the `ActiveRecord::Base` class. Ruby script generated with example ruby command is listed in following listing.

```
class Catalog < ActiveRecord::Base

end
```

A controller class may be created with the following ruby command.

```
C:/ruby/catalog>ruby     script/generate     controller
catalog
```

A controlller class, which extends the `ApplicationController` class gets generated. Controller ruby script is shown in following listing.

```
class CatalogController < ApplicationController

end
```

Scaffolding may be added to the controller class by adding `scaffold:catalog`.

```
class CatalogController < ApplicationController

scaffold:catalog

end
```

By default, actions and views listed below get generated: `index`, `list`, `show`, `new`, `create`, `edit`, `update`, `destroy`. If the default actions views are to be overridden, create view templates corresponding to the actions. For example, to override the default view for edit action, create a view template edit.rhtml in the views/catalog directory of the Rails application.

3.11.2 Creating Scaffolding with Scaffold Generator

The rails framework provides the scaffold generator to create a controller class and a model class and add scaffolding to the controller class. Scaffolding is an interface to the data in the database. The interface is used to create new entries in the database, retrieve entries, update entries and delete entries. The syntax of the scaffold generator class is as follows.

```
C:/ruby/catalog>ruby script/generate scaffold
modelname, controllername,  action1, action2..
```

In the schema generator command, variable *modelname* specifies the model class and variable *controllername* specifies the controller class. Specifying controllername is optional. *Action1, action2..* specify the actions in the controller class and are optional to be specified. If the controller is not specified the plural form of the model name is used to create the controller class. Model name and controller name should not be suffixed with 'Model' or 'Controller'.

In the Ruby console window run the scaffold generator with the following command.

```
C:\ruby\catalog>ruby script/generate scaffold catalog
```

A model class, a controller class and view templates get generated. By default, actions and views listed below get generated: index, list, show, new, create, edit, update, destroy. Model class `Catalog` extends the ActiveRecord::Base class. The model class, Catalog, is shown in following listing.

```
class Catalog < ActiveRecord::Base
  end
```

The controller class created has the plural form of the model class. The controller class extends the ApplicationController class. The controller class `CatalogsController` is shown below.

```
class CatalogsController < ApplicationController
  def index
    list
    render :action => 'list'
  end
```

```ruby
  # GETs should be safe (see
http://www.w3.org/2001/tag/doc/whenToUseGet.html)
  verify :method => :post, :only => [ :destroy,
:create, :update ],
         :redirect_to => { :action => :list }

  def list
    @catalog_pages, @catalogs = paginate :catalogs,
:per_page => 10
  end

  def show
    @catalog = Catalog.find(params[:id])
  end

  def new
    @catalog = Catalog.new
  end

  def create
    @catalog = Catalog.new(params[:catalog])
    if @catalog.save
      flash[:notice] = 'Catalog was successfully
created.'
      redirect_to :action => 'list'
    else
      render :action => 'new'
    end
  end

  def edit
    @catalog = Catalog.find(params[:id])
  end

  def update
    @catalog = Catalog.find(params[:id])
    if @catalog.update_attributes(params[:catalog])
      flash[:notice] = 'Catalog was successfully
updated.'
      redirect_to :action => 'show', :id => @catalog
    else
      render :action => 'edit'
    end
  end

  def destroy
    Catalog.find(params[:id]).destroy
```

```
    redirect_to :action => 'list'
  end

  end
```

With the scaffolding the following actions (methods) get generated in the controller class :index, list, show, new, create, edit, update, destroy. The default view templates may be overridden with view templates in the views directory. For example, a custom view template edit.rhtml may be provided in the views/catalogs directory. A stylesheet *app/public/stylesheets/scaffold.css* also gets generated. A layout *catalogs.rhtml* gets generated in the *views/layouts* directory. Next, we shall run the Ruby on Rails application in WeBrick web server. Start the WEBrick server with the following command.

```
C:\ruby\catalog>ruby script/server
```

The WeBrick server gets started. Access the WeBrick web server with URL http://localhost:3000 as shown in Figure 3.9.

Fig. 3.9 WeBrick Console

Display the list of catalog entries with the `list` view template, which is invoked with the URL http://localhost:3000/catalogs/list. To create a new catalog entry click on the New catalog link as shown in Figure 3.10.

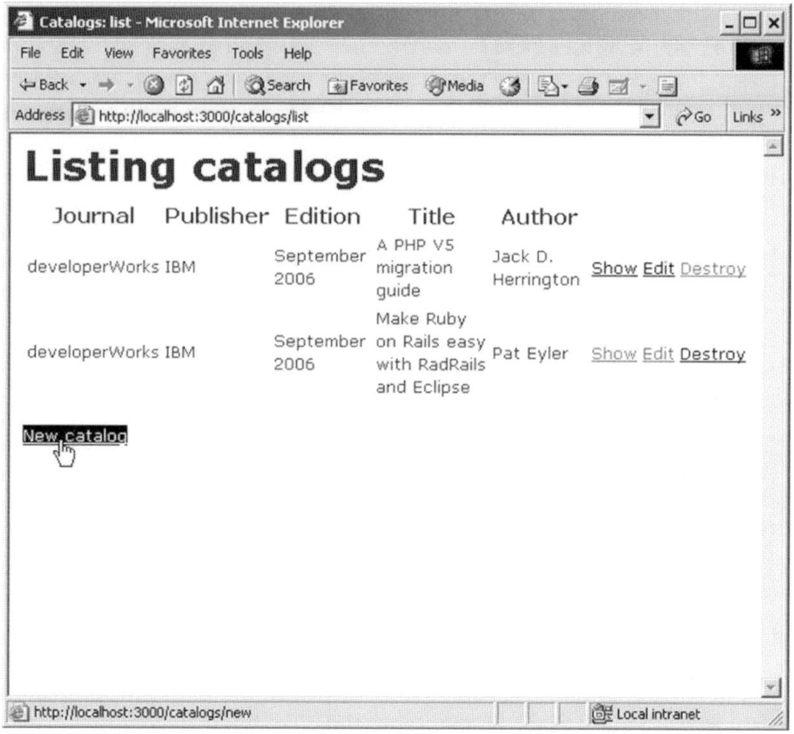

Fig. 3.10 Listing Catalog Entries

In the `new` view template add a catalog entry and click on the Create button as shown in Figure 3.11.

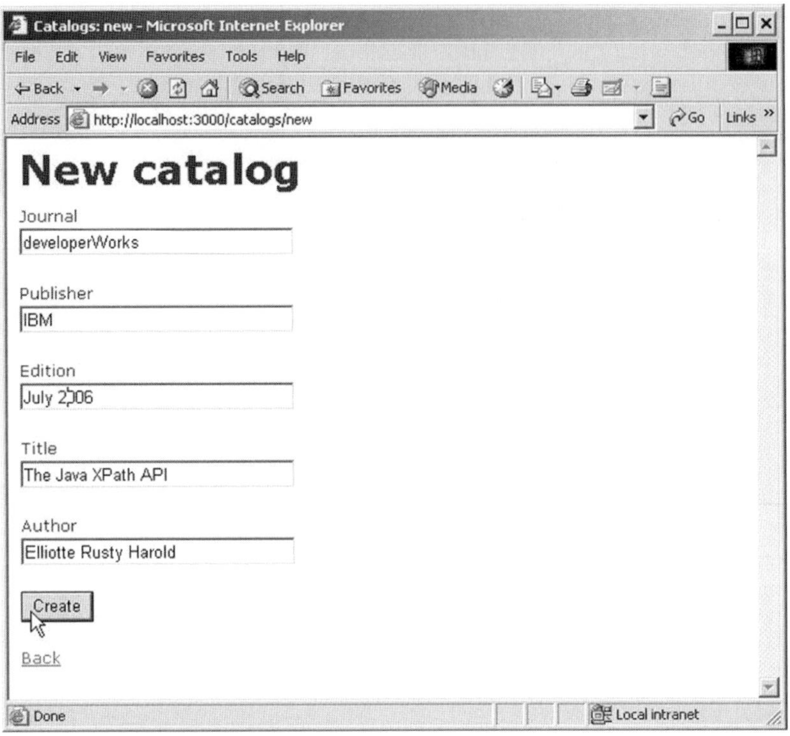

Fig. 3.11 Creating a New Catalog Entry

A new catalog entry gets added as shown in the list view template. To show a catalog entry click on the Show link. To delete a catalog entry click on the Destroy link. To edit a catalog entry click on the Edit link as shown in Figure 3.12.

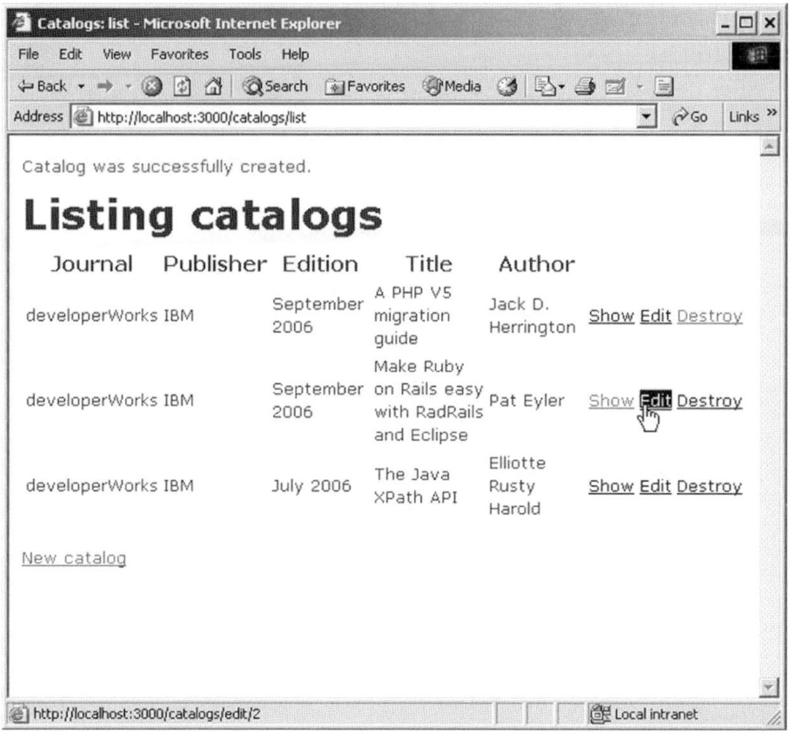

Fig. 3.12 Selecting Edit

In the edit view template modify the catalog entry, for example, modify the title and click on the Edit button as shown in Figure 3.13.

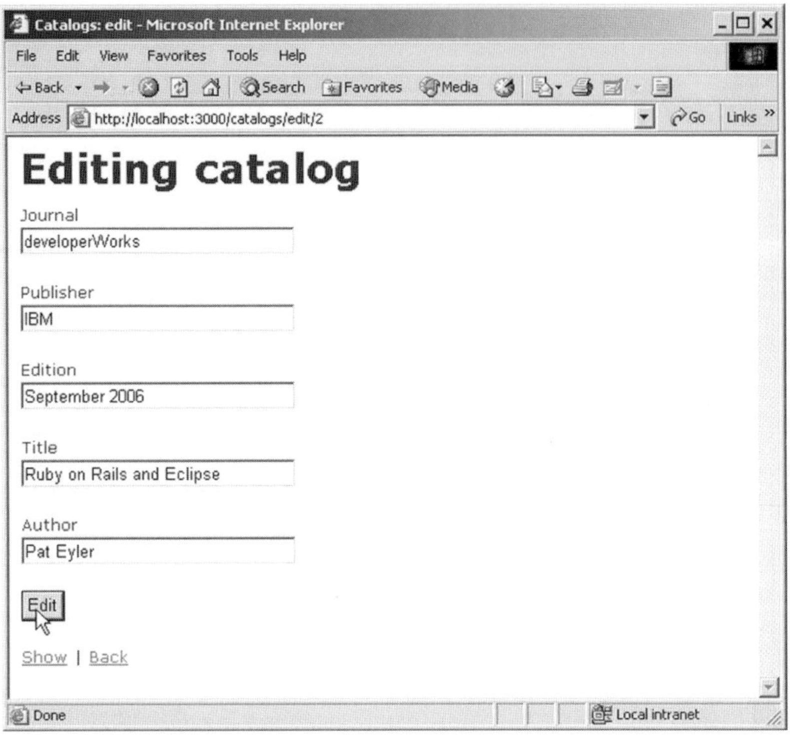

Fig. 3.13 Editing a Catalog Entry

Catalog entry gets updated as shown in Figure 3.14.

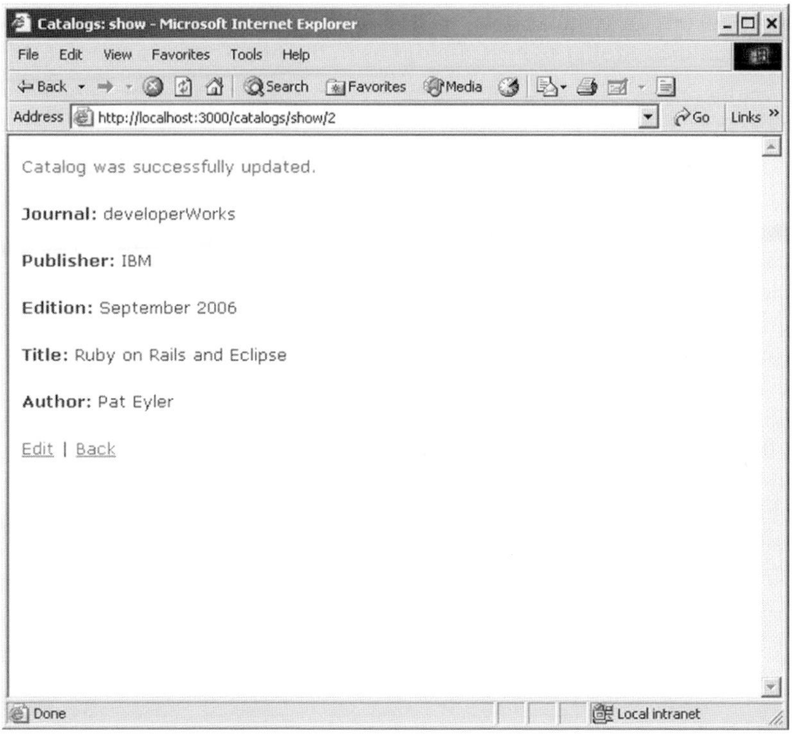

Fig. 3.14 Updated Catalog Entry

3.12 Ajax Scaffolding

We shall be discussing Ajax with Ruby on Rails in the next chapter. But, because the Ajax functionality may be added to scaffolding we shall introduce Ajax in this chapter. Ajax is a web technique with which XML data may be transferred between a browser and a server without reloading the web page. To add Ajax functionality to the scaffolding install the `ajax_scaffold_generator` gem. Run the following command while connected to the internet.

```
C:/ruby>gem install ajax_scaffold_generator
```

Gem ajax_scaffold_generator.3.1.10 gets installed. Create a rails application, modify the database.yml and create a catalogs table using migrations as in the non Ajax scaffolding example. Run the Ajax scaffold generator on the database table "catalogs". We shall use model name Catalog and controller name Catalogs as in the non-Ajax example.

```
C:/ruby/railsapp> ruby script/generate ajax_scaffold
Catalog
```

Controller class `CatalogsController` in Ruby script `catalogs_controller.rb` gets generated. The controller actions new, create, update, list, cancel, edit, destroy and view templates new.rjs, create.rjs, update.rjs, list.rhtml, cancel.rjs, edit.rjs, destroy.rjs get generated. CSS stylesheets for the view templates also get generated. Start the WEBrick web server and invoke the URL http://localhost:3000/catalogs. The catalogs table entries get displayed in the `list` action view template. The CRUD view templates use Ajax for addition, update, and delete operations. To create a new catalog entry click on the Create New link as shown in Figure 3.15.

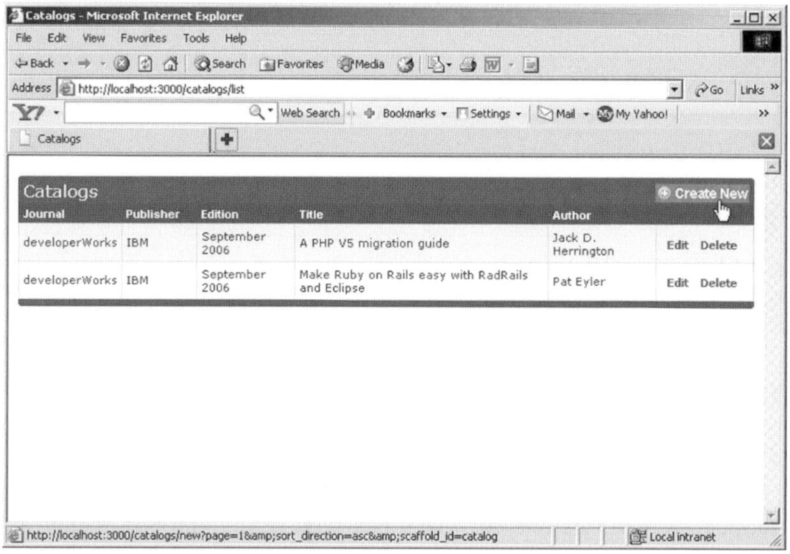

Fig. 3.15 Create New

The Create Catalog window opens in the same view template with Ajax. In the Create Catalog frame specify values for a new catalog entry and click on Create as shown in Figure 3.16.

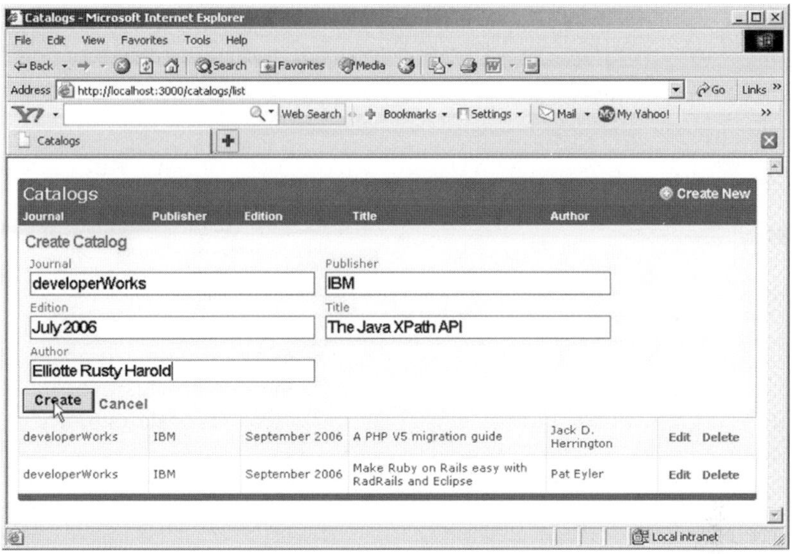

Fig. 3.16 Creating new Catalog Entry

A new catalog entry gets added to the catalogs table and gets displayed in the list action view template. To edit a catalog entry click on Edit as shown in Figure 3.17.

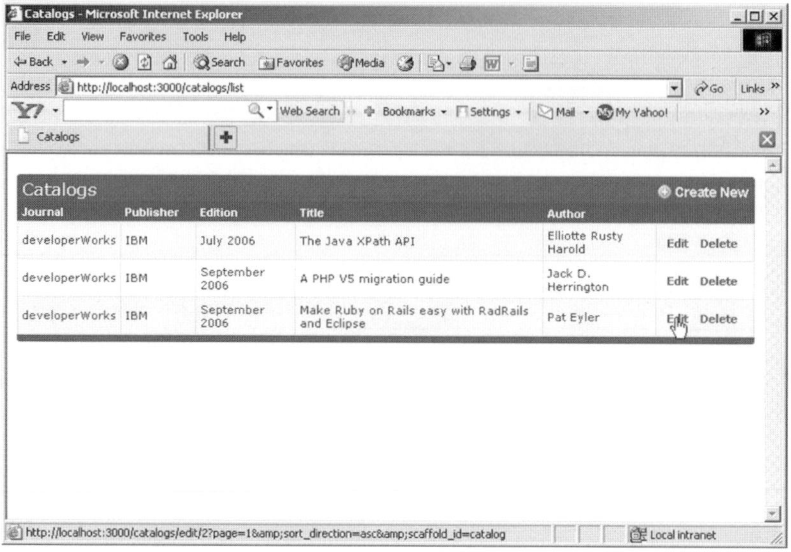

Fig. 3.17 Editing Catalog Entry

In the Update Catalog frame modify the field values and click on Update as shown in Figure 3.18.

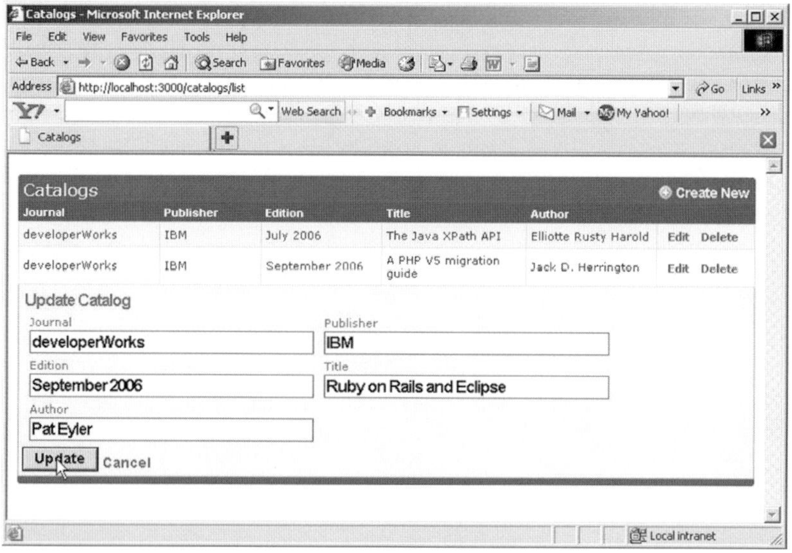

Fig. 3.18 Updating Catalog

The catalog entry gets modified. To delete a catalog entry click on Delete as shown in Figure 3.19.

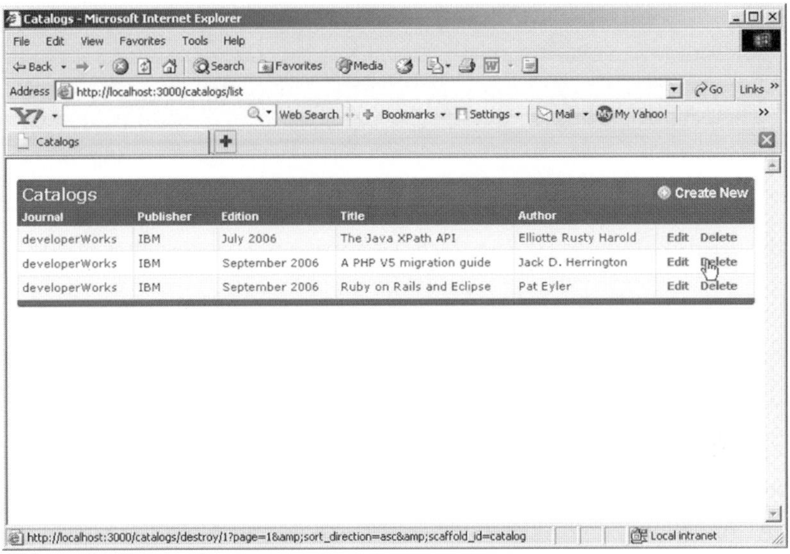

Fig. 3.19 Deleting Catalog Entry

The catalog entry gets deleted as shown in Figure 3.20. A difference between the Ajax scaffolding example and the non-Ajax scaffolding example is that in the Ajax scaffolding example only the list action view template is displayed and the catalog entry addition, update and delete operations are performed using .rjs templates. In the non-Ajax scaffolding example the view templates for the different controller actions are displayed.

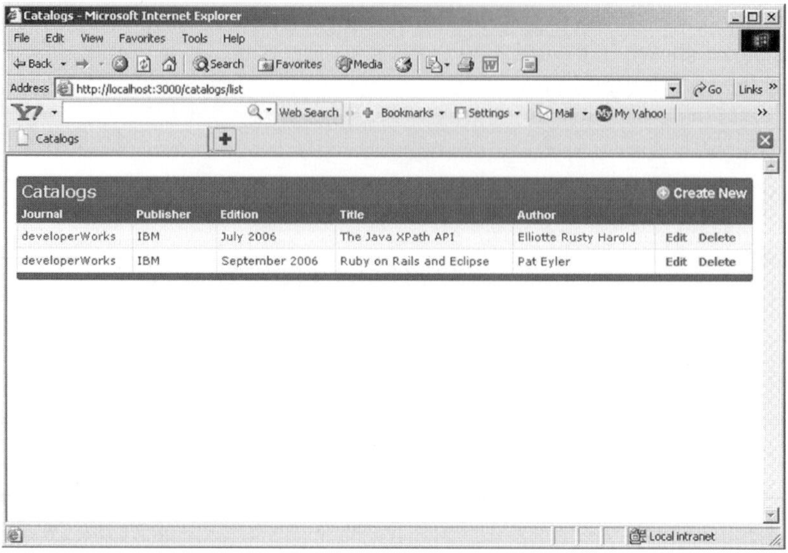

Fig. 3.20 Catalogs table with an entry deleted

3.13 Validations

The Rails framework has the provision to validate fields. For example, set the journal field as a required field. To the catalog.rb script model class Catalog add the following line.

```
validates_presence_of :journal
```

In the views/catalogs/_form.rhtml modify the following line.

```
<label  for="catalog_journal">Journal</label>
```

Modify the line to the following.

```
<label                                class="required"
for="catalog_journal">Journal*</label>.
```

Invoke the Ajax scaffolding with the url http://localhost:3000/catalogs. Click on Create New to create a new catalog entry. The Journal field has a asterix indicating that the field is a required field. Specify values for all the fields except the Journal field and click on Create as shown in Figure 3.21.

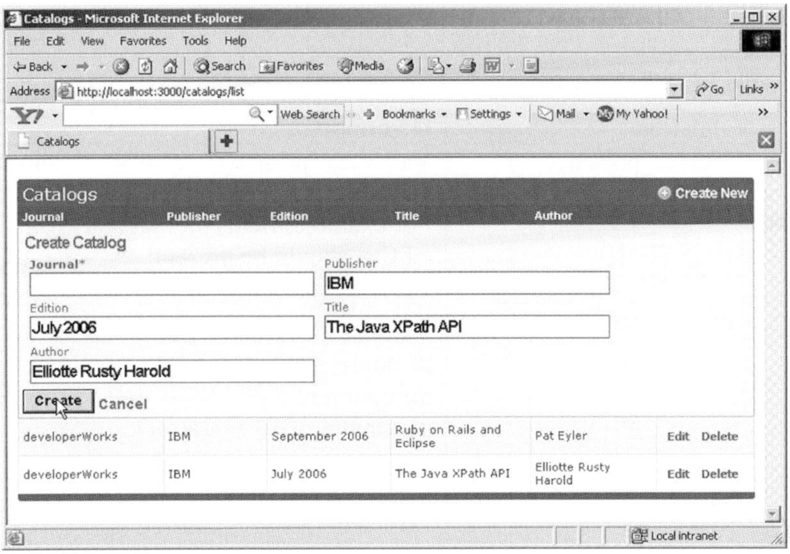

Fig. 3.21 Validating Fields

An error message gets displayed indicating that the Journal field may not be empty as shown in Figure 3.22.

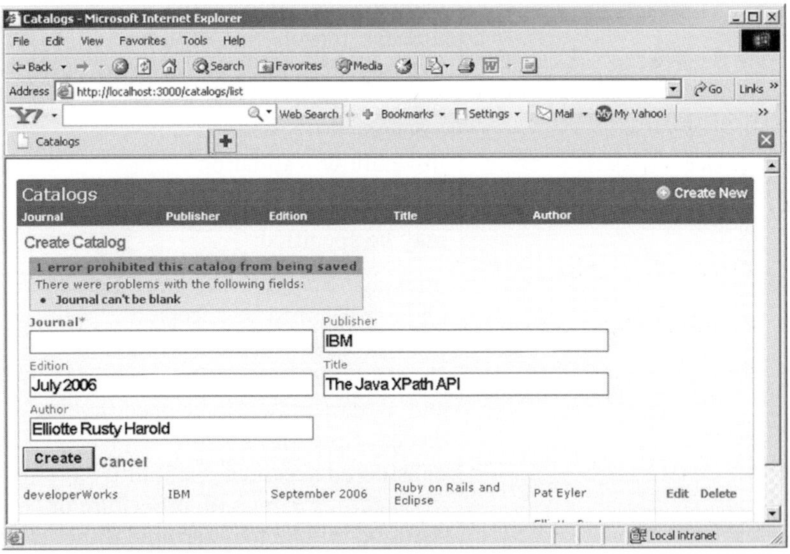

Fig. 3.22 Validation Error

The Rails Validations that may be specified are discussed in Table 3.2.

Table 3.2 Rails Validations

Validation	Description
validates_presence_of	Validates presence of one or more fields. For example, fields journal and edition should be present: validates_presence_of:journal, :edition
validates_length_of	Validates length of a field. For example, catalogid should be minimum of 8 characters and maximum of 16 characters: validates_length_of :catalogid, :minimum => 8 :maximum => 16
validates_acceptance_of	Validates the acceptance of a condition. For example, a checkbox, license_terms, should accept the value "1". validates_acceptance_of :license_terms, :message => "must be accepted", :on =>:save, :accept=>"1", :if=>:allow_validation The following configuration options may be specified: :message-Specifies the error message. Default is "must be accepted". :on-Specifies when the validation should occur. Default is :save. :create and :update may also be specified. :accept-Specifies a value that is considered accepted. Default is "1". :if-Specifies a method, procedure or string to invoke to determine if the validation should occur.

Table 3.2 (continued)

Validation	Description
validates_confirmation_of	Validates confirmation of a field. For example, validate confirmation of user_name field:
	validates_confirmation_of :user_name, :message => "doesn't match confirmation", :on=>:save, :if=>:allow_validation
	Fields user_name and user_name_confirmation are presented in the user view. The following configuration options may be specified:
	:message-Specifies the error message. Default is "doesn't match confirmation". :on-Specifies when the validation should occur. Default is :save. :create and :update may also be specified. :if-Specifies a method, procedure or string to invoke to determine if the validation should occur.
validates_uniqueness_of	Validates uniqueness of a field. For example, catalogid should be unique:
	validates_uniqueness_of :catalogid

Table 3.2 (continued)

Validation	Description
validates_format_of	Validates format of a field. For example, zip code should match a specified regular expression: validates_format_of :zipcode :with => /(^\d{5}$)\|(^\d{5}-\d{4}$)/
validates_numericality_of	Validates that a field is a number. For example, the catalogid field should be an integer: validates_numericality_of :catalogid,:on => :create,:message=>"is not an integer",:only_integer=>true, :allow_nil=>false, :if=>:allow_validation The following configuration options may be specified: :message - Specifies a custom error message. Default is "is not a number". :on- Specifies when the validaion should occur. Default is :save. :create and :update may also be specified. :only_integer-Specifies whether the value is required to be an integer. Default is false. :allow_nil-Specifies if nil values may be specified. Default is false. :if -Specifies a method, procedure or string to invoke to determine if the validation should occur.

Table 3.2 (continued)

Validation	Description
validates_inclusion_in	Validates if the field value is included in the specified list of values. For example, journal value should be one of developerWorks, DB2 Magazine or WebSphere Journal:
	validates_inclusion_of :journal, :in=>%w(developerWorks,DB2 Magazine,WebSphere Journal), :message=>"is not included in the list", :allow_nil=>false, :if=>:allow_validation
	The following configuration options may be specified:
	:in-Enumeration of values. :message - Specifies a custom error message. Default is "is not included in the list". :allow_nil-Specifies if nil values may be specified. Default is false. :if -Specifies a method, procedure or string to invoke to determine if the validation should occur.

Table 3.2 (continued)

Validation	Description
validates_exclusion_of	Validates that field value is not in the specified enumeration. For example, the cataloged should not be in the range of 0-10.
	validates_exclusion_of :catalogid, :in=>0..10, :message =>"is reserved", :allow_nil=>false, :if=>:allow_validation
	The configuration options are the same as for validates_inclusion_in.The default error message is "is reserved".
validates_associated	Validates if associated objects are also valid.

3.14 Summary

In this chapter we discussed the   scaffolding for CRUD operations provided by the Rails framework. We discussed the different types of scaffoldings and created a CRUD application to create, read, update and delete catalog entries in MySQL database. We also configured Rails with Oracle and SQL Server 2005 databases. We discussed the Ajax scaffolding, which adds Ajax to the CRUD. We also discussed Rails validations. Ruby on Rails is simpler than J2EE and PHP for developing MVC CRUD applications. JSPs/HTMLs, servlets, EJBs, and configuration fields that are required in a J2EE application are not required for a Ruby on Rails application. A connection with the database is not required to be obtained and SQL statements are not required to be run as in PHP and Java.

4 Ajax on Rails

4.1 Introduction

Ajax is an XMLHttpRequest based web technique with which data may be transferred between a client application and a web server and sections of the web page updated with the XMLHttpRequest response without reloading the web page. Rails facilitates the development of a dynamic web application by supporting Ajax functions with which an XMLHttpRequest request may be made to a web server. In this chapter we shall develop an Ajax application using the Rails framework and MySQL database.

4.2 Overview of Ajax

Asynchronous JavaScript and XML (Ajax) is a web technique for developing asynchronous web applications. Ajax combines the XMLHttpRequest object with JavaScript and XML Document Object Model (DOM) technologies to provide asynchronous interaction between a web client and a server. Asynchronous implies that a HTTP request send() method returns immediately, thus providing dynamic interaction between a web page and a server. The XMLHttpRequest object is used to implement the Asynchronous JavaScript for XML (Ajax) web technique. The XMLHttpRequest object transfers XML data between a client and a server. XMLHttpRequest object was introduced as an ActiveX object in IE5, and is a window object property in IE7. Asynchronous communication between a client and a server in a web application has various applications. Google's Gmail is an example of an Ajax application. Some of the other Ajax applications are listed below.

1. Dynamic Form Data Validation. As an example, suppose a user fills out a form to register with a web site. The validity of data in the form

is not checked till the form is submitted. With Ajax, the data added to the form is dynamically validated using business logic in a server application. Thus, a complete form does not have to be posted to the server to check if data in the form is valid.

2. Auto completion. As a user adds some data to a form, the remaining form gets auto completed.

3. Refreshing data on a page. Some web pages require that data be refreshed frequently, a weather web site for example. Using the AJAX technique, a web page may poll the server for latest data and refresh the web page without reloading the page.

4.3 Overview of XMLHttpRequest

XMLHttpRequest object provides asynchronous communication between a client application, which may be an HTML/JavaScript page, and a server application, which may be a Java Servlet. With the XMLHttpRequest object, XML data may be submitted to a server and retrieved from the server response without reloading a web page. The XML data received in a response may be rendered on the client side using XML DOM and XSLT. Microsoft in IE 5 introduced XMLHttpRequest for Windows as an ActiveX component. Internet Explorer 6 also implements XMLHttpRequest as an ActiveX object. In IE 7, XMLHttpRequest was introduced as a window object property. The XMLHttpRequest object provides various attributes/properties and methods to implement HTTP client functionality. The XMLHttpRequest attributes/properties are discussed in Table 4.1. In subsequent sections we shall discuss the procedure to use these attributes in a web application.

Table 4.1 XMLHttpRequest Attributes

Attribute/Property	Description
onreadystatechange	Specifies the callback method for asynchronous requests
readyState	Retrieves the current state of a HTTP request
responseText	Retrieves the server response as text
responseXML	Retrieves the server response as an XML DOM object.

Table 4.1 (continued)

Attribute/Property	Description
responseBody	Retrieves the response body
status	Retrieves the HTTP status code[1] of the request.
statusText	Retrieves the text of the HTTP status.

The XMLHttpRequest object methods are used to create an XMLHttpRequest object, open a request, set request headers, get and set response headers, and send a request. XMLHttpRequest methods are discussed in Table 4.2.

Table 4.2 XMLHttpRequest Methods

Method	Description
abort()	Cancels the current HTTP request.
getAllResponseHeaders()	Retrieves all the response headers if readyState value is 3 or 4. Returns null if readyState is 0, 1, or 2.
getResponseHeader(string header)	Returns a specified response header if readyState value is 3 or 4. Returns null if readyState is 0, 1, or 2.
open(string method, string url[, boolean asynch][,string username][, string password])	Opens a HTTP request with a specified method and URL
send(data)	Sends a HTTP request to the server and recieves an XML response.
setRequestHeader(string headerName, string headerValue)	Sets HTTP request headers if readyState value is 1.

---

[1] Status Code Definitions- http://www.w3.org/Protocols/rfc2616/rfc2616-sec10.html

4.4 Creating an XMLHttpRequest Object

Before a client application may send a HTTP request, an XMLHttpReuest is required to be created. XMLHttpRequest is implemented as an ActiveX component in IE 5 and 6, and as a window object property in IE 7. An XMLHttpRequest object is created in IE 6 with the following script, which may be specified in a client application.

```
<script>
if (window.ActiveXObject) {
var req = new ActiveXObject("Microsoft.XMLHTTP");
</script>
```

In Internet Explorer 7, XMLHttpRequest is implemented as a window object property. An XMLHttpRequest object in IE7 is created with the following script that may be specified in a JavaScript application.

```
<script>
if (window.XMLHttpRequest) {
var req = new XMLHttpRequest();
}
</script>
```

After an XMLHttpRequest object has been created, the readyState property is set to 0. At this stage, an XMLHttpRequest object has been created, but not initialized.

4.5 Opening an HTTP Request

After an XMLHttpRequest object has been created, open an HTTP request using the open(string method, string url[, boolean asynch][, string username][, string password]) method. The open() method initializes a HTTP request, but does not send the request. HTTP method and server URL are required parameters of the open() method. The URL may be relative or absolute. Boolean parameter asynch specifies if the HTTP request is asynchronous or synchronous. The default value of the asynch is true. In the following example, an HTTP request is opened with HTTP method GET and a relative URL to an JSP page, *validate.jsp*. The userId parameter is included   in   the   URL.   JavaScript   method encodeURIComponent(String) is used to encode userId value.

```
<script>
var userId=document.getElementById("userId");
req.open("GET", "validate.jsp?userId="+
encodeURIComponent(userId), true);
</script>
```

After the open() method has been invoked, the `readyState` property is set to 1. Attributes `responseText`, `responseXML`, status, and `statusText` are set to their initial values.

4.6 Sending an HTTP Request

After opening a HTTP request, register a callback method using the `onreadystatechange` property. The callback method is invoked when the value of the readyState property changes. In the following example callback event handler *requestCallback* is registered with the XMLHttpRequest object using the `onreadystatechange` property.

```
<script>
req.onreadystatechange=requestCallback;
</script>
```

Next, send an HTTP request with the `send(data)` method. The data parameter may be a string, an array of unsigned bytes, or an XML DOM object. The data may be set to `null`. The `send()` method is asynchronous if the boolean parameter asynch of the open() method is set to true, and synchronous if the asynch is set to false. A asynchronous method returns immediately, a synchronous method does not return till the HTTP request is complete and the entire response has been received.

```
<script>
req.send(null);
</script>
```

After the `send()` method has been invoked, the readyState property value is set to 2. At this stage, the status and headers are not available. When the HTTP request has completed, the readyState property is set to 4.

4.7 Processing an HTTP Response

In the previous section a callback method was registered with the XMLHttpRequest object. The callback method gets invoked when the readyState property changes. A readyState value of 3 indicates that some data has been received, but response headers and status are not completely available. At this stage, the responseXML property value is null. The responseText property value contains partial response data.   A readyState property value of 4 indicates that response headers are completely set and all the data has been received. In the requestCallback method, check the value of the readyState property. If the readyState property value is 4 and the status is 200, which corresponds to "Ok", invoke the JavaScript function *response()* as shown in following script.

```
<script>
function requestCallback(){
  if(req.readyState==4){
    if(req.status==200){

      response();
      }
    }
  }
</script>
```

In the response() function, the values of the responseXML, responseBody, and responseText properties may be retrieved to modify the page content on the page that initiated the HTTP request. The responseXML property contains an XML DOM object that may be processed to obtain element and attribute values.

```
<script>
function response(){
var  xmlResponse=req.responseXML;
var  textResponse=req.responseText;
...
}
</script>
```

4.8 Ajax with PHP

Various Ajax frameworks for PHP are available, for example, Xajax and Sajax. Xajax is used to communicate asynchronously between a client application and a server side application comprised of PHP scripts. Xajax generates JavaScript wrapper functions for PHP functions on the server side that may be accessed from a client application. When a client application invokes the wrapper functions, an XMLHttpRequest object is initiated and an XMLHttpRequest request is sent to the server. On the server, the Xajax object receives the XMLHttpRequest request and invokes the PHP functions corresponding to the JavaScript wrapper functions. The default request type of PHP functions registered through Xajax is POST. The PHP functions process the data and return an XML response that is returned to the client application by the Xajax object. Based on the instructions in the XML response, the Xajax's JavaScript message pump updates the content of the client input page. Xajax has a feature that, data is updated only if data has been modified.

4.9 Ajax with Java

Similar to PHP, various Ajax frameworks are available for Java, some of which are AjaxTags, Direct Web Remoting (DWR), and Google Web Toolkit (GWT). AjaxTags is a tag library for implementing the Ajax web technique in a JSP page. AjaxTags provides various tags to implement the Ajax functionality some of which are ajax:anchors, ajax:select, ajax:autocomplete, ajax:htmlContent and ajax:updateField. For example, ajax:htmlContent fills a DOM element with the HTML content returned by the server. Direct Web Remoting (DWR) is a Java open source library for developing Ajax applications. DWR consists of two components: JavaScript running in the browser that sends requests and dynamically updates the web page with the response, and a Servlet running on the server that processes requests and sends response back to the browser. Remoting in DWR implies that Java class methods are remoted as JavaScript functions in the browser. DWR dynamically generates JavaScript corresponding to Java classes and the JavaScript may be run in the browser just as any other JavaScript class library. The JavaScript functions generated corresponding to Java class methods have a callback function as one of the parameters. The remote methods are invoked in the browser using a callback function and the request is sent to the server using Ajax. When the request is complete a response is returned to the browser using Ajax. The callback function specified in the remote method gets invoked with the data returned from the server and the web page may be updated with the server response. Google Web Toolkit (GWT) is a Java framework for developing Ajax applications. Ajax being a JavaScript based web technique, GWT generates the required JavaScript and HTML from the Java classes. GWT provides a library of dynamic, reusable user interface (UI) components for UI applications. Only a front-end Java class is required to be specified to create a GWT application.

4.10 Support for Ajax in Rails

Rails provides support for Ajax in the Prototype JavaScript Framework, which is a set of methods that return the required JavaScript to implement the method. The Prototype helpers are provided in the `ActionView::Helpers::PrototypeHelper` class. Using Ajax, controller methods may be invoked from JavaScript code in a view without posting a web page to the server. Some of the methods in the Prototype JavaScript framework are discussed in Table 4.3.

Table 4.3 Rails Prototype JavaScript Methods

Prototype Method	Description
link_to_remote	Returns a link to a remote object
form_remote_tag	Returns a form tag that will submit using XMLHttpRequest.
submit_to_remote	Returns a button input that will submit a form with XMLHttpRequest.
observe_field	Observes a field with a specified DOM ID and invokes a specified url using XMLHttptRequest. Updates innerHTML of a specified DOM ID with XMLHttpRequest response text.
observe_form	Similar to observe_field, but for a form.
update_page	Updates a web page using XMLHttpRequest.

Table 4.3 (continued)

Prototype Method	Description
periodically_call_remote	Periodically invokes a specified url using XMLHttpRequest and updates a specified div with XMLHttpRequest response text.
update_element_function	Returns a JavaScript function that will update a specified element using XMLHttpRequest.

We shall discuss each of these functions in some detail. Callback functions may be invoked at various stages of the Ajax request. Callback functions are specified using callback options. The callback options that are used with the ActionView::Helpers::PrototypeHelper class are discussed in Table 4.4.

Table 4.4 Callback Options

Callback Option	Description
:uninitialized	Invoked when an XMLHttpRequest object has been created, but not yet initialized; readyState value is 0.
:loading	Invoked when the open() method on the XMLHttpRequest object has been invoked, but the send() method has not yet been invoked. ReadyState value is 1.
:loaded	Invoked when the send() method has been invoked. The readyState value is 2.
:interactive	Invoked when the response has not completely been received. The readyState value is 3.

Table 4.4 (continued)

Callback Option	Description
:success	Invoked when XMLHttpRequest is completed and the HTTP status code is in the range of 2xx.
:failure	Invoked when the XMLHttpRequest is completed and the HTTP status is not in the range of 2xx.
:complete	Invoked when the XMLHttpRequest is completed and the :failure or :success callbacks have been invoked, if present.

4.10.1 link_to_remote

The link_to_remote method returns a link, which is invoked using XMLHttpRequest, to a remote action specified with the :url option. The XMLHttpRequest response may be used to update a DOM object whose id may be specified using the :update option. The callback options may be used to invoke JavaScript functions. For example, a link to controller action *update_catalog* may be created that updates div *catalog*.

```
link_to_remote    "Update    Catalog",    :update    =>
"catalog",:url    =>    {    :action    =>"update_catalog",
:id=>catalog.id }
```

The :position option may be used to specify how the target DOM is to be updated. The :position option may have a value of :before, :top, :bottom, or :after. By default the remote request is asynchronous during which the callbacks may be invoked. Callbacks are invoked with the XMLHttpRequest object "request".

Browser side invocation logic may be customized with JavaScript code snippets invoked using some optional parameters, discussed in Table 4.5.

Table 4.5 Browser Optional Parameters

Parameter	Description
:confirm	Adds a confirmation dialog.
:condition	Perform remote request conditionally using the specified condition.
:before	Invoked before request is invoked.
:after	Invoked after request is initiated and before :loading
:submit	Submit using the specified DOM ID as the container element for the form elements, instead of the form element.

4.10.2 form_remote_tag

The `form_remote_tag` method returns a form tag that submits using XMLHttpRequest instead of HTTP POST. The :url and callback options are the same as for link_to_remote. For example, invoke the *process_form* action when a form is submitted. When the XMLHttpRequest is completed, invoke the *processResponse* function. In the controller class the form elements are available in `params` hash.

```
form_remote_tag  :url => { :action =>"process_form",
:id=>catalog.id } :complete=>"processResponse"
```

4.10.3 submit_to_remote

The `submit_to_remote` method returns a button input tag that will submit using XMLHttpRequest. The same options as in the form_remote_tag may be specified. For example a form has fields journal

and edition and buttons Create and Update, which are created using the
submit_to_remote tag.

```
<form>
    <label for="journal">Journal:</label> <input
id="journal"
 type="text" name="journal" /><br />
    <label for="edition">Edition:</label> <input
id="edition"
 type="text" name="edition" /><br />
    <%= submit_to_remote 'button', 'Create', :url =>
{ :action =>
 'create' } %>
    <%= submit_to_remote 'button', 'Update', :url =>
{ :action =>
 'update' } %>
    </form>
```

4.10.4 observe_field

The `observe_field` method observes a field with the specified DOM
ID and sends an Ajax request when the field value has changed. Either the
:url or the :function option is required. The :url option invokes a
controller action and the :function option invokes a function using
XMLHttpRequest. Additional options that may be specified are discussed
in Table 4.6.

Table 4.6 observe_field Options

Option	Description
:frequency	Specifies the frequency in seconds after which the field is polled. If value specified is –ve, 0 or a value is not specified, event based observation is used instead of time based observation.
:update	Specifies the DOM ID whose innerHTML is to be update with XMLHttpRequest response text.

Table 4. 6 (continued)

Option	Description
:with	Specifies a JavaScript expression that contains the XMLHttpRequest request parameters. Defaults to 'value', which refers to the field value.
:on	Specifies the event handler to observe. By default is set to "changed" for form fields and text areas and "click" for radio buttons and checkboxes. Another event handler such as "blur" and "focus" may be set with :on.

4.10.5 observe_form

The `observe_form` method is similar to observe_field except that the entire form is observed instead of a field. The options are the same as for observe_field, except the :with option default value, which is set to a string containing the field names and field values in the form.

4.10.6 periodically_call_remote

The `periodically_call_remote` method is used to invoke a controller action, specified in the :url option, periodically (default is 10 seconds) and update a div, specified with the :update option, using the XMLHttpRequest response. The :url and callback options are the same as for link_to_remote.

4.10.7 update_element_function

The `update_element_function` returns a JavaScript function that updates a DOM element. The options that may be used with the update_element_function are discussed in Table 4.7.

Table 4.7 Options for update_element_functions

Option	Description
:content	The content to use for updating. The :content option may contain Ruby variables set in the controller class.
:action	Specifies the action to be performed on the element. Values that may be specified are :update, :empty, or :remove. The default value is :update. The :empty value empties the element. The :remove value removes the element.
:position	If the :action option is set to :update, specifies the position at which the content is updated. Specified value may be :before, :top, :bottom, :after

For example, update the journal element with the *@journal* variable set in the controller class. Position the update value after the current value in the element.

```
<%= update_element_function(
        "journal", :action => :update, :position =>
:after,:content => "<p>#{@journal.name}</p>")) %>
```

4.10.8 update_page

The update_page method is used to update multiple elements in a page using the JavaScriptGenerator. Returns JavaScript code in the Ajax response.

4.11 Creating a Ruby on Rails Application

In this section we shall create a Ruby on Rails Ajax application using the Model-View-Controller pattern.   Install MySQL 5.0 database if not already installed and create a database instance. Create a Rails application, *ajaxrails*, with the following command.

```
c:/ruby>rails ajaxrails
```

A Rails application directory structure gets generated. The root directory of the Rails application is `ajaxrails`. The `app` directory consists of sub-directories `models`, `views` and `controllers` for model classes, view templates and controller classes respectively. The `config` directory consists of a `database.yml` configuration file in which a database configuration is defined. By default the MySQL database is configured. The `db` directory consists of a sub-directory `migrate` that consists of migrations that will be discussed in the next section.

4.12 Creating a Database Table

In this chapter we shall develop a Rails application with the Prototype JavaScript framework, which implements the Ajax functionality in Rails. The example application consists of a Catalog search form that retrieves an article list using `XMLHttpRequest`. First, create a database table and add data to the table using ActiveRecord migrations. A migration is a class that extends the ActiveRecord::Migration class. The procedure to create a table and add table data is as follows.

1. Create a migration.
2. Edit the migration code.
3. Run the migration.

Before creating and running a migration, modify the database.yml configuration file in the config directory of the example Rails application ajaxrails with the MySQL database. A migration may be run in development environment (default), production environment or test environment. Modify the development environment settings in database.yml file to as shown below.

```
development:
 adapter: mysql
  database: test
  username: root
  password: rootpw
  host: localhost
```

Add a space between the ':' and the configuration values. For example, specify `adapter: mysql` instead of `adapter:mysql`. If the root user does not require a password specify `password:` without a value. If the Oracle database is used modify the development environment in database.yml as follows.

```
development:
 adapter: oci
  database: ORCL
  username: OE
  password: password
  host:
```

If Oracle database is used we also need to install Ruby oci8 driver as discussed in Chap. 3.

If SQL Server 2005 database is used modify the development environment in database.yml to as shown in following listing.

```
development:
adapter: sqlserver
database: tempdb
username: sqlserver
password: sqlserver
host: localhost, portnumber
mode: DBI:ADO
```

Variable portnumber is obtained from the SQL Server configuration Manager as explained in chapter 3. Also, as explained in Chap. 3, we need to install the ADO driver to use the SQL Server adapter.

We shall generate a migration by generating a model class. Create a model, Catalog, using the following command from the ajaxrails directory.

```
c:/ruby/ajaxrails>ruby  script/generate model Catalog
```

A Ruby script, catalog.rb, which consists of a model class, Catalog, which extends the ActiveRecord::Base class gets generated and is listed below. The '<' notation indicates that the Catalog class extends the ActiveRecord::Base class.

```
class Catalog < ActiveRecord::Base
  end
```

A migration script, 001_create_catalogs.rb, which consists of CreateCatalogs class also gets generated. The migration class, CreateCatalogs, extends the ActiveRecord::Migration class. A default migration consists of methods self.up and self.down. Method self.up consists of transformations to implement the migration and self.down consists of transformations to rollback a migration. In the CreateCatalogs class, self.up consists of a transformation create_table that creates a *catalogs* table. Active Record uses pluralization to map model classes to database tables. The model class is singular and capitalized and the database table is plural and lowercase. For example, if the model class is Catalog, the table name is catalogs. The self.down method in CreateCatalog migration class consists of a drop_table transformation that drops database table catalogs. Next, we shall modify the migration class to create a table, add columns to the table and add data to the table. To the catalogs table add columns section, title, and url of type string and size 255. The example migration script uses the block form of create_table.

```
create_table :catalogs do |t|
    t.column :section, :string, :limit => 255
    t.column :title, :string, :limit => 255
    t.column :url, :string, :limit => 255
end
```

Valid column types that may be added are integer, float, datetime, timestamp, time, text, string, binary and boolean. Add data to the catalogs table with ActiveRecord::Base class method create. An example row is added as shown below.

```
Catalog.create :section => "XML", :title => "JAXP
validation", :url =>
 http://www-128.ibm.com/developerworks/xml/library/x-
jaxpval.html
```

The complete migration script is listed below.

```
class CreateCatalogs < ActiveRecord::Migration
  def self.up
    create_table :catalogs do |t|
    t.column :section, :string, :limit => 255
    t.column :title, :string, :limit => 255
    t.column :url, :string, :limit => 255
    end


Catalog.create :section => "XML", :title => "JAXP
validation", :url =>
"http://www-128.ibm.com/developerworks/xml/library/x-
jaxpval.html"
Catalog.create :section => "XML", :title => "The Java
XPath API", :url =>
"http://www-128.ibm.com/developerworks/xml/library/x-
javaxpathapi.html"
Catalog.create :section=> "Open Source",
:title => "Make Ruby on Rails easy with RadRails and
Eclipse", :url =>
```

```
"http://www-
128.ibm.com/developerworks/opensource/library/os-ecl-
radrails/"

   end

   def self.down
   drop_table :catalogs
   end
   end
```

Next, run the migration with `rake`. Rake is similar to Java's ant. Rails has a target called `migrate` to run migrations.

```
c:/ruby/ajaxrails>rake db:migrate
```

A database table *catalogs* gets generated.

4.13 Sending a Request

In this section we shall send an HTTP request from a catalog search form using Ajax. Ajax is implemented by the `XMLHttpRequest` functionality provided by the prototype JavaScript library. We shall use a Ruby on Rails application to develop the Ajax application. The example Rails application consists of the following Ruby and configuration files.

1. index.rhtml in the views directory (the view template).
2. catalog.rb in the models directory (the model class).
3. catalog_controller.rb in the controllers directory (the controller class)
4. database.yml file in the config directory.

A database.yml file gets created when a rails application is created. We configured the database.yml file with the MySQL database and created a table in the database in the previous section. A model script, catalog.rb, was created in the previous section. In this section we shall create a controller script, define a controller action `index` and create a view template `index.rhtml`. Create a controller class, a controller action index, and a view template index.rhtml with the following command.

```
c:/ruby/ajaxrails>ruby    script/generate    controller
catalog index
```

A catalog_controller.rb Ruby file gets generated in the controllers directory. The controller script includes a controller action index. Add controller actions get_articles and get_article_list to process HTTP requests from a view template. The controller script is shown in the following listing.

```
class CatalogController < ApplicationController

  def index
  end

  def get_articles
  end

  def get_article_list
  end
end
```

A catalog directory gets generated in the views directory for view templates. A view template, index.rhtml, gets generated in the views/catalog directory. HTTP requests using XMLHttpRequest are initiated from the index.rhtml view template and processed by the Action Controller framework.

Each controller class method either renders a corresponding view template with a matching name (the default, *index.rhtml* matches index action in controller class), renders another view template, redirects to an action in the controller class, renders an action in the controller class, renders a file, or renders text in the view template that invoked the method.

Next we shall initiate an XMLHttpRequest in index.rhtml view template. The Ajax functionaility is implemented in the Prototype JavaScript framework, therefore, include the prototype library with the following declaration in the <head> </head> section of the index.rhtml file.

```
<%= javascript_include_tag "prototype" %>
```

An XMLHttpRequest may be initiated using one of the methods discussed in Table 4.3. We shall discuss two of these methods, form_remote_tag and observe_field.

4.13.1 Sending a Request with form_remote_tag Method

In the form_remote_tag version of index.rhtml add a form with the form_remote_tag method.

```
<%=form_remote_tag(:update=>"article_list",
:url=>{:action=>:get_article_list}) %>
```

The form_remote_tag returns a <form> tag that is submitted using XMLHttpRequest instead of HTTP POST or GET. The :update option specifies a form id to be updated. The :url option specifies the controller action to invoke when the form is submitted. Add a label, and a text field to the form with `text_field_tag` method. Method text_field_tag is included in the ActionView::Helpers::FormTagHelper module. The text field is included in the form to specify a section for catalog search. When the form is submitted, an XMLHttpRequest request is sent to get_article_list action of the controller class and the article_list div in the form is updated with XMLHttpRequest response text that consists of an article list retrieved from the database.

```
<label>Search by Section:</label>
<%=text_field_tag:section %>
```

Add a submit button with the submit_tag method.

```
<%=submit_tag "Search" %>
```

Add a div that is to be updated and add form end tag with the end_form_tag method. The end_form_tag method outputs the </form> tag.

```
<div id="article_list"></div>
<% end_form_tag %>
```

The index.rhtml view template that generates a form with the form_remote_tag method is listed below.

```
<html>
  <head>
    <title></title>
    <%= javascript_include_tag "prototype" %>
  </head>
  <body>
    <h3>Catalog Search Form</h3>

<%=form_remote_tag(:update=>"article_list",
:url=>{:action=>:get_article_list}) %>
<label>Search by Section:</label>
    <%=text_field_tag:section %>
<%=submit_tag "Search" %>
<div id="article_list"></div>
<% end_form_tag %>


  </body>
</html>
```

4.13.2 Sending a Request with observe_field Method

In the observe_field version of index.rhtml the text field used to specify a catalog section is polled at a specified frequency and an XMLHttpRequest request is sent to the web server. The get_articles controller action is invoked periodically. An article_list div in the web page is updated with XMLHttpRequest response text, which consists of an article list retrieved from the database. Add a text field with text_field_tag method.

```
<%=text_field_tag:section %>
```

Specify the text field to observe and the div to update with the observe_field method.

```
<%= observe_field(:section, :frequency=>0.1,
:update=>"article_list",
:url=>{:action=>:get_articles})%>
```

The observe_field method specifies that the :section text field is to observed. The :frequency option of the observe_field method specifies the frequency (in seconds) with which the text field is to be polled. The :update option specifies the div to be updated with XMLHttpRequest reponse text. The :url option specifies the controller action to invoke at the specified frequency.

The index.rhtml view template that includes a text field observed with the observe_field method is listed below.

```
<html>
  <head>
    <title></title>
    <%= javascript_include_tag "prototype" %>
  </head>
  <body>
    <h3>Catalog Search Form</h3>


<label>Search by Section:</label>
    <%=text_field_tag:section %>
<%= observe_field(:section, :frequency=>0.1,
:update=>"article_list",
:url=>{:action=>:get_articles})%>
<div id="article_list"></div>

  </body>
  </html>
```

4.14 Processing a Request

The procedure to initiate a request and process a response is as follows.

1. A request is initiated from a prototype library method in the view template. Examples of methods that may initiate a request are form_remote_tag and observe_field.
2. The view template method invokes an action in the controller class with XMLHttpRequest.
3. The controller class retrieves the value/s specified in the view and queries the database using the model class to create a connection with the database and obtain data from the database. The controller action processes the data by applying a business logic and renders text that is sent to the view that invoked the controller action.
4. The XMLHttpRequest response text is processed in the view. In the example application the response text is used to update a div with an article list for a specified section.

In the example application, an XMLHttpRequest is initiated from view template index.rhtml. If the form_remote_tag method is used to send a request, the get_article_list action in the controller is invoked. If the observe_field method is used to send a request the get_articles action in the controller class is invoked. The controller class obtains a data result set using a SQL query created from the section value specified in the view and outputs a list of retrieved articles. The controller class, CatalogController, obtains data using the model class, Catalog. The model class Catalog was generated in the Creating a Database Table section. By default, the Rails framework uses the plural of the model class with the first letter lowercased as the table name. The table name may also be specified using set_table_name method of ActiveRecord::Base class as explained in this section. By default, the rails framework uses the connection parameters specified in the database.yml file to establish a connection in the database. A connection may also be specified using the establish_connection method as we shall discuss in this section. If the default connection configuration specified in database.yml is to be used the catalog.rb is not required to be modified. In the example application the connection configuration is set in the catalog.rb file to discuss the provision to override the default connection configuration. Setting the connection configuration in the model class may be used when multiple models and controllers are used. Modify the catalog.rb Ruby file to create a database connection. In the Catalog class set table name from which data is to be retrieved with set_table_name method of ActiveRecord::Base class.

```
class Catalog < ActiveRecord::Base
set_table_name "catalogs"
end
```

Next, establish a connection with the database with the establish_connection method. For a connection with the MySQL database, specify :adapter value as "mysql" in lowercase.

```
ActiveRecord::Base.establish_connection(
    :adapter   => "mysql",
    :host      => "localhost",
    :database  => "test",
    :username  => "root",
    :password  =>  "rootpw"
  )
```

The complete listing for the catalog.rb model class is listed below.

```
require 'rubygems'
require 'active_record'

class Catalog < ActiveRecord::Base
set_table_name "catalogs"
end

ActiveRecord::Base.establish_connection(
   :adapter   => "mysql",
   :host      => "localhost",
:database => "test",
   :username => "root",
   :password => "rootpw"
 )
```

The controller class CatalogController (catalog_controller.rb file) integrates the model with the view. A controller class is a sub class of the ApplicationController class, which is a sub class of the ActionController::Base class. The controller class consists of actions (methods) that are invoked from a view. A controller class action is either mapped to a view template with a matching name, redirected to a view template, redirected to another controller action, or renders text in the view that invoked the action. CatalogController consists of actions index, get_articles, and get_article_list. The index action has a corresponding view template in the views directory. The get_articles and get_article_list actions send response text to the index.rhtml view template.

The get_article_list action gets invoked from index.rhtml view template if the template consists of the form_remote_tag method. In the get_article_list method retrieve the value of the section text field.

```
@section=params[:section]
```

If Oracle database is used retrieve the value of the section text field and convert the value to upper case as the values in the database table are uppercase.

```
@section=params[:section].upcase
```

Create a variable, @catalogList, for a list of articles retrieved from the database for the specified section.

```
@catalogList="<ol>"
```

The ActiveRecord::Base class provides various finder methods to query a database. These finder methods are discussed in Table 4.8.

Table 4.8 ActiveRecord::Base Finder Methods

Finder Method	Description	Options
find(*args)	Retrieves database data using one of the following retrieval approaches. Find by id-Finds by id. Example, find(1,options). Find first-Returns the first record matched by the specified options. Example, find(:first,options). Find all- Returns the complete result set. Example, find(:all,options).	Some of the commonly used options are as follows. :conditions-An SQL fragment, Example, :conditions=>"section='Developer'". :limit-An integer that specifies the limit on the number of rows to return. :offset-An offset determining from where the rows should be fetched. If value is 3, the first 2 rows are skipped. :select-A SELECT query. The default is SELECT * FROM. :from-Specifies the table name or database view. Set if the default table name is not to be used. :readonly-Specifies if the result is read only.
find_by_sql(sql)	Runs a SQL statement to select data.	-

Table 4.8 (continued)

Finder Method	Description	Options
find_by_ find_all_by_ find_or_create_by_ find_or_initialize_by_	Dynamic attribute-based finders. Dynamic finders are cleaner than the SQL based finder. Dynamic finders are used by appending the attribute name to the finder method. For example, to find by section use: find_by_section(section). To create a record if a record does not exist use find_or_create_by_. Multiple attributes may be specified in a finder by including an "and". For example to find by section and tile use find_by_section_and_tit le (section, title). To return a new record, if the record does not exist, without saving the record use find_or_initialize_by.	Same as for find(). The Complete Interface for find_by_section is find_by_section (section, options).

Using dynamic finders such as find_by_attribute makes the code more readable and maintainable, but slows down the query and reduces efficiency as the dynamic methods have to be generated dynamically by the ActiveRecord and the SQL query has to be built from the dynamic finder. Using find_by_sql directly is more efficient and is recommended if SQL queries are to be optimized.

Next, select database table data using the find_by_sql method and a SELECT statement SQL query. A database connection was obtained in the model script (catalog.rb) and the database table was also specified in the model script. Iterate over the result set array to construct a list of articles that match the specified section.

```
Catalog.find_by_sql("SELECT * from catalogs WHERE
SECTION='"+@section+"'").
each do|catalog|
@catalogList+="<li><a href=\""+catalog.url+"\">"
+catalog.title+ "</a></li>"
end
```

Send a response with render:text method.

```
render:text =>@catalogList
```

The get_articles controller class action gets invoked if observe_field method is used in the index.rhtml view template. Retrieve the value of the section text field.

```
@section=request.raw_post
```

Due to a bug in the raw_post a '=' might get appended to the string value. Use the following to obtain the string value from raw_post.

```
@section=request.raw_post[0, request.raw_post.length-
1]
```

If Oracle database is used retrieve the value of the section text field and convert the value to upper case.

```
@section=request.raw_post.upcase
```

Construct a local variable, *@catalogList*, for a list of articles retrieved for a section.

```
@catalogList="<ol>"
```

The result set for a section may be obtained by one of the finder methods.

```
Catalog.find(:all, :conditions => ["section = ?",
@section])
Catalog.find_all_by_section(@section)
Catalog.find_by_sql("SELECT * from catalogs WHERE
SECTION='"+@section+"'")
```

We shall run a SQL query with a SELECT statement with a specified section value using the find_by_sql method and iterate over the result set to construct a list of articles that match the section value.

```
Catalog.find_by_sql("SELECT * from catalogs WHERE
SECTION='"+@section+"'").each
do|catalog|
@catalogList+="<li><a href=\""+catalog.url+"\">"
+catalog.title+ "</a></li>"
end
```

Return a response to the index.rhtml view with render:text.

```
render:text=> @catalogList
```

The controller script, catalog_controller.rb is listed below.

```
class CatalogController < ApplicationController

def index
end

def get_articles
 @section=request.raw_post

  @catalogList="<ol>"
Catalog.find_by_sql("SELECT * from catalogs WHERE
SECTION='"+@section+"'").
each do|catalog|
@catalogList+="<li><a href=\""+catalog.url+"\">"
+catalog.title+ "</a></li>"
   end
  @catalogList+="</ol>"
render:text=> @catalogList

end


def get_article_list
 @section=params[:section]
  @catalogList="<ol>"

Catalog.find_by_sql("SELECT * from catalogs WHERE
SECTION='"+@section+"'").
each do|catalog|
@catalogList+=">li>>a href=\""+catalog.url+"\">"
+catalog.title+ ">/a>>/li>"
   end
```

```
   @catalogList+="</ol>"
 render:text =>@catalogList
 end

   end
```

4.15 Processing the Response

The response from the controller class is used to update the article_list div specified in the :update option of the form_remote_tag method or observe_field method.

```
<%=form_remote_tag(:update=>"article_list",
:url=>{:action=>:get_article_list}) %>

<%= observe_field(:section, :frequency=>0.1,
:update=>"article_list",
  :url=>{:action=>:get_articles})%>
```

Next we shall run the MVC Ruby on Rails application. First, start the WEBrick web server.

```
c:/ruby/ajaxrails>ruby script/server
```

The web server may be accessed at url http://localhost:3000/ as shown in Figure 4.1.

Fig. 4.1 Ruby on Rails Console

We shall run the Rails Ajax application with each of the view templates, index.rhtml, discussed in the Sending a Request section. One of the view templates uses the form_remote_tag method to send a request and another uses the observe_field method to send a request. Copy index.rhtml for the form_remote_tag method to views/catalog directory of the ajaxrails directory. Invoke the index action of the Catalog controller with url http://localhost:3000/Catalog/index in a web browser. A input form gets displayed as shown in Figure 4.2.

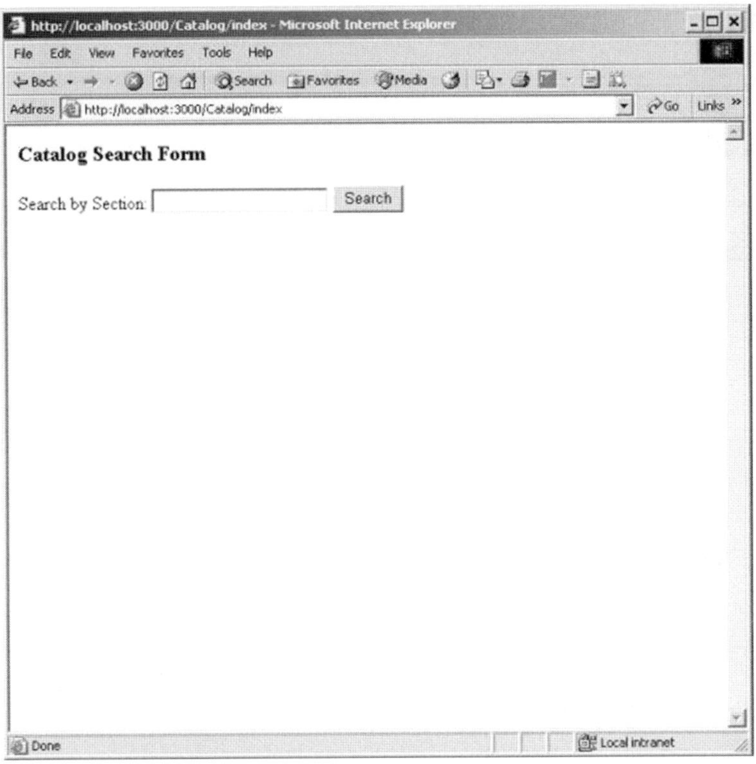

Fig. 4.2 Catalog Search Form

Specify a value in the Search by section field, "Open Source" for example. The section value may be uppercase or lowercase or mixedcase. Click on the Search button as shown in Figure 4.3.

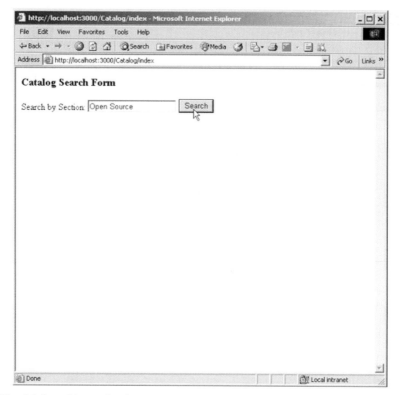

Fig. 4.3 Searching a Catalog

An XMLHttpRequest request gets sent and a view page `div` gets updated with the response text, which consists of a list of articles that match the specified section. The article list gets displayed without posting the form to the web server as shown in Figure 4.4.

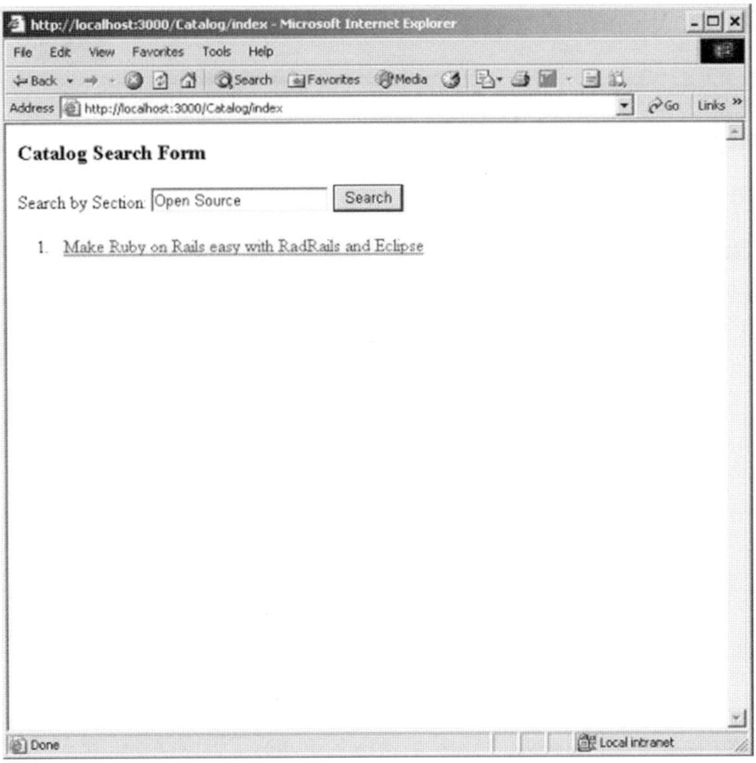

Fig. 4.4 Catalog Search Result

Next, we shall run the Rails application with observe_field method in the view template. Copy index.rhtml for the observe_field method to the views/catalog directory of the ajaxrails directory. Invoke the index action in the controller class with url http://localhost:3000/Catalog/index. A search form gets displayed as shown in Figure 4.5. The search form has only an input text field that is polled at regular intervals and the field value is sent to the web server with XMLHttpRequest.

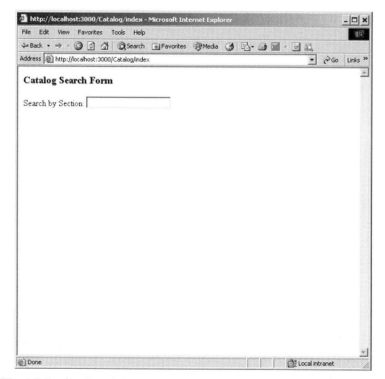

Fig. 4.5 Catalog Search Form

Specify a section field value. If the specified section value does not match a section value in the database an article list is not displayed as shown in Figure 4.6.

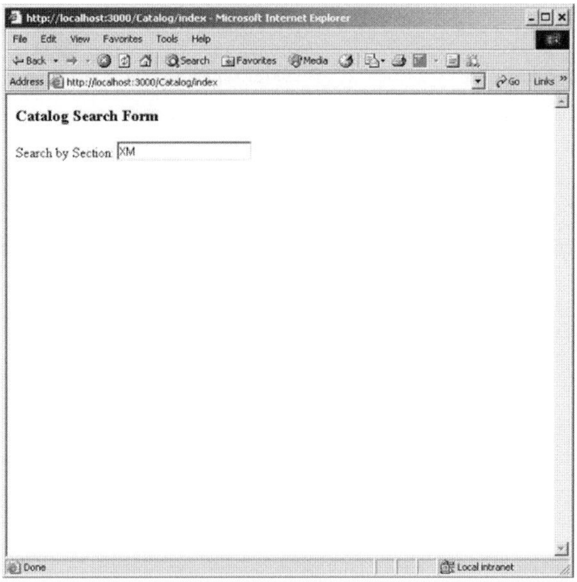

Fig. 4.6 Specifying an Input Value

Specify a section value that matches a section in the database table `catalogs`. Specify "XML" for example. A list of articles that match the specified section gets displayed without clicking on a button as shown in Figure 4.7.

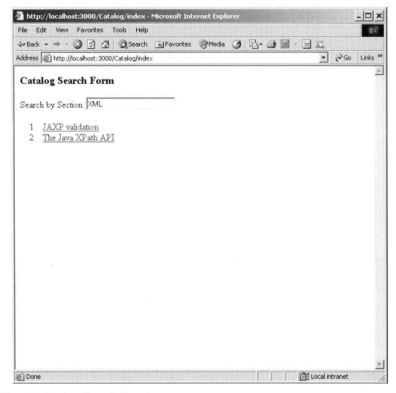

Fig. 4.7 Catalog Search Result

4.16 Summary

In this chapter we discussed the Ajax web technique. The Rails framework provides the Ajax functionality in the PrototypeHelper   class. The advantages of the Ruby on Rails framework may be combined with the dynamic interaction between a client and a server provided by Ajax to develop easy to develop dynamic web applications.

5 Creating PDF and Excel Reports

5.1 Introduction

Portable Document Format (PDF) is a file format created by Adobe Systems for electronic information exchange. PDF is widely used to capture, view, and print information from any application and on any platform. PDF documents preserve the source file information including text, drawings, 3D, full-color graphics, photos, and business logic. Adobe has submitted PDF 1.7 to ISO for a formal, open standard ISO 32000. Various tools are available to generate a PDF document with Ruby on Rails. Some of these PDF tools are listed below.

1. HTMLDOC is an application that converts HTML documents to Adobe PostScript or Adobe PDF files.
2. PdfWriter is a function library, available as a pdf_writer.rb file, to generate PDF documents.
3. PDF::Writer is a tool to generate PDF documents.
4. Ruby FPDF is a ruby file that may be used to generate PDF files.
5. JasperReports is a Java reporting tool that may be integrated with Rails.
6. Rails PDF Plugin.

Often data is required to be presented in a spreadsheet. Excel is a spreadsheet program by Microsoft to analyze, exchange, and present information in a row-column-cell format. Ruby provides various libraries to generate an Excel spreadsheet. Some of these Ruby libraries are discussed below.

1. The Builder ruby library may be used to export XML to Excel spreadsheet.
2. Apache POI Ruby Bindings may be used to generate an XML Document
3. The Ruby Spreadsheet library.

In this chapter we shall create PDF and Excel spreadsheet documents using Ruby on Rails. For comparison, we shall also briefly discuss how one would create a PDF document and an Excel spreadsheet in PHP and Java.

5.2 Creating a PDF with PHP

In PHP a PDF document is created using one of the PHP class libraries for PDF such as PDFLib or ClibPDF. For example, with ClibPDF, first one would open a new PDF document using the `cpdf_open()` function.

```
$cpdf=cpdf_open(0);
```

Start a new page using the cpdf_page_init() function. In which, page size, page number, and page orientation may be specified. A bookmark may be added using the cpdf_add_outline() function. Text is added to the PDF document using the cpdf_begin_text() function.

```
cpdf_begin_text($cpdf);
```

Set font using the cpdf_set_font() function and text position with the cpdf_set_text_pos() function. Specify text rendering mode with the cpdf_set_text_rendering() function. Text may be rendered in fill mode or stroke mode. Add text to the PDF document using the cpdf_text() function.

```
cpdf_text($cpdf,"PDF Document created with PHP");
```

The text section is ended with the cpdf_end_text() function.

```
cpdf_end_text($cpdf);
```

The ClibPDF class library also provides functions to add a line or add a JPEG to the PDF document.

5.3 Creating a PDF with Java

A PDF document is created using the Apache FOP API. The Formatting Objects Processor (FOP) API converts a XSL Formatting Objects (XSL-FO) object to a PDF object. For example, if an XML document is to be converted to a PDF document, first we need to transform the XML document to an XSL-FO file, foFile, using a Transformer object. Create a FOP driver object.

```
org.apache.fop.apps.Driver                    driver=new
org.apache.fop.apps.Driver();
```

Set the PDF renderer on the Driver object.

```
driver.setRenderer(Driver.RENDER_PDF);
```

Specify an InputStream for the XSL-FO document.

```
InputStream input=new FileInputStream(foFile);
driver.setInputSource(new InputSource(input));
```

Specify an OutputStream for the PDF document.

```
OutputStream output=new FileOutputStream(pdfFile);
driver.setOutputStream(output);
```

Run the FOP driver to generate a PDF document.

```
driver.run();
```

5.4 Creating a PDF File with Ruby on Rails

We shall create example PDF files with the `PDF::Writer` tool. We need to install PDF::Writer and dependencies with the package manager RubyGems. The ruby command to install PDF::Writer is as follows.

```
c:/ruby>gem install pdf-writer
```

All gem install commands are required to be run while connected to the Internet. PDF::Writer gets installed including the dependencies as shown in Figure 5.1.

Fig. 5.1 Installing PDF-Writer Gem

Some of the commonly used methods of the PDF::Writer class are discussed in Table 5.1.

Table 5.1 PDF::Writer Methods

Method	Description
add_content(content)	Adds content to the PDF::Writer object.
add_internal_link(label, x0, y0, x1, y1)	Adds an internal link.
add_link(uri, x0, y0, x1, y1)	Adds a link.
add_text(x, y,size = nil,text, angle = 0, word_space_adjust = 0)	Adds text to the document at specified location. Size defaults to current font_size and word_space_adjust is an internal parameter.
add_text_wrap(x, y, width, text, size = nil, justification = :left, angle = 0, test = false)	Adds text within the specified width and returns the remaining text.
insert_page(page = nil)	Returns or sets the insert page property. For example, insert_page(25) sets the insert page as 25 and insert_page(:last) sets the insert page as the last page.
margins_cm(top, left = top, bottom = top, right = left)	Defines the margins in cm.
new(options = {})	Creates a new PDF document. Accepts the following parameters: :paper-Specifies the size of the default page. :orientation-Specifies page orientation to long (:portrait) or wide (:landscape).
render(debug = false)	Returns the PDF stream as string.
save_as(name)	Saves PDF as a file.
select_font(font, encoding = nil)	Loads the specified font if not already loaded and sets the font as the current font.
start_columns(size = 2, gutter = 10)	Starts multi column output.

Table 5.1 (continued)

Method	Description
size()	Returns the number of PDF objects in the document.
start_columns(size = 2, gutter = 10)	Starts multi column output.
start_new_page(force = false)	Creates a new page. If multi column output is set, changes the column or creates a new page. If force set to true creates a new page even if multi column output is set.
start_page_numbering(x, y, size, pos = nil, pattern = nil, starting = nil)	Starts page numbering.
text(text, options = {})	Adds text. The following options may be specified. :font_size-Specifies font size. :left-Space to leave from left margin. :right-Space to leave from right margin. :absolute_left-Absolute left position, overrides :left. :absolute_right-Absolute right position-overrides :right. :justification-:left, :right, :center or :full. :leading-Height taken by the line. :spacing-Word spacing.

Next, we shall create an example PDF document. First, create a rails application for the PDF document with the following command.

```
C:/ruby>rails pdfwriter
```

We need to create a controller Ruby script to generate a PDF document with following command; also create a controller action called *createPDF*.

```
C:/ruby/pdfwriter>ruby    script/generate    controller
pdfwriter createPDF
```

A controller script *pdfwriter_controller.rb* gets generated in the *C:\ruby\pdfwriter\app\controllers* directory. In the controller script add a require statement for PDF::Writer.

```
require 'pdf/writer'
```

In the createPDF action we need to create a PDF::Writer object.

```
pdfWriter = PDF::Writer.new
```

We need to select the font to be used in the PDF document using the select_font method. Also specify the page margins and page numbering using the margins_cm and start_page_numbering methods.

```
pdfWriter.select_font 'Times-Roman'
 pdfWriter.margins_cm(5, 5, 5, 5);
pdfWriter.start_page_numbering(300,  10,  10,  pos  =
:center, pattern = nil, starting = nil)
```

Output text using the text method in which the font size and justification may also be set.

```
pdfWriter.text "This PDF document is created with PDF
Writer.", :font_size => 72, :justification => :center
```

Output the PDF document to a file output.pdf using the send_data method of the ActionController::Streaming module.

```
send_data      pdfWriter.render,      :filename      =>
'output.pdf', :type => "application/pdf"
```

The complete controller script, pdfwriter_controller.rb, is listed below.

```
class PdfwriterController < ApplicationController
  require 'pdf/writer'

 def createPDF
   pdfWriter = PDF::Writer.new
   pdfWriter.select_font 'Times-Roman'
   pdfWriter.margins_cm(5, 5, 5, 5);
   pdfWriter.start_page_numbering(300,  10,  10,  pos
 = :center, pattern = nil, starting = nil)

   pdfWriter.text  "This  PDF  document  is  created
with  PDF  Writer.", :font_size => 25, :justification
=> :center
   send_data      pdfWriter.render,      :filename      =>
'output.pdf', :type => "application/pdf"
```

```
      end
    end
```

We need to start the WEBrick web server with the following command.

```
C:/ruby/pdfwriter>ruby script/server
```

To create the PDF document we need to invoke the createPDF action in the controller script with URL http://localhost:3000/pdfwriter/createPDF. A PDF document gets created as shown in Figure 5.2.

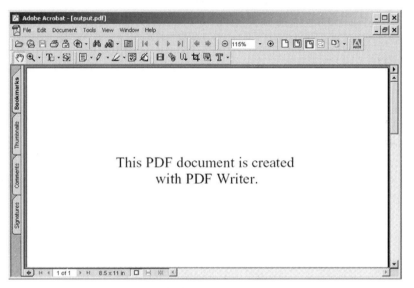

Fig. 5.2 PDF Document Generated with PDF::Writer

Ruby on Rails may also be used to generate graphics with the PDF::Writer::Graphics class, charts with the PDF::Charts::StdDev class, and tables with the PDF::SimpleTable class. In the next section we shall create a table.

5.5 Creating a Table in PDF

The PDF::SimpleTable class is used to create a table in PDF. Method new of the class is used to create a new table. Method render_on is used to render a table on a PDF::Writer object. Some of the commonly used attributes of the PDF::SimpleTable class are discussed in Table 5.2.

Table 5.2 PDF::SimpleTable Attributes

Attribute	Description
column_gap	Space in PDF user units to the left and right sides of each cell. Default value is 5.
column_order	Specifies the order of the columns.
columns	An array that specifies columns and column options.
data	Specifies an array of Hash entries; each entry being a key-value pair in the same order as specified in the column_order attribute.
font_size	Font size; defaults to 10 points.
heading_color	Text color of the heading.
heading_font_size	Heading Font size;defaults to 12 points.
inner_line_style	Specifies inner line style.
line_color	Specifies line color.
maximum_width	Maximum width of the table.
orientation	Table orientation relative to position. The following values may be used: :left-Left of position. :right-Right of position. :center-Centered at position.
outer_line_style	Outer line style.
position	Specifies position of the table. :left-Aligned with the left margin. :right-Aligned with the right margin. :center-Aligned with center, the default value.
row_gap	Gap between the text and cell lines at the top and bottom in each row.

Table 5.2 (continued)

Attribute	Description
show_headings	Specifies if heading are to be shown, defaults to true.
show_lines	Specifies if lines are to be shown in the table. :none-Shows no lines. :outer-Shows outer lines. :inner-Shows inner lines. :all-Shows all lines
split_rows	Specifies if rows are to be split across page pundaries. Defaults to false.
text_color	Text color of table text.
title	Table title.
title_color	Title color.
title_font_size	Font size of title.
title_gap	Specifies gap between title and table. Defaults to 5 units.
width	width

PDF::SimpleTable also provides the render_on method to render a table on a PDFWriter object. A column in a table is represented with the PDF::SimpleTable::Column class. The PDF::SimpleTable::Column class provides method new to create a new column. Some of the attributes of the Column class are discussed in Table 5.3.

Table 5.3 Attributes of PDF::SimpleTable::Column

Attribute	Description
heading	Specifies column heading. Value is a PDF::SimpleTable::Column::Heading class object.
justification	Column justification- :left, :right, :center, or :full
name	Column name
width	Column width

To create a table in a PDF document we need to create a Rails application, *pdftable*.

```
C:/ruby>rails pdftable
```

We also need to create a controller ruby script and a controller action, *createPDFTable*.

```
C:/ruby>ruby    script/generate    controller    pdftable
createPDFTable
```

A controller script *pdftable_controller.rb* gets generated. Controller class PdfwriterController gets generated in the controller script as shown below.

```
class PdftableController < ApplicationController

 def createPDFTable
 end

end
```

To the controller class we need to add `require` statements for pdf writer and simple table.

```
require 'pdf/writer'
require 'pdf/simpletable'
```

In the controller action, createPDFTable, we need to create a PDF::Writer object and select the font to be used in the PDF::Writer object.

```
pdfWriter = PDF::Writer.new
pdfWriter.select_font("Times-Roman")
```

To create a table in PDF, we need to create a SimpleTable object.

```
PDF::SimpleTable.new do |table|
end
```

In the table set the table title using the `title` attribute.

```
table.title = "Journal Catalog"
```

The column order is set using the column_order attribute.

```
table.column_order.push(*%w(Journal Publisher Edition
Title Author))
```

Next, we shall create column objects and set the column headings. For example the Journal column is created as follows.

```
table.columns["Journal"]                              =
PDF::SimpleTable::Column.new("Journal") { |column|
        column.heading = "Journal"
    }
```

Show table lines and table headings using the show_lines and show_headings attributes respectively.

```
table.show_lines    = :all
table.show_headings = true
```

The table orientation and table position may be set using the orientation and position attributes respectively.

```
table.orientation    = :center
table.position       = :center
```

We need to specify a data array and set the data on the table.

```
data = [
        {"Journal"=>"Oracle            Magazine",
"Publisher"=>"Oracle Publishing","Edition" => "July-
August   2005","Title"=>"Tuning    Undo    Tablespace",
"Author" => "Kimberly Floss" },
        {"Journal"=>"Oracle            Magazine",
"Publisher"  =>  "Oracle  Publishing","Edition"  =>
"September-October 2005", "Title" => "Creating Search
Pages", "Author" => "Steve Muench" },
        ]
```

```
table.data.replace data
```

To create a PDF document, first, we need to render the table on the PDF::Writer object using the render_on method.

```
table.render_on(pdfWriter)
```

We need to output the PDF::Writer object to a PDF file using the send_data method.

```
send_data     pdfWriter.render,     :filename    =>
'catalog.pdf', :type => "application/pdf"
```

The complete controller script, pdftable_controller.rb, is listed below.

```
class PdfwriterController < ApplicationController
    require 'pdf/writer'
    require 'pdf/simpletable'

  def createPDFTable
      pdfWriter = PDF::Writer.new
```

```
pdfWriter.select_font("Times-Roman")

        PDF::SimpleTable.new do |table|
        table.title = "Journal Catalog"
        table.column_order.push(*%w(Journal
Publisher Edition Title Author))

        table.columns["Journal"]                    =
PDF::SimpleTable::Column.new("Journal") { |column|
            column.heading = "Journal"
        }
        table.columns["Publisher"]                   =
PDF::SimpleTable::Column.new("Publisher") { |column|
            column.heading = "Publisher"
        }
        table.columns["Edition"]                     =
PDF::SimpleTable::Column.new("Edition") { |column|
            column.heading = "Edition"
        }
        table.columns["Title"]                       =
PDF::SimpleTable::Column.new("Title") { |column|
            column.heading = "Title"
        }
        table.columns["Author"]                      =
PDF::SimpleTable::Column.new("Author") { |column|
            column.heading = "Author"
        }

        table.show_lines    = :all
        table.show_headings = true
        table.orientation   = :center
        table.position      = :center

        data = [
          {"Journal"=>"Oracle              Magazine",
"Publisher"  =>  "Oracle  Publishing","Edition"  =>
"July-August 2005","Title"=>"Tuning Undo Tablespace",
"Author" => "Kimberly Floss" },
          {"Journal"=>"Oracle              Magazine",
"Publisher"  =>  "Oracle  Publishing","Edition"  =>
"September-October 2005", "Title" => "Creating Search
Pages", "Author" => "Steve Muench" },
          ]

        table.data.replace data
        table.render_on(pdfWriter)
      end
```

```
send_data      pdfWriter.render,      :filename      =>
'catalog.pdf', :type => "application/pdf"
        end
        end
```

Start the WEBrick server if not already started.

```
C:/ruby/pdftable>ruby script/server
```

To create a table in a PDF document we need to invoke the controller action createPDFTable with the following URL.

```
http://localhost:3000/pdftable/createPDFTable
```

A PDF file catalog.pdf gets generated. PDF file catalog.pdf is shown in Figure 5.3.

Fig. 5.3 catalog.pdf

5.6 Creating a Spreadsheet with PHP

A spreadsheet is created in PHP with the Spreadsheet_Excel_Writer class library, which is available as a PEAR module. A spreadsheet workbook is created with the Spreadsheet_Excel_Writer() constructor.

```
$workbook                        =                  new
Spreadsheet_Excel_Writer('workbook.xls');
```

A worksheet is added to the workbook with the Workbook::&addWorksheet() function.

```
$worksheet =& $workbook->addWorksheet('worksheet1');
```

A format is added to a worksheet with the Workbook::&addFormat () function and text is added to the worksheet with the Worksheet::write(row, column, text, format) function.

```
$format_row =& $workbook->addFormat();
$format_title->setBold();
$worksheet->write(1,  2,  'Second  row,  third  column',
$format_row);
```

Close the workbook with the Workbook::close () function.

5.7 Creating a Spreadsheet with Java

The Apache POI API is used to create an Excel document. First, import the Apache POI HSSF package.

```
import  org.apache.poi.hssf.usermodel.*;
```

Create a HSSFWorkbook object, which represents an excel workbook.

```
HSSFWorkbook wb=new HSSFWorkbook();
```

Create an Excel spreadsheet from the workbook.

```
    HSSFSheet
spreadSheet=wb.createSheet("spreadSheet");
```

To set cell style create a HSSFCellStyle object.

```
HSSFCellStyle cellStyle=
    wb.createCellStyle();
```

For a cell style, set the cell border.

```
cellStyle.setBorderRight(
    HSSFCellStyle.BORDER_MEDIUM);
cellStyle.setBorderTop(
  HSSFCellStyle.BORDER_MEDIUM);
```

Column width may be specified using the setColumnWidth() method of the HSSFSheet object. For example, the column width of the first column is set as follows.

```
spreadSheet.setColumnWidth((
short)0,   (short)(256*25));
```

Create a row in the spreadsheet with the createRow() method of HSSFSheet. Rows, columns and cells are 0 based.

```
HSSFRow row=spreadSheet.createRow((short)0);
```

Create a row cell with the createCell() method of HSSFRow.

```
HSSFCell cell=row.createCell((short)0);
```

Set the cell style on a row cell.

```
cell.setCellStyle(cellStyle);
```

Set the cell value.

```
cell.setCellValue("column1");
```

Create an OutputStream to output the Excel workbook.

```
FileOutputStream output=new FileOutputStream(new
File("Excel.xls"));
```

Output the Excel workbook.

```
wb.write(output);
 output.flush();
 output.close();
```

5.8 Creating an Excel Spreadsheet with Ruby on Rails

In this section we shall create an Excel spreadsheet from MySQL database. MS Excel defines an XML Schema to create a spreadsheet in XML format. We shall use the builder Ruby gem to export an XML document to a spreadsheet. First, we need to create a rails application for generating an Excel spreadsheet from a database.

```
C:/ruby>rails rubyexcel
```

Modify the development mode settings in database.yml file to specify the database as 'test'. The development mode settings for MySQL database are shown in following listing.

```
development:
adapter: mysql
database: test
username: root
password: mysql
```

```
host: localhost
```

We shall use ActiveRecord migrations to create a database table. We need to create a migration script by creating a model script as follows.

```
C:\ruby\rubyexcel> ruby script/generate model catalog
```

A model script app/models/catalog.rb and a migration script db/migrate/ 001_create_catalogs.rb get created. Modify the migration script 001_create_catalogs.rb to create a database table and add data to the table. In the create_table transformation create a table catalogs with columns journal, publisher, edition, title, author as shown below.

```
class CreateCatalogs < ActiveRecord::Migration
  def self.up
   create_table :catalogs do |t|
   t.column :journal, :string, :limit => 255
   t.column :publisher, :string, :limit => 255
   t.column :edition, :string, :limit => 255
    t.column :title, :string, :limit => 255
   t.column :author, :string, :limit => 255

end

Catalog.create :journal => "Oracle Magazine", :publisher => "Oracle
Publishing", :edition => "July-August 2005", :title=> "Tuning Undo
Tablespace",:author=>"Kimberly Floss"
Catalog.create :journal => "Oracle Magazine", :publisher => "Oracle
Publishing", :edition => "September-October 2005", :title=> "Creating
Search Pages",:author=>"Steve Muench"

  end

  def self.down
   drop_table :catalogs
  end
end.
```

The migration script is run with `rake` and the db:migrate target.

```
C:/ruby/rubyexcel>rake db:migrate
```

Database table 'catalogs' gets created in MySQL database. Next, we shall generate an Excel Spreadsheet from the database. We need to create a controller script to retrieve data from the database and generate an Excel spreadsheet from the data. Also create a controller action gen_excel as shown below.

```
C:/ruby/rubyexcel>ruby    script/generate    controller
catalog gen_excel
```

A controller script catalog_controller.rb gets generated in the app/controllers directory. A gen_excel.rxml view template gets generated in the to the app/views/catalog directory

We need to set the Content-Type, Content-Disposition, and Cache-Control headers. The Content-Type header sets the content type to MS Excel. The Content-Disposition header specifies the Excel file that is generated. Set the Cache-Control header to nil, setting which does not generate the "Internet Explorer was not able to open this internet site" error.

```
headers['Content-Type'] = "application/vnd.ms-excel"
headers['Content-Disposition']='attachment;
filename="catalog.xls"'
headers['Cache-Control'] = ''
```

Retrieve data from the database using a finder method and define a Ruby instance variable for the result set. Instance Variables defined in the controller script are available in the view template.

```
@catalogs = Catalog.find(:all)
```

We shall be generating an Excel spreadsheet in XML format. A Builder::XmlMarkup object is available by default in .rxml view templates. We need to create a gen_excel.rxml view template in the views/catalog directory and delete the gen_excel.rhtml view template.

In the view template we shall create an Excel spreadsheet in XML format. MS Excel defines an XML Spreadsheet Schema (XMLSS) to create an Excel spreadsheet in XML format. Elements in the XMLSS schema are in the `urn:schemas-microsoft-com:office:spreadsheet` namespace. The top-most element in an XML Spreadsheet is ss:Workbook. A worksheet in an XML Spreadsheet document is represented with the ss:Worksheet element. Some of the commonly used elements in the XMLSS schema are discussed in Table 5.4.

Table 5.4 XMLSS Schema Elements

Element	Description	Attributes	Sub-Elements
ss:Workbook	Top-most element in an XML Spreadsheet document.	-	ss:Worksheet (required) ss:Styles
ss:Styles	Contains the style definitions.	-	ss:Style
ss:Style	Defines a style.	ss:ID(required)	ss:Alignment ss:Borders ss:Font ss:Interior ss:NumberFormat ss:Protection
ss:Alignment	Specifies the font alignment.	ss:Horizontal – Specifies horizontal alignment of text. ss:Vertical- Specifies vertical alignment of text. ss:Indent- Specifies the indentation of text. ss:VerticalText- Specifies if text is vertically drawn. ss:WrapText- Specifies if text is to be wrapped.	-
ss:Borders	Defines the borders.	-	ss:Border
ss:Interior	Defines the fill properties.	ss:Color ss:Pattern ss:PatternColor	ss:Interior

Table 5.4 (continued)

Element	Description	Attributes	Sub-Elements
ss:NumberFormat	Defines the number format.	ss:Format	ss:Number Format
ss:Border	Defines a border.	ss:Position(required)-Specifies the border type;left, right, top, bottom. ss:Color –Specifies border color. ss:LineStyle-Specifies line style. ss:Weight-Specifies border thickness.	-
ss:Font	Defines the font of a style.	ss:Bold ss:Color ss:FontName ss:Italic ss:Size ss:StrikeThrough ss:Underline	-
ss:Protection	Specifies if a spreadsheet is editable.	ss:Protected, x:HideFormula	-
ss:Worksheet	Defines a worksheet.	ss:Name(required) ss:Protected	ss:Table x:WorksheetOptions
ss:Table	Defines a table.	ss:DefaultColumnWidth ss:DefaultRowHeight ss:LeftCell –Specifies the column index. ss:StyleID ss:TopCell-Specifies the row index.	ss:Column ss:Row

Table 5.4 (continued)

Element	Description	Attribute	Sub-Elements
ss:Column	Defines the formatting of one or more columns.	c:Caption ss:AutoFitWidth ss:Hidden ss:Index ss:StyleID ss:Width	-
ss:Row	Defines formatting and data of one ore more rows.	c:Caption ss:AutoFitHeight ss:Height ss:Hidden ss:Index ss:StyleID	ss:Cell
ss:Cell	Defines a cell.	ss:Formula ss:HRef ss:Index ss:StyleID	ss:Data
ss:Data	Specifies the data in a cell.	ss:Type	B Font I S Span Sub Sup U
x:WorksheetOptions	Specifies worksheet options.		x:PageSetup
x:PageSetup	Specifies the print options.	-	x:Footer x:Header x:Layout x:PageMargins
x:Footer	Specifies the footer of a printed page.	x:Margin (required) x:Data	-
x:Header	Specifies the header of a printed page.	x:Margin (required) x:Data	-

Table 5.4 (continued)

Element	Description	Attributes	Sub-Elements
x:Layout	Specifies the layout of the page setup.	x:CenterHorizontal x:CenterVertical x:Orientation x:StartPageNumber	-
x:PageMargins	Specifies margins of a printed page.	x:Bottom (required) x:Left (required) x:Right (required) x:Top(required)	-

In the gen_excel.rxml view template we shall create an XML document using the @xml Builder::XmlMarkup object, which is available in .rxml templates by default. Elements are created with Builder::XmlMarkup by invoking methods on the @xml object. Methods sent to the @xml object are converted to equivalent XML markup. For example the following @xml method invocation generates the element `<catalog>Oracle Magazine</catalog>`.

```
@xml.catalog("Oracle Magazine")
```

We shall discuss more about creating an XML document in Chap. 6. We need to create the XML declaration, using the instruct! method, and create the root element Workbook. The namespace declarations required for a spreadsheet document in XML format are also set in the root element.

```
@xml.instruct!:xml,:version=>"1.0",:encoding=>"UTF-8"
   @xml.Workbook({
     'xmlns'=>"urn:schemas-microsoft-
com:office:spreadsheet",
     'xmlns:o'=>"urn:schemas-microsoft-
com:office:office",
     'xmlns:x'=>"urn:schemas-microsoft-
com:office:excel",
     'xmlns:html'=>"http://www.w3.org/TR/REC-html40",
     'xmlns:ss'=>"urn:schemas-microsoft-
com:office:spreadsheet"
     }) do

   end
```

We need to add the Styles element.

```
@xml.Styles do
end
```

We also need to define the default style. We shall use the Verdana font.

```
  @xml.Style   'ss:ID'   =>   'Default',   'ss:Name'   =>
'Normal' do
  @xml.Alignment                 'ss:Vertical'=>'Bottom',
'ss:Horizontal' => 'Center'
  @xml.Borders
  @xml.Font 'ss:FontName' => 'Verdana'
   @xml.Interior
   @xml.NumberFormat

  end
```

We also need to define a style for the header, for which we shall use the Arial Bold style.

```
@xml.Style 'ss:ID' => 'header' do
@xml.Alignment       'ss:Vertical'       =>       'Bottom',
'ss:Horizontal' => 'Center'
@xml.Font 'ss:FontName' => 'Arial',   'ss:Bold'=>'1'

end
```

A spreadsheet is represented with the Worksheet element. Therefore, we need to add the Worksheet element.

```
@xml.Worksheet 'ss:Name' => 'Catalog' do
end
```

We also need to add a table to the worksheet.

```
@xml.Table                'ss:DefaultColumnWidth'=>'100',
'ss:DefaultRowHeight' => '15' do
end
```

Next, we shall add the header row to the table.

```
@xml.Row 'ss:StyleID' => 'header' do
      for column in Catalog.content_columns do
         @xml.Cell do
            @xml.Data   column.human_name,   'ss:Type'
=> 'String'
         end
       end
     end
```

To add data to the spreadsheet iterate over the result set retrieved from the database in the instance variable @catalogs and add a row to the table for each row in the result set.

```
for catalog in @catalogs
       @xml.Row do
           for column in Catalog.content_columns do
              @xml.Cell do
                   @xml.Data catalog.send(column.name),
    'ss:Type' => 'String'
              end
           end
       end
    end
```

The complete gen_excel.rxml template is listed below.

```
   @xml.instruct!          :xml,           :version=>"1.0",
:encoding=>"UTF-8"
  @xml.Workbook({
     'xmlns'                => "urn:schemas-microsoft-
com:office:spreadsheet",
     'xmlns:o'              => "urn:schemas-microsoft-
com:office:office",
     'xmlns:x'              => "urn:schemas-microsoft-
com:office:excel",
     'xmlns:html'      =>     "http://www.w3.org/TR/REC-
html40",
     'xmlns:ss'             => "urn:schemas-microsoft-
com:office:spreadsheet"
    }) do

    @xml.Styles do
     @xml.Style 'ss:ID' => 'Default', 'ss:Name' =>
'Normal' do
        @xml.Alignment  'ss:Vertical'  => 'Bottom',
'ss:Horizontal' => 'Center'
        @xml.Borders
        @xml.Font 'ss:FontName' => 'Verdana'
        @xml.Interior
        @xml.NumberFormat

    end

    @xml.Style 'ss:ID' => 'header' do
        @xml.Alignment  'ss:Vertical'  => 'Bottom',
'ss:Horizontal' => 'Center'
```

```ruby
        @xml.Font       'ss:FontName'      =>      'Arial',
'ss:Bold'=>'1'

    end


  end

  @xml.Worksheet 'ss:Name' => 'Catalog' do
    @xml.Table        'ss:DefaultColumnWidth'=>'100',
'ss:DefaultRowHeight' => '15' do

      # Header
      @xml.Row 'ss:StyleID' => 'header' do
        for column in Catalog.content_columns do
          @xml.Cell do
            @xml.Data   column.human_name,  'ss:Type'
=> 'String'
          end
        end
      end

      # Rows
      for catalog in @catalogs
        @xml.Row do
          for column in Catalog.content_columns do
          @xml.Cell do
            @xml.Data   catalog.send(column.name),
'ss:Type' => 'String'
            end
          end
        end
      end

    end
  end

  end
```

Next, we shall run the rubyexcel rails application. Start the WEBrick web server.

```
C:/ruby/rubyexcel>ruby script/server
```

To generate the spreadsheet invoke the gen_excel controller action with URL http://localhost:3000/catalog/gen_excel.

An Excel spreadsheet gets generated. Because the Spreadsheet is in XML format, it requires MS Excel 2003 to open. Download and install Excel[1]. The spreadsheet generated is shown in Figure 5.4.

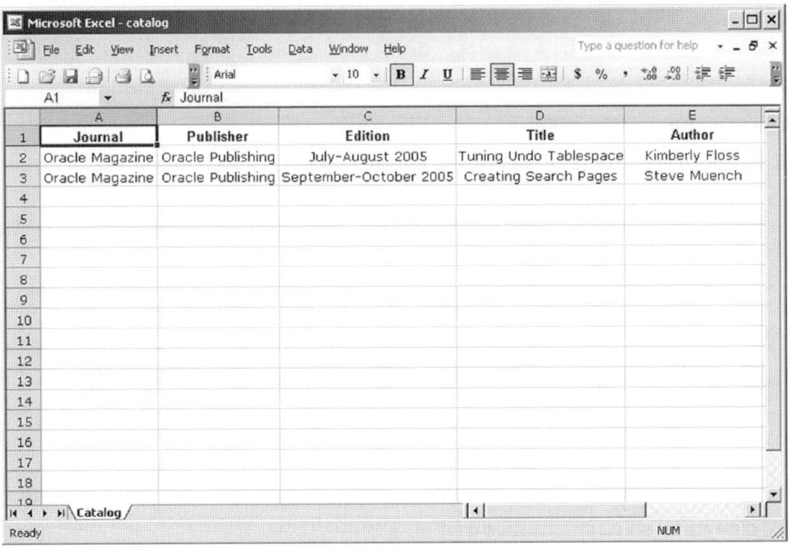

Fig. 5.4 Spreadsheet Generated with Ruby on Rails

5.9 Creating a Spreadsheet with Ruby Spreadsheet

In this section we shall create an Excel spreadsheet using the Ruby Spreadsheet library. Download the Spreadsheet TAR file[2]. Extract the file to the c:/ruby directory, in which Ruby on Rails is installed. Run the following commands to install the Spreadsheet library.

```
ruby spreadsheet-excel.gemspec
gem install spreadsheet-excel-0.3.4.gem
```

The Spreadsheet Ruby library gets installed. Output from the installation is shown in Figure 5.5.

---

[1] MS Excel- http://office.microsoft.com/en-us/excel/FX100487621033.aspx
[2] Spreadsheet Library- http://rubyforge.org/projects/spreadsheet

Fig. 5.5 Installing Spreadsheet Ruby Library

We need to create a rails application to generate a spreadsheet with the spreadsheet library.

```
C:/ruby>rails spreadsheet
```

We also need to create a controller script, including a controller action, to generate an Excel spreadsheet.

```
c:/ruby/spreadsheet>ruby  script/generate  controller
spreadsheet spreadsheet
```

The spreadsheet ruby library provides various classes, which are discussed in Table 5.5 to generate a spreadsheet.

Table 5.5 Spreadsheet Library Classes

Class	Description	Methods
Excel	Represents a .xls File	new() creates an Excel object.
Workbook	Represents a workbook.	add_worksheet(sheet_name)-Adds a worksheet to the workbook. add_format(attributes/format_object) -Adds a format to the workbook. close-Closes the workbook.
Format	Defines a worksheet format.	new() creates a Format object.

Table 5.5 (continued)

Class	Description	Methods
Worksheet	Represents a worksheet.	write(row,column,value,format=nil) –Adds data to the specified cell. write_row(row,column,Array,format =nil)-Adds a row of data. write_column(row,column,Array,for mat=nil)-Adds a column of data. format_row(int/range,height=nil,for mat=nil) –Applies formatting to an entire row or range of rows. format_column(int/range,width=nil,f ormat=nil)-Applies formatting to a column or range of columns.

Next we shall modify the controller script to create a spreadsheet. Add a `require` and an `include` statement for the spreadsheet library. With the include statement a class may be used without the package prefix.

```
require "spreadsheet/excel"
include Spreadsheet
```

We need to create a Workbook object in the controller action spreadsheet.

```
workbook = Excel.new("catalog.xls")
```

We need to define a format for the header row and a format for the spreadsheet data and add the formats to the Workbook.

```
format1 = Format.new(
    :color     => "blue",
    :bold      => true,
    :underline => true
)

format2 = Format.new(
    :color     => "blue",
    :bold      => false,
    :underline => false
)
workbook.add_format(format1)
workbook.add_format(format2)
```

We need to add a worksheet to the workbook, which may be done with the add_worksheet method.

```
worksheet1 = workbook.add_worksheet
```

Next, we shall add the header row. For example a header column at index 0,0 is added as follows.

```
worksheet1.write(0,0,"Journal",format1)
```

A row of data is added to worksheet with the `write` method. For example, the data at index 1,0 is added as follows.

```
worksheet1.write(1,0,"Oracle Magazine",format2)
```

The complete controller script, controller_spreadsheet.rb, is listed below.

```
class SpreadsheetController < ApplicationController

require "spreadsheet/excel"
include Spreadsheet
def spreadsheet
workbook = Excel.new("catalog.xls")

format1 = Format.new(
    :color     => "blue",
    :bold      => true,
    :underline => true
)

format2 = Format.new(
    :color     => "blue",
    :bold      => false,
    :underline => false
)
workbook.add_format(format1)
workbook.add_format(format2)

worksheet1 = workbook.add_worksheet
# Add a header row
worksheet1.write(0,0,"Journal",format1)
worksheet1.write(0,1,"Publisher",format1)
worksheet1.write(0,2,"Edition",format1)
worksheet1.write(0,3,"Title",format1)
worksheet1.write(0,4,"Author",format1)
#Add a data row
worksheet1.write(1,0,"Oracle Magazine",format2)
worksheet1.write(1,1,"Oracle Publishing",format2)
worksheet1.write(1,2,"July-August 2005",format2)
worksheet1.write(1,3,"Tuning                              Undo
Tablespace",format2)
```

```
worksheet1.write(1,4,"Kimberly Floss",format2)

#Add a data row
worksheet1.write(2,0,"Oracle Magazine",format2)
worksheet1.write(2,1,"Oracle Publishing",format2)
worksheet1.write(2,2,"September-October
2005",format2)
worksheet1.write(2,3,"Creating Search Pages",format2)
worksheet1.write(2,4,"Steve Muench",format2)

workbook.close
end
end
```

Start the WEBrick web server.

```
C:/ruby/spreadsheet>ruby script/server
```

We need to invoke the spreadsheet controller action, spreadsheet, with URL http://localhost:3000/spreadsheet/spreadsheet. A spreadsheet gets generated in the rails application directory. The spreadsheet may be opened with Excel Viewer or Excel 2003 as shown in Figure 5.6.

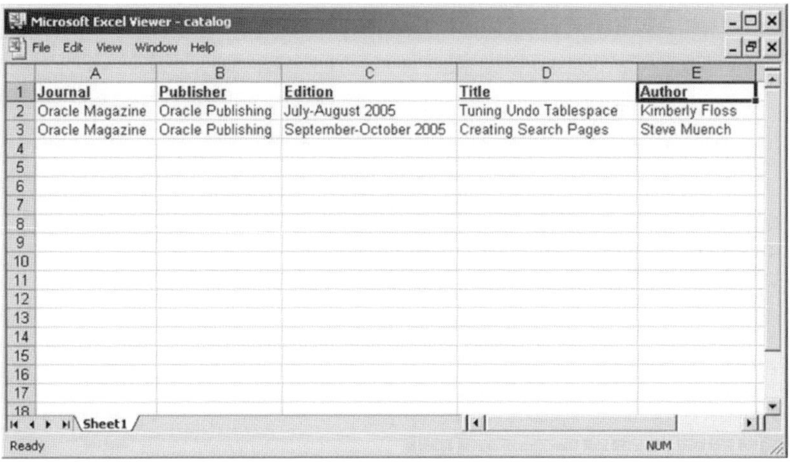

Fig. 5.6 Spreadsheet Generated with Spreadsheet Library

5.10 Summary

Ruby provides various RubyGems gems to create PDF and Excel spreadsheet documents. In this chapter we create a PDF document using the PDF::Writer Ruby library and added a table to a PDF document using the PDF::SimpleTable class. We create an Excel spreadsheet by exporting an XML document, which conforms to the XML Spreadsheet Schema (XMLSS) XML Schema. We also create an Excel spreadsheet using the Ruby Spreadsheet library.

6 XML On Rails

6.1 Introduction

Ruby on Rails is a database based web framework. XML is the standard medium for data exchange. An XML document may be created and parsed with Ruby on Rails. Rails provides a ruby library called `Builder` to generate XML markup. The Builder package contains class `Builder::XmlMarkup` to generate an XML document. REXML is an XML toolkit for Ruby that may be used to parse an XML document. In this chapter we shall create an XML document with the Builder library. We shall also create an XML document from Oracle database. Subsequently we shall parse an XML document with REXML using XPath.

6.2 Processing XML with PHP 5

PHP 5 provides XML extensions for parsing, transforming, XPath navigation, and validation of XML documents. Using the DOM extension an XML document an XML document may be created and parsed, navigated with XPath, and validated with an XML Schema. SimpleXML extension in PHP 5 simplifies parsing by converting an XML document to a PHP object that may be accessed with property selectors and array iterators. The XSL extension in PHP 5 is used to transform an XML document.

An XML document in PHP 5 is represented with DOMDocument class, which extends DOMNode class. In PHP, first create a DOMDocument object.

```
$dom = new DOMDocument();
```

Create root element catalog with createElement() function. Add the root element to the DOMDocument object with appendChild() function. Create an attribute with createAttribute() function. Output the XML DOMDocument generated using saveXML() function.

```
echo $dom->saveXML();
```

For XPath evaluation, the DOMXPath class is used to evaluate an XPath expression in the context of an XML document node. An XML document is validated with an XML schema with the schemaValidate() function. With the PHP 5 extension, an XML document is transformed using an XSLTProcessor. Create an XSLTProcessor.

6.3 Processing XML with Java

An XML document is created and parsed using the Java API for XML Parsing (JAXP). First, we need to create a DocumentBuilderFactory object. From the factory object, create a DocumentBuilder object.

```
DocumentBuilder              builder              =
factory.newDocumentBuilder();
```

Create a new Document object, which represents an XML document, from the DocumentBuilder object.

```
Document document=builder.newDocument();
```

Add elements and attributes to the Document object using the createElement()and createAttribute() methods. To output the XML document, create a TransformerFactory object and subsequently create a Transformer object. Create a DOMSource object for the Document object and a StreamResult object for the output. Output the Document object using the Transformer object.

```
transformer.transform(source, result);
```

An XML document may be parsed using the XPath API in the javax.xml.xpath package in JDK 5.0. First, we need to create an XPathFactory object.

```
XPathFactory factory=XPathFactory.newInstance();
```

Create an XPath object.

```
XPath xPath=factory.newXPath();
```

The element or attribute whose value is to be retrieved is selected using XPath. Create and compile an XPathExpression. Create an InputSource for an XML document. Evaluate the XPath expression using the evaluate() method.

6.4 Installing XML Builder

Builder is installed with the package manager RubyGems. Run the following command while connected to the Internet to install Builder 2.0.0.

```
C:/ruby>gem install builder
```

Builder gets installed as shown in Figure 6.1.

Fig. 6.1 Installing Builder

The Builder::XmlMarkup provides methods discussed in Table 6.1.

Table 6.1 Builder::XmlMarkup Methods

Method	Description
cdata!(text)	Adds a CDATA section.
comment!(comment_text)	Adds a comment.
declare!(inst, *args, &block)	Adds a declaration. args specifies 0 or more arguments.
instruct!(directive_tag=:xml, attrs={})	Adds a processing instruction. Attributes are specifies with an array of hash entries.
target!()	Returns target of Builder object.

Table 6.1 (continued)

Method	Description
new(options={})	Creates a XML markup Builder object. The following options may be specified in an array of hash entries. :target=>targetObject, :indent=>indentation :margin=>initial_indentation

We shall use some of these methods in creating an XML document in this chapter. Download and install the Oracle Database 10g. We also need to install Ruby oci8 driver[1], which is required to connect to Oracle database from a Ruby on Rails application. Download the ruby-oci8-0.1.16-mswin32.rb file. Cd to the c:/ruby directory and run the Ruby application ruby-oci8-0.1.16-mswin32.rb.

```
c:/ruby>ruby ruby-oci8-0.1.15-mswin32.rb
```

6.5 Creating an XML Document with Ruby on Rails

In this section we shall generate an example XML document, catalog.xml, listed below.

```
<?xml version="1.0" encoding="UTF-8"?>
<!DOCTYPE catalogs [
    <!ELEMENT catalogs (catalog+)>
    <!ELEMENT catalog (journal, publisher, title,
author)>
    <!ELEMENT journal (#PCDATA)>
    <!ATTLIST journal (edition CDATA)>
    <!ELEMENT publisher (#PCDATA)>
    <!ELEMENT title (#PCDATA)>
    <!ELEMENT author (#PCDATA)>
  ]>
<!--Journal Catalog -->

<catalogs>
<catalog>
<journal edition="July-August 2005">
```

---

[1] Ruby oci8 Driver- http://rubyforge.org/frs/?group_id=256

```
Oracle Magazine</journal>
<publisher>Oracle Publishing</publisher>
<title>Tuning Undo Tablespace</title>
<author>Kimberly Floss</author>
</catalog>

<catalog>
<journal edition="September-October 2005">
Oracle Magazine</journal>
<publisher>Oracle Publishing</publisher>
<title>Creating Search Pages</title>
<author>Steve Muench</author>
</catalog>
</catalogs>
```

We need to create a rails application, *xmlbuilder*, for generating an XML document with Builder 2.0.0.

```
C:/ruby>rails xmlbuilder
```

We also need to create a controller, *xmlbuilder*, including a controller action *gen_xml* to run the ruby code to generate an XML document.

```
C:/ruby>xmlbuilder>ruby  script/generate  controller
xmlbuilder gen_xml
```

A controller class XmlbuilderController, including a controller action gen_xml, gets generated as shown in following listing.

```
class XmlbuilderController < ApplicationController

  def gen_xml
  end
end
```

In the controller script we need to add a `require` statement for the Builder package.

```
require 'builder'
```

In the controller class create a Builder::XmlMarkup object. Set output to STDOUT and specify indentation in the XML output.

```
xml_markup                                              =
Builder::XmlMarkup.new(:target=>STDOUT,  :indent=>2)
```

We need to add an XML declaration to the XML document using the instruct! method.

```
xml_markup.instruct!        :xml,        :version=>"1.0",
:encoding=>"UTF-8"
```

Also add a DOCTYPE declaration using the declare! method.

```
xml_markup.declare!        :DOCTYPE,        :catalogs        do
|catalogs| end
```

To the DOCTYPE add ELEMENT declarations. For example, ELEMENT declaration for *catalogs* element is added as follows.

```
catalogs.declare! :ELEMENT, :catalogs, :"(catalog+)"
```

Add a comment with the comment!("comment text") method.

```
xml_markup.comment! "Journal Catalog"
```

Add XML markup for root element catalogs.

```
xml_markup.catalogs{}
```

To the catalogs element add *catalog* elements. XML markup for a catalog element is added as shown in following listing.

```
xml_markup.catalog { |catalog|
catalog.journal("Oracle Magazine", "edition"=>"July-
August 2005"); catalog.publisher("Oracle
Publishing"); catalog.title("Tuning Undo
Tablespace");catalog.author("Kimberly Floss")};
```

The complete controller ruby script, *xmlbuilder_controller.rb*, is shown below.

```
require 'builder'
class XmlbuilderController < ApplicationController
  require_gem 'builder'

def gen_xml
  xml_markup                                          =
Builder::XmlMarkup.new(:target=>STDOUT, :indent=>2)
    xml_markup.instruct!    :xml,    :version=>"1.0",
:encoding=>"UTF-8"

  xml_markup.declare!    :DOCTYPE,    :catalogs    do
|catalogs|
      catalogs.declare!      :ELEMENT,      :catalogs,
:"(catalog+)"
      catalogs.declare!      :ELEMENT,      :catalog,
:"(journal, publisher, title, author)"
      catalogs.declare!      :ELEMENT,      :journal,
:"(#PCDATA)"
```

```
        catalogs.declare!        :ATTLIST,        :journal,
:"(edition CDATA)"
        catalogs.declare!        :ELEMENT,        :publisher,
:"(#PCDATA)"
        catalogs.declare!         :ELEMENT,          :title,
:"(#PCDATA)"
        catalogs.declare!        :ELEMENT,          :author,
:"(#PCDATA)"

    end
  xml_markup.comment! "Journal Catalog"
  xml_markup.catalogs{
  xml_markup.catalog              {              |catalog|
catalog.journal("Oracle Magazine", "edition"=>"July-
August        2005");        catalog.publisher("Oracle
Publishing");        catalog.title("Tuning        Undo
Tablespace");catalog.author("Kimberly Floss")};

  xml_markup.catalog              {              |catalog|
catalog.journal("Oracle              Magazine",
"edition"=>"September-October              2005");
catalog.publisher("Oracle              Publishing");
catalog.title("Creating              Search
Pages");catalog.author("Steve Muench")}

}
    end
  end
```

In the app/views/xmlbuilder directory of the xmlbuilder rails application a gen_xml.rhtml file gets generated when the controller class is created. The gen_xml.rhtml file is the view template for the controller action gen_xml. Template gen_xml.rhtml may be kept empty. In the example gen_xml.rhtml file add text "XML Document Generated". Start the WEBrick server with the following ruby command.

```
C:/ruby/xmlbuilder>ruby script/server
```

To generate the XML document we need to invoke the gen_xml controller action with URL http://localhost:3000/xmlbuilder/gen_xml. XML document gets output to the STDOUT as shown in Figure 6.2.

```
Command Prompt - ruby script/server                          _ □ ×
<?xml version="1.0" encoding="UTF-8"?>
<!DOCTYPE catalogs [
  <!ELEMENT catalogs (catalog+)>
  <!ELEMENT catalog (journal, publisher, title, author)>
  <!ELEMENT journal (#PCDATA)>
  <!ATTLIST journal (edition CDATA)>
  <!ELEMENT publisher (#PCDATA)>
  <!ELEMENT title (#PCDATA)>
  <!ELEMENT author (#PCDATA)>
]>
<!-- Journal Catalog -->
<catalogs>
  <catalog>
    <journal edition="July-August 2005">Oracle Magazine</journal>
    <publisher>Oracle Publishing</publisher>
    <title>Tuning Undo Tablespace</title>
    <author>Kimberly Floss</author>
  </catalog>
  <catalog>
    <journal edition="September-October 2005">Oracle Magazine</journal>
    <publisher>Oracle Publishing</publisher>
    <title>Creating Search Pages</title>
    <author>Steve Muench</author>
  </catalog>
</catalogs>
```

Fig. 6.2 STDOUT XML Document

The following message gets displayed in the browser.

```
XML Document Generated
```

6.6 Creating an XML Document from a Database

Rails supports the Active Record pattern to model database table columns as model object attributes. Thus, a object relational mapping (ORM) between business objects and database tables is provided. In this section we shall create an XML document from an Oracle database table. We need to create a rails application, *databasexml*, for generating an XML document from a database.

```
C:/ruby>rails databasexml
```

We need to modify the development mode settings in database.yml file to specify the database as 'ORCL'. The development mode settings for Oracle database are shown in following listing.

```
development:
adapter: oci
database: ORCL
username: OE
password:  password
host:
```

We shall use ActiveRecord migrations to create a database table. Create a migration script by creating a model script as follows.

```
C:\ruby\databasexml>    ruby    script/generate    model
catalog
```

A model script app/models/catalog.rb and a migration script db/migrate/ 001_create_catalogs.rb get created. The migration script class, CreateCatalogs, extends the ActiveRecord::Migration class.

The default migration script consists of methods self.up and self.down. The self.up method is is invoked to apply a migration and create a database table. The create_table transformation of class ActiveRecord::Migration is used to create a database table catalogs. ActiveRecord uses pluralization to map a model class to a database table. The model class is singular and upper case and the database table is plural and lower case. In the example Ruby on Rails application, the model class is *Catalog* and the database table is *catalogs*.

We need to modify the migration script 001_create_catalogs.rb to create a database table and add data to the table. In the create_table transformation create a table catalogs with columns journal, publisher, edition, title, author as shown below.

```
class CreateCatalogs < ActiveRecord::Migration
  def self.up
    create_table :catalogs do |t|
    t.column :journal, :string, :limit => 255
    t.column :publisher, :string, :limit => 255
    t.column :edition, :string, :limit => 255
     t.column :title, :string, :limit => 255
    t.column :author, :string, :limit => 255

  end

  Catalog.create   :journal   =>   "Oracle   Magazine",
:publisher => "Oracle Publishing", :edition => "July-
August    2005",    :title=>    "Tuning    Undo
Tablespace",:author=>"Kimberly Floss"
  Catalog.create   :journal   =>   "Oracle   Magazine",
:publisher   =>   "Oracle   Publishing",   :edition   =>
"September-October 2005", :title=> "Creating Search
Pages",:author=>"Steve Muench"

  end

  def self.down
    drop_table :catalogs
  end
end
```

We need to run the migration script with the rake command and the db:migrate target.

```
C:/ruby/databasexml>rake db:migrate
```

Database table catalogs gets created in Oracle database. Next, we need to create a controller script to generate an XML document from the database table. Specify controller class as *catalog* and define a controller action *gen_xml*.

```
C:/ruby/databasexml>ruby script/generate controller
catalog gen_xml
```

Controller script app/controllers/catalog_controller.rb gets created as shown below.

```
class CatalogController < ApplicationController

  def gen_xml
  end
end
```

In the controller class we need to create a Builder::XmlMarkup object. The indentation is set with the :indent option and the margin is set with the :margin option.

```
@xml = Builder::XmlMarkup.new (:indent=>2,
:margin=>4)
```

An XmlMarkup object is not required to be created. An XmlMarkup object, @xml, is available by default in an .rxml view template. An XmlMarkup object may be created to specify additional options such as :indent and :margin. Next, retrieve data from Oracle database table catalogs, which was set in the model script using the find(:all) method. The result set of the database query is stored in instance variable @catalogs, which would be available in view templates for the catalog controller.

```
@catalogs=Catalog.find(:all)
```

The complete controller script, catalog_controller.rb, is listed below.

```
class CatalogController < ApplicationController
    def gen_xml
    @xml = Builder::XmlMarkup.new (:indent=>2,
:margin=>4)
    @catalogs=Catalog.find(:all)
    end
end
```

We need to replace the gen_xml.rhtml view template in the views/catalog directory with a gen_xml.rxml template. In the RXML template create an XML document from data retrieved from the database. We shall use instance variable @xml, which represents an XmlMarkup object, to create the XML document. We need to add an XML declaration using the instruct! Method. Version is specified using the :version option.

```
@xml.instruct! :xml, :version=>"1.0"
```

An XML document has a root element. Therefore, add root element 'catalogs'.

```
@xml.catalogs{}
```

In the root element iterate over the data retrieved from the database and create a 'catalog' element for each row of data in the result set.

```
for catalog in @catalogs
    @xml.catalog do
        @xml.journal(catalog.journal)
        @xml.publisher(catalog.publisher)
        @xml.edition(catalog.edition)
        @xml.title(catalog.title)
        @xml.author(catalog.author)
    end
```

The complete gen_xml.rxml file is listed below.

```
@xml.instruct! :xml, :version=>"1.0"

@xml.catalogs{
   for catalog in @catalogs
     @xml.catalog do
         @xml.journal(catalog.journal)
         @xml.publisher(catalog.publisher)
         @xml.edition(catalog.edition)
         @xml.title(catalog.title)
         @xml.author(catalog.author)
     end
   end
}
```

Next, run the rails application to generate an XML document. Start the WEBrick web server if not already started.

```
C:/ruby/databasexml>ruby script/server
```

To generate the XML document invoke the gen_xml controller action with the URL http://localhost:3000/catalog/gen_xml. An XML document gets generated as shown in Figure 6.3.

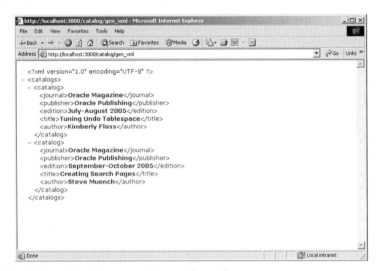

Fig. 6.3 Invoking the gen_xml controller action

6.7 Parsing an XML Document with REXML

REXML is an XML toolkit for Ruby. REXML supports XPath with which node values may be selected. The REXML::XPath class is used to parse an XML document with XPath. REXML::XPath class methods are discussed in Table 6.2.

Table 6.2 REXML::XPath Class Methods

Method	Description
each(element, path=nil, namespaces={})	Iterates over nodes that match the XPath expression specified with path. 'element' specifies to context element.
first(element, path=nil, namespaces={})	Returns the first node that matches the specified XPath expression.
match(element, path=nil, namespaces={})	Returns an array of nodes that match the specified XPath expression.

In this section we shall parse an example XML document with REXML. We need to create a rails application, *rexml*, for REXML.

```
C:/ruby>rails rexml
```

We need to create a controller, *rexml*, for the rails application and define a controller action *xpath* to parse an XML document with XPath using REXML.

```
C:/ruby/rexml>ruby script/generate controller rexml
xpath
```

The controller class with a controller action gets created as shown below.

```
class RexmlController < ApplicationController

  def xpath
  end
end
```

We need to add a `require` statement for REXML.

```
require "rexml/document"
```

We need to specify the XML document to be parsed as a string.

```
string = <<EOF
<catalogs>
<catalog>
<journal>Oracle Magazine</journal>
<publisher>Oracle Publishing</publisher>
<edition>July-August 2005</edition>
<title>Tuning Undo Tablespace</title>
```

```
<author>Kimberly Floss</author>
</catalog>

<catalog>
<journal>Oracle Magazine</journal>
<publisher>Oracle Publishing</publisher>
<edition>September-October 2005</edition>
<title>Creating Search Pages</title>
<author>Steve Muench</author>
</catalog>
</catalogs>
EOF
```

We need to create a REXML::Document object from the XML string. A REXML::Document object represents a complete XML document.

```
doc = REXML::Document.new string
```

Next, we shall retrieve element values from the XML document and create a table. Define an instance variable for a table and create a header row for a table.

```
@catalogList="<table><tr><th>Journal</th><th>Publish
er</th><th>Edition</th><th>Title</th><th>Author</th>
</tr>"
     …
@catalogList+="</table>"
```

We need to iterate over the catalog elements and add a row for each catalog element in the XML document. The REXML::XPath class is used to iterate over a node set with the each() method.

```
REXML::XPath.each(doc,"/catalogs/catalog") { |row|
@catalogList+="<tr>"
…
…
@catalogList+="</tr>"
}
```

Iterate over each catalog node to add a table column value in the table row. For example, a Journal column value is added as shown below.

```
REXML::XPath.each(row,"journal") { |journal|
@catalogList+="<td>"+journal.text+"</td>"

}
```

The complete controller script, rexml_controller.rb, is listed below.

```ruby
require "rexml/document"

class RexmlController < ApplicationController

  def xpath

    string = <<EOF
<catalogs>
<catalog>
<journal>Oracle Magazine</journal>
<publisher>Oracle Publishing</publisher>
<edition>July-August 2005</edition>
<title>Tuning Undo Tablespace</title>
<author>Kimberly Floss</author>
</catalog>

<catalog>
<journal>Oracle Magazine</journal>
<publisher>Oracle Publishing</publisher>
<edition>September-October 2005</edition>
<title>Creating Search Pages</title>
<author>Steve Muench</author>
</catalog>
</catalogs>
EOF
    doc = REXML::Document.new string

@catalogList="<table><tr><th>Journal</th><th>Publishe
r</th><th>Edition</th><th>Title</th><th>Author</th></
tr>"

  REXML::XPath.each(doc,"/catalogs/catalog") { |row|
  @catalogList+="<tr>"
  REXML::XPath.each(row,"journal") { |journal|
  @catalogList+="<td>"+journal.text+"</td>"

}
  REXML::XPath.each(row,"publisher") { |publisher|
  @catalogList+="<td>"+publisher.text+"</td>"

}

  REXML::XPath.each(row,"edition") { |edition|
  @catalogList+="<td>"+edition.text+"</td>"
```

```
}
REXML::XPath.each(row,"title") { |title|
@catalogList+="<td>"+title.text+"</td>"
}
REXML::XPath.each(row,"author") { |author|
@catalogList+="<td>"+author.text+"</td>"

}
@catalogList+="</tr>"
}
@catalogList+="</table>"
  end
end
```

A view template xpath.rhtml gets created in the app/views/rexml directory when the controller class is generated. In the xpath.rhtml view template specify the following Ruby output embedding.

```
<%= @catalogList %>
```

Start the WEBrick web server if not already started.

```
C:/ruby/rexml>ruby script/server
```

To parse the XML document with XPath and generate a table we need to invoke the controller action xpath with URL http://localhost:3000/rexml/xpath. A table gets generated from the XML document as shown in Figure 6.4.

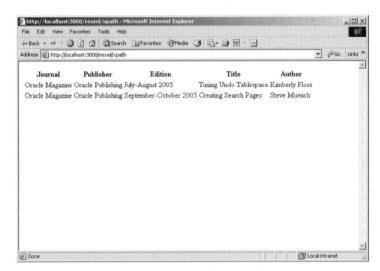

Fig. 6.4 Table Generated from XML Document with XPath

6.8 Summary

XML is the standard medium of data exchange. Ruby provides the RubyGems builder gem to create an XML document. We created an XML document with the builder gem. We also created an XML document from a database using the MVC Rails framework. Subsequently, we parsed an XML document using the REXML toolkit.

7 PHP On Rails

7.1 Introduction

Ruby on Rails is a web framework for developing database based web applications. Ruby on Rails applications are based on the Model-View-Controller pattern. PHP is a commonly used scripting language and provides various frameworks based on the Ruby on Rails framework. Some of the PHP ports of Ruby on Rails framework are Zend Framework, Akelos Framework and PHP On Trax. PHP On Trax is an open source web application and persistence framework, based on Ruby on Rails, to develop database-based web applications according to the Model-View-Controller pattern. In this chapter we shall develop a MVC application using the PHP On Trax framework.

7.2 Installing PHP

Download the Apache HTTP Server 2.0[1]. Install the Apache HTTP server by double-clicking on the Apache web server application, *apache_2.0.55-win32-x86-no_ssl*. Next, install PHP 5. Download PHP 5.2.0[2]. Extract the PHP zip file *php-5.1.2-Win32.zip* to an installation directory, C:/PHP for example.To the PATH environment system variable add C:/PHP, the directory in which PHP 5 is installed. Modify the *php.init-recommended* file in the C:/PHP directory to *php.ini*.

Enable the MySQL extension in php.ini configuration file. Set the extension directory by specifying `extension_dir = "./ext"`. Activate the MySQL extension by removing the ';' from the following line.

```
extension=php_mysql.dll
```

---

[1] Apache2 HTTP Server- http://httpd.apache.org/
[2] PHP 5.2- http://www.php.net/

Set error reporting[3] in php.ini file to E_ERROR.

```
error_reporting  =  E_ERROR
```

Install   PHP   5   in   the   Apache   HTTP   server.   To   the
<Apache2>\conf\httpd.conf file add the following .

```
# For PHP 5
LoadModule php5_module "C:/PHP/php5apache2.dll"
AddType application/x-httpd-php .php

# configure the path to php.ini
  PHPIniDir "C:/PHP/"
```

<Apache2> is the directory in which Apache 2 web server is installed,
and is C:/Apache2 in this chapter. If the directory in which PHP 5 is
installed is other than C:/PHP, replace C:/PHP with the directory in which
PHP 5 is installed. The PHPIniDir directive specifies the directory
containing the php.ini configuration file. We also need to install the MDB2
driver MySQL, which is available as a PEAR module. First, install PEAR.
Download go-pear.php[4] and run the following command to install PEAR.

```
C:/PHP>PHP go-pear.php
```

Download the MDB2 driver for MySQL *MDB2_Driver_mysql-1.2.2.tgz*
file. Copy the .tgz file to the C:/PHP directory. Install the MDB2 driver
with the following command.

```
C:/PHP>pear install -o MDB2_Driver_mysql-1.2.2.tgz
```

7.3 Installing PHPOnTrax

PHPOnTrax is available as a PEAR module. Download the PHPOnTrax[5]
pear module and install the module with the pear installer. Run the
following command to install PHPOnTrax.

```
pear install -o PHPonTrax-266svn.tgz
```

PHPonTrax gets installed as shown in Figure 7.1.

---

[3] Error Reporting- http://ca3.php.net/error_reporting
[4] go-pear.php-http://go-pear.org/
[5] PHPOnTrax- http://www.phpontrax.com/

Fig. 7.1 Installing PHPOnTrax

A PHPonTrax directory gets created in the C:\PHP\PEAR directory. Create a *trax.bat* file in the C:/PHP directory, which is in the PATH environment variable. To the trax.bat file add the following code.

```
php C:\PHP\PEAR\PHPonTrax\trax.php %1
```

The trax.bat file shall be used to create a PHPOnTrax application.

7.4 Creating a Trax Application

In this section we shall create a PHPonTrax application. Create an application catalog in the Apache web server root with the following command.

```
C:\Apache2\htdocs >trax catalog
```

A trax application with an application structure similar to a Ruby on Rails application gets created. The app directory consists of the controllers directory for the controller PHP scripts, the models directory for the model scripts and the views directory for the views templates. Instead of the controllers/application.rb of a Ruby on Rails application a controllers/application.php PHP script gets generated. The application.php script is shown below.

```
<?php
class ApplicationController extends ActionController
{

}
    ?>
```

PHPOnTrax being a direct port of the Rails framework you would notice the similarity of the PHP controller script with a Ruby controller script.

Instead of a database.yml file in a Ruby on Rails application, a database.ini database configuration file gets created in the config directory. Modify the config/environment.php directory to specify the PHP directory and the trax root directory. Define variables PHP_LIB_ROOT, TRAX_ROOT, and TRAX_ENV as shown in following listing.

```
define("PHP_LIB_ROOT",     "C:/PHP/PEAR");
define("TRAX_ROOT",
"C:/Apache2/Apache2/htdocs/catalog");
define("TRAX_ENV",     "development");
```

The public/.htaccess file specifies configuration directives for the Apache HTTP server. The configuration directives in the .htaccess file apply to the directory in which the .htaccess file is placed and the subdirectories of the directory. Modify the public/.htaccess file. Replace the following line:

```
php_value                              include_path
.:C:\Apache2\Apache2\htdocs\catalog/config
```

with the following line:

```
php_value                              include_path
.;C:\Apache2\Apache2\htdocs\catalog/config
```

The include_path directive specifies a list of directories and is used to locate files. Access the Trax application console with the URL http://localhost/catalog/public as shown in Figure 7.2.

Fig. 7.2 PHP On Trax Console

Modify the C:\Apache2\conf\httpd.conf file so that the directives in the .htaccess file may override earlier access information. Activate the mod_rewrite module by removing the '#' before the following line.

```
LoadModule rewrite_module modules/mod_rewrite.so
```

The mod_rewrite module provides rules based rewriting engine to rewrite requested URLs. Also set the AllowOverride directive to All.

```
AllowOverride All
```

The AllowOverride directive specifies which directives in the .htaccess may override earlier access information. Modify all the AllowOverride directives in the httpd.conf file. Modify the DocumentRoot directive in httpd.conf to the following.

```
DocumentRoot "C:/Apache2/htdocs/catalog/public"
```

Restart the Apache server. Next, we shall create a Trax application. Create a file *model.bat* in the htdocs/catalog directory and copy the following code to the directory.

```
php ./script/generate.php model  %1
```

The model.bat file is used to create model scripts. A model class models data in a database table. Create a file controller.bat in the htdocs/catalog directory and copy the following code to the batch file.

```
php ./script/generate.php controller  %1 %2 %3 %4
```

The controller.bat file is used to generate controller scripts. A controller class integrates a model class with the view templates. Generate a PHP model script, catalog, with the following command.

```
C:\Apache2\htdocs\catalog>model catalog
```

A model script catalog.php gets created in the catalog/app/models directory. PHP script catalog.php is shown below.

```
<?php
class Catalog extends ActiveRecord {
}
?>
```

Create a PHP controller, *catalog,* with the following command. Also create a controller action *phprails*.

```
C:\Apache2\htdocs\catalog>controller catalog phprails
```

A   catalog_controller.php   script   gets   created   in   the catalog/app/controllers directory. The controller script includes a function phprails(). Modify the phprails() function to output a message to the browser as shown in the following listing.

```php
<?php
class CatalogController extends ApplicationController
{
        function phprails() {

            echo "PHP on Rails";
        }
}
    ?>
```

A view template phprails.phtml gets created in the views/catalog directory. The phprails.phtml file may be edited; modify the phprails.phtml file to the following.

```
<h3>PHP on Rails</h3>
```

Invoke the phprails controller action with the URL http://localhost/catalog/phprails as shown in Figure 7.3.

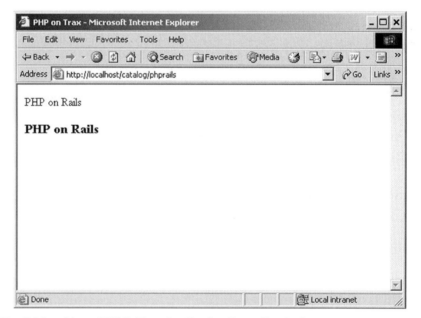

Fig. 7.3 Invoking a PHPOnTrax Application Controller Action

7.5 Creating a CRUD Application

In this section we shall create a CRUD application with PHP. First, modify the `config/database.ini` file for the MySQL database. We shall be using the `development` mode as follows.

```
[development]
    phptype = mysql
    database = test
    hostspec = localhost
    username = root
    password =
    persistent = true
```

We shall generate a model class and the scaffolding for the model class, which models a database table, with the scaffold generator. Create a *scaffold.bat* file in the C:\Apache2\htdocs\catalog directory. Copy the following code to the scaffold.bat file.

```
php ./script/generate.php scaffold  %1 %3
```

Before we create the scaffolding, create a database table `catalogs` in the MySQL database with the SQL script shown in the next listing. The primary key field should be "id" and of type `INT`.

```
CREATE TABLE catalogs(id INT PRIMARY KEY, Journal
VARCHAR(255), Publisher VARCHAR(255),
 Edition VARCHAR(255), Title Varchar(255), Author
Varchar(255));

INSERT INTO catalogs VALUES(1, 'developerWorks',
'IBM', 'September 2006',
'A PHP V5 migration  guide', 'Jack D. Herrington');

INSERT INTO catalogs VALUES(2, 'developerWorks',
'IBM', 'September 2006',
'Make Ruby on Rails easy with RadRails and Eclipse',
'Pat Eyler');
```

Delete the controllers/catalog_controller.php file and the models/catalog.php file, which were created for an example application in previous section. Create a scaffolding for the catalogs table with the following command.

```
C:\Apache2\htdocs\catalog>scaffold catalog catalog
```

A model class catalog.php gets generated in the models directory as shown below.

```php
<?php

class Catalog extends ActiveRecord {
}

?>
```

A controller script catalog_controller.php gets created in the controllers directory. The controller script is shown below.

```php
<?php

class CatalogController extends ApplicationController
{

    function index() {
      $catalog = new Catalog();
      $this->catalogs = $catalog->find_all();
      $this->content_columns = $catalog-
>content_columns;
    }

    function show() {
      $catalog = new Catalog();
      $this->catalog = $catalog-
>find($_REQUEST['id']);
    }

    function add() {
      $this->catalog = new
Catalog(array_key_exists('catalog',$_REQUEST) ?
                    $_REQUEST['catalog'] : null );
        if($_POST) {
            if($this->catalog-
>save($_POST['catalog'])) {
              Session::flash('notice', "Catalog was
successfully created.");
                $this->redirect_to =
url_for(array(":action" => "index"));
            } else {
              Session::flash('error', "Error adding
catalog to the database.");
            }
        }
    }

    function edit() {
```

```
      $catalog = new Catalog();
      $this->catalog = $catalog-
>find($_REQUEST['id']);
        if($_POST) {
             if($this->catalog-
>save($_POST['catalog'])) {
                Session::flash('notice', "Catalog was
successfully updated.");
                $this->redirect_to =
url_for(array(":action" => "show",
                     ":id" => $this->catalog));
             } else {
                Session::flash('error', "Error saving
catalog to the database.");
             }
        }
    }

    function delete() {
        if($_REQUEST['id'] > 0) {
             $catalog = new Catalog();
             $catalog = $catalog-
>find($_REQUEST['id']);
             if($catalog->delete()) {
                Session::flash('notice', "Catalog was
successfully deleted.");
             } else {
                Session::flash('error', "Error deleting
catalog from the database.");
             }
        }
        $this->redirect_to = url_for(array(":action"
=> "index"));
    }
}

  ?>
```

View templates _form.phtml, edit.phtml, index.phtml, add.phtml, and
show.phtml get created in the views directory. Modify the _form.phtml
view template. Add the following line as the first line in the _form.phtml
file.

```
<p><label for="catalog_id">Id:</label><br/>
  <?= text_field("catalog", "id") ?></p>
```

The default URL for a URL action is http://localhost/controller/action. Custom URLs may also be defined in the config/routes.php file. For example the index controller action of catalog controller may be invoked by specifying a custom router in the config/routes.php file.

```
$router->connect( "catalog",
       array(":controller" => "catalog",
       ":action" => "index") );
```

Next, we shall use the scaffolding for the catalogs table to add, modify and delete catalog entries. Invoke the index controller action with the URL http://localhost/catalog/index. The catalogs listing gets displayed. To create a new listing click on the New hyperlink as shown in Figure 7.4.

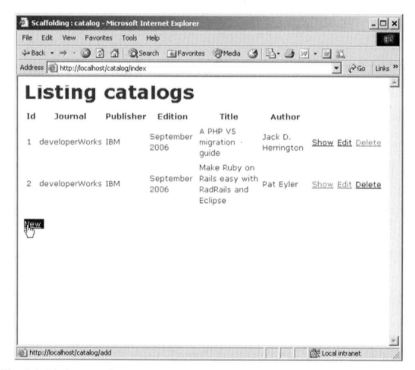

Fig. 7.4 Listings catalogs

In the New catalog view template, create a new catalog entry and click on the Create button as shown in Figure 7.5.

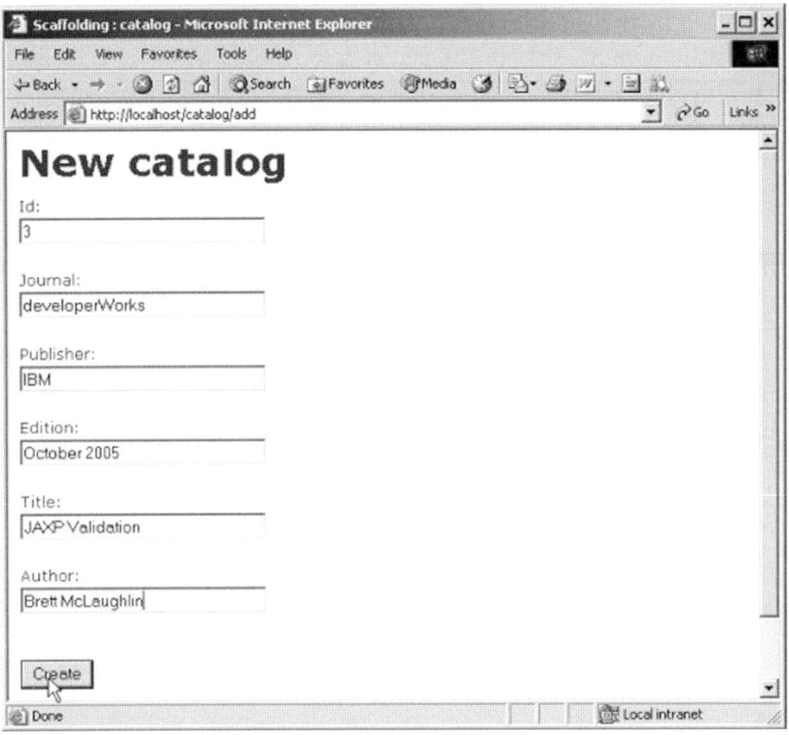

Fig. 7.5 Creating a new catalog entry

A new catalog entry gets added to the database table `catalogs` and gets listed in the "Listing catalogs". To edit a catalog entry, click on the Edit hyperlink as shown in Figure 7.6.

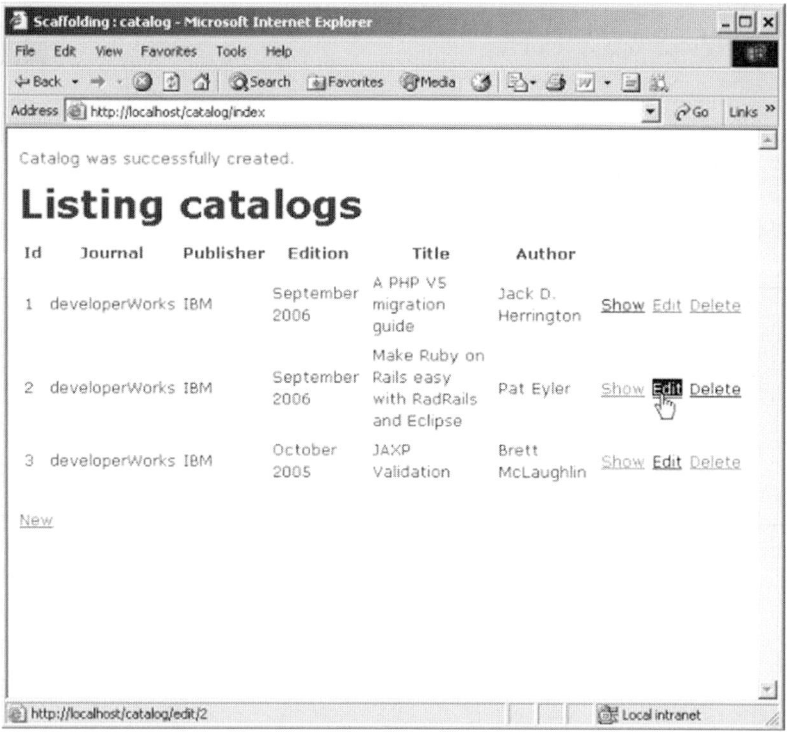

Fig. 7.6 Invoking the edit controller action

Next, modify the catalog entry, for example modify the title and click on the Edit button as shown in Figure 7.7. The primary key field, id should not be modified.

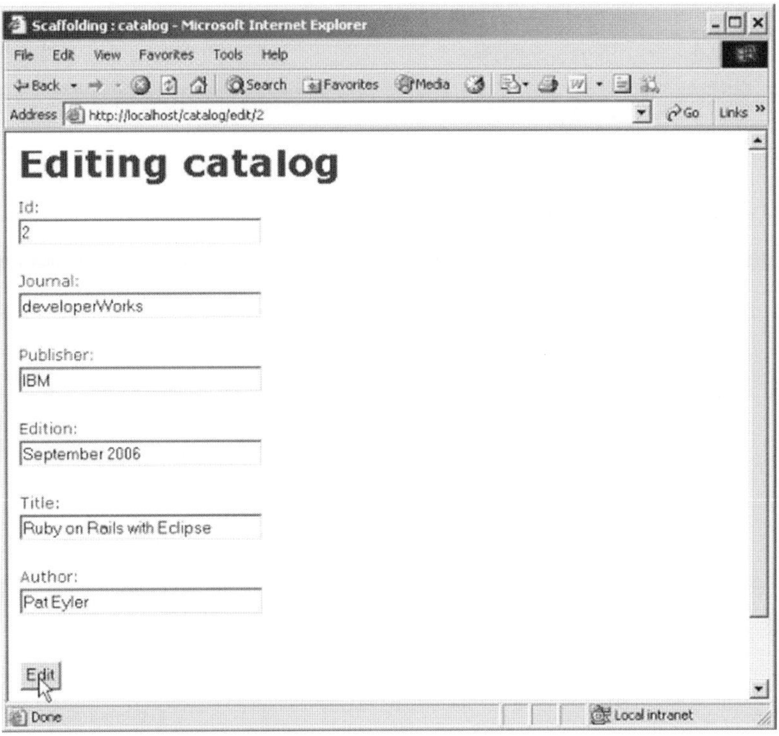

Fig. 7.7 Modifying a catalog entry

The catalog entry gets updated. Click on the Back hyperlink to display the modified listings. To display a catalog entry, click on the Show hyperlink as shown in Figure 7.8.

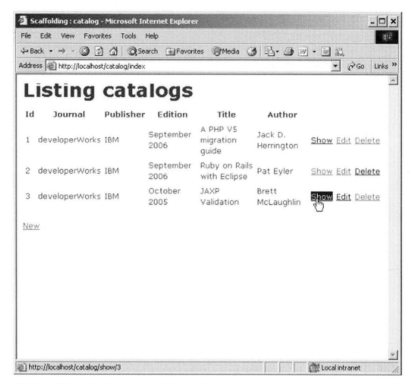

Fig. 7.8 Invoking the show controller action

The catalog entry gets displayed as shown in Figure 7.9.

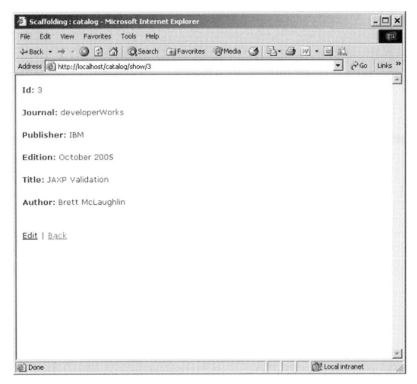

Fig. 7.9 Displaying Catalog Entry

To delete a catalog entry, click on the Delete hyperlink as shown in Figure 7.10.

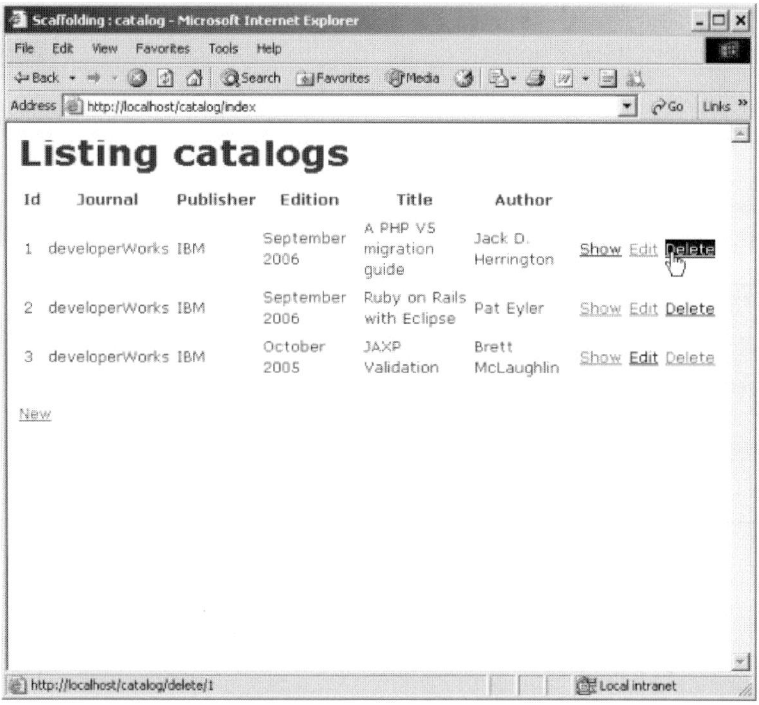

Fig. 7.10 Deleting a Catalog Entry

Catalog entry gets deleted from the database and the Listing catalogs as shown in Figure 7.11.

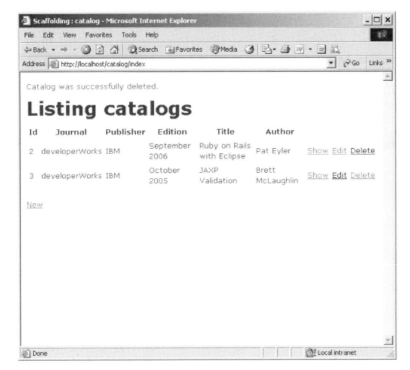

Fig. 7.11 Listings catalog

7.6 Summary

PHP provides various frameworks that are based on the Ruby on Rails framework. In this chapter we discussed one such PHP framework PHP On Trax to create a CRUD application with MySQL database.

8 LDAP On Rails

8.1 Introduction

A directory service is an application/s that stores, retrieves and modifies information about network resources such as network users. The actual data is stored in a database; a database service is an abstract layer on top of the database. Lightweight Directory Access Protocol (LDAP) is a lightweight protocol for accessing directory services. LDAP is based on entries; an entry is a set of attributes identified by a globally unique Distinguished Name (DN). Each of a directory entry's attributes has a type and one or more values. The attributes in a directory entry's distinguished name(DN) are arranged in a hierarchy from right to left with the rightmost attribute as the top entry and with the leftmost attribute/s that are unique at its level called as Relative Distinguished Name (RDN). A DN is a sequence of RDNs. Some examples of attribute types are discussed in Table 8.1.

Table 8.1 Attribute Types

Attribute Type	Description
o	Organization
dc	Domain component
ou	Organizational unit
cn	Common name
uid	Userid
dn	Distinguished name
mail	Email address

An entry in a directory is identified by a distinguished name (DN). An example of a directory entry's distinguished name is as follows.

```
cn=dvohra,ou=People,dc=example,dc=com
```

In the example DN, the base entry/root is "dc=example,dc=com". The relative distinguished name is "cn=dvohra". LDAP defines operations for adding, searching, modifying and deleting directory entries. A LDAP server is required to provide a LDAP directory service. Some of the commonly used LDAP servers are OpenLDAP, Tivoli Directory Server, and Oracle Internet Directory. We shall discuss the procedure to install OpenLDAP, Tivoli Directory Server and Oracle Internet Directory. We shall use the Oracle Internet Directory to create a directory service.

8.2 Installing OpenLDAP

We shall discuss the procedure to install the windows version of the OpenLDAP directory server.   Download OpenLDAP[1] for Windows operating system. Double-click on the OpenLDAP application *openldap-2.2.29-db-4.3.29-openssl-0.9.8a-BDB_ONLY-win32_Setup.exe.*   The OpenLDAP Setup wizard gets started as shown in Figure 8.1. Click on Next button.

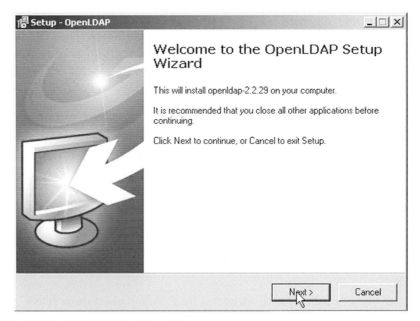

Fig. 8.1 OpenLDAP Setup Wizard

---

[1] OpenLDAP- http://download.bergmans.us/openldap/

Accept the license agreement and click on Next button. Select the default destination, C:\Program Files\OpenLDAP, and click on Next button. Select components BDB-tools and OpenLDAP-slapd as NT service and click on Next as shown in Figure 8.2.

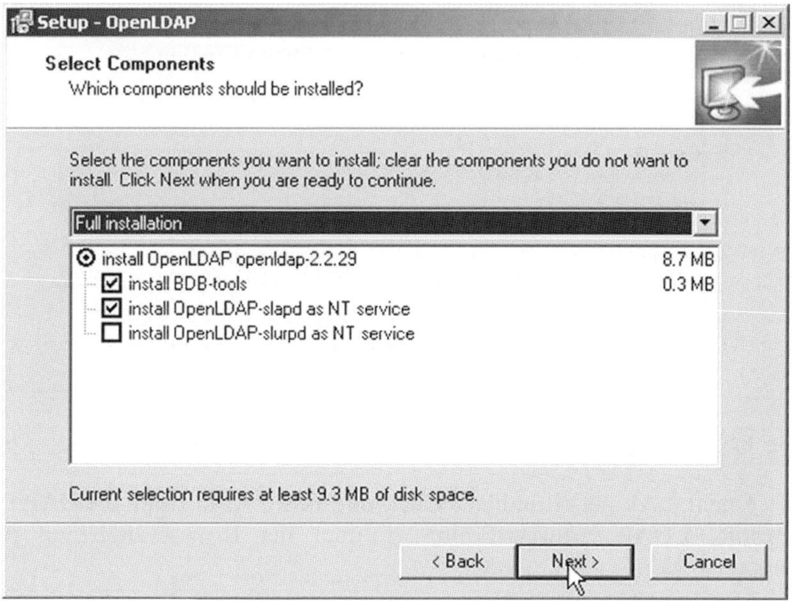

Fig. 8.2 Selecting OpenLDAP Components

Specify a Start Menu Folder and click on Next. Select additional tasks such as "automatically start OpenLDAP NT service after reboot" and "Create a desktop item" and click on Next. Click on the Install button to install OpenLDAP as shown in Figure 8.3.

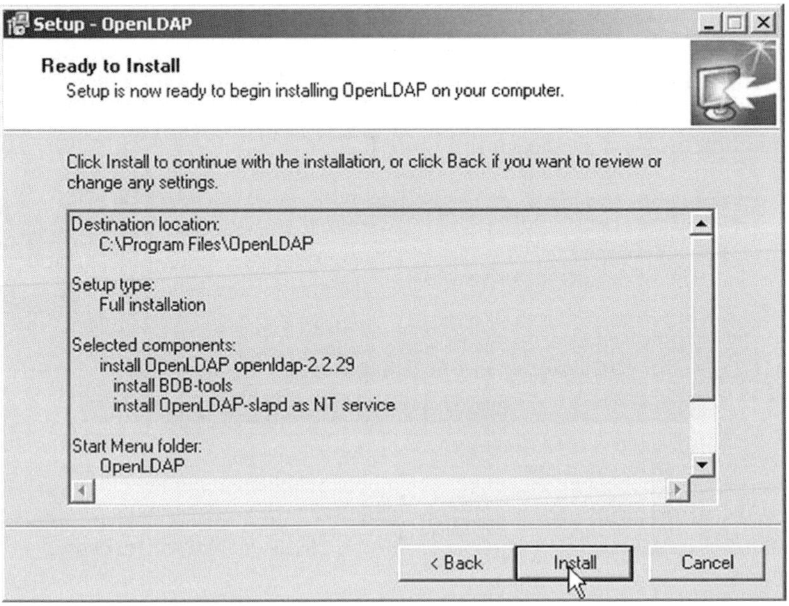

Fig. 8.3 Installing OpenLDAP

OpenLDAP gets installed. Click on Finish. Also install a LDAP GUI console, LDAP Browser/Editor[2]. Extract the Browser282b2.zip to a directory.

Configuration for a `slapd` server is specified in the `slapd.conf` configuration file. Configuration information is of three types: global, back-end and database. The configuration information is specified with directives; the global directives precede the back-end directives, which precede the database directives.

The global directives apply to all backends and database types. Some of the commonly used global directives are discussed in Table 8.2.

Table 8.2 Global Directives

Directive	Description
idletimeout <integer>	Specifies the number of seconds after which an idle connection is closed.

---

[2] LDAP Browser- http://www-unix.mcs.anl.gov/~gawor/ldap/

Table 8.2 (continued)

Directive	Description
loglevel<integer>	Specifies level at which debug information and other statistics are logged. Value of −1 enables all debugging and 0 disables debugging.
sizelimit <integer>	Specifies the maximum number of entries to return from a search operation. Default value is 500.
timelimit <integer>	Specifies the maximum number of seconds spent on a request. Default value is 3600.

Backend directives specify a backend and apply to all database instances in a backend. The commonly used backend directive is as follows.

```
backend <type>
```

The backend directive specifies a backend declaration. Some of the backend types are bdb (Berkley DB transactional backend) and sql (SQL programmable backend).

Database directives specify information about a database instance. Some of the commonly used database directives are discussed in Table 8.3.

Table 8.3 Database Directives

Directive	Description
database <type>	Specifies a database instance declaration. Some of the types are bdb and sql.
readonly {on|off}	Specifies a readonly database.
rootdn <DN>	Specifies a superuser DN that may bypass directory access and administrative restrictions.
rootpw <password>	Specifies the password for rootdn DN.
suffix <dn suffix>	Also known as 'root' or 'base', specifies the topmost entry in a DIT (Directory Information Tree).

Table 8.3 (continued)

Directive	Description
directory	Specifies the directory in which Berkley DB database files are located.

Next, we shall modify the directives in the slapd.conf file in the C:\Program Files\OpenLDAP   directory of the OpenLDAP server we installed earlier.   The database directive is already set to bdb for the Berkley DB database. Set the suffix, rootdn, and rootpw as shown in following listing.

```
database   bdb
suffix     "dc=example,dc=com"
rootdn     "cn=Manager,dc=example,dc=com"
rootpw     netldap
directory ./data
```

Start/Restart the OpenLDAP Directory service. LDAP entries are represented in LDAP Data Interchange Format (LDIF) in a .ldif format. The format of an entry in a LDIF file is as follows.

```
#comment
dn: <distinguished name>
<attrdesc>: <attrvalue>
<attrdesc>: <attrvalue>
```

Next, we shall add attributes to the base dn. Create an .ldif file (*baseentry.ldif*) in the C:\Program Files\OpenLDAP directory and copy the following ldif listing to the file.

```
dn: dc=example,dc=com
objectClass: top
objectClass: dcObject
objectClass: organization
dc :example
o: NetLDAP
```

Next, start the OpenLDAP slapd server with the following command from the OpenLDAP installation directory.

```
C:\Program Files\OpenLDAP> .\slapd -d 1
```

OpenLDAP provides the ldapadd tool to add a directory entry. Run the ldapadd command on the *baseentry.ldif* file as shown below. The –d argument specifies the bind DN for authenticating connection to the directory. The –w argument specifies the password for authenticating to the bind DN. The –file argument specifies the LDIF file that contains the directory entries.

```
C:\Program Files\OpenLDAP>ldapadd   -D
"cn=Manager,dc=example,dc=com" -v -w netldap   -f
baseentry.ldif
```

Double click on the *lbe.bat* file to start the LDAP Browser. In the Connect frame specify the following parameters for the different fields.

```
Host: localhost
Port: 389
Base DN: dc=example,dc=com
User DN: cn=Manager
```

Select the "append base DN" and click on the Connect button as shown in Figure 8.4.

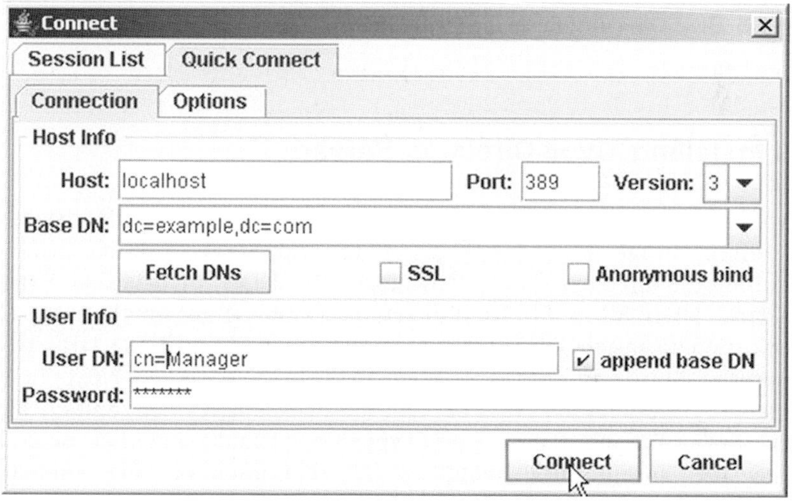

Fig. 8.4 Connecting to the LDAP Browser

The LDAP Browser displays the base directory entry as shown in Figure 8.5. Directory entries may be added to the base entry using Ruby on Rails.

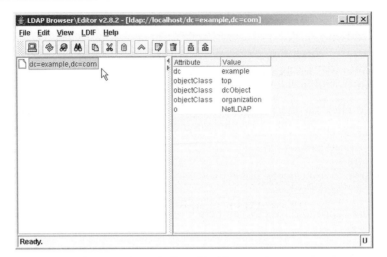

Fig. 8.5 Base Directory Entry in OpenLDAP

8.3 Installing Tivoli Directory Server

Tivoli Directory Server 6.0 is built on top of DB2 UDB database. Therefore, install DB2 UDB 8.1 Enterprise Server Edition prior to installing the directory server. Download DB2 UDB 8.1 database. Extract the DB2 UDB 8 zip file to a directory. Double-click on the setup.exe application to install DB2 UDB 8. In the Setup Wizard, the DB2 UDB Enterprise Server Edition is selected by default. Click on Next. In the Welcome page click on Next. Accept the license agreement and click on Next. Select the installation type (Typical by default) and click on Next. Select the "Install DB2 Enterprise Server Edition on this computer" checkbox and click on Next. Select the default installation directory , C:\Program Files\IBM\SQLLIB by default, and click on Next. Specify username (db2 for example) and password (db2admin for example) for DB2 Administration Server and click on Next. Select the default administration contact list settings and click on Next. Select the default DB2 instance, DB2, and click on Next. Select the default settings in Prepare the DB2 tools catalog frame and click on Next. Select "Defer the task.. " in the "Specify a contact .." frame and click on Next. In the "Enable operating system security for DB2 objects" uncheck the checkbox "Enable operating system security. Click on Next. Click on Install to install DB2 UDB 8 database. The DB2 database gets installed. Click on Finish.

Next, create the sample database. In the IBM DB2 First Steps Launchpad frame click on Create Sample Database. In the Create Sample Database frame check the DB2 UDB sample checkbox and click on OK. The SAMPLE database gets created.

Next, we shall install the Tivoli Directory Server 6.0. Download Tivoli Directory Server 6.0. Extract the zip file *6.0.0.3-TIV-ITDS-Win32-IF0002.zip* To a directory. Double-click on Setup.exe to install the Tivoli Directory Server. In the Install wizard for Tivoli Directory Server 6.0 click on Next as shown in Figure 8.6.

Fig. 8.6 Tivoli Directory Server InstallShield Wizard

Accept the license agreement and click on Next. The DB2 8.1 gets listed in the "The following applications have been identified on your system" frame. Click on Next. Specify the installation directory, C:\Program Files\IBM\LDAP by default, and click on Next. Select the Tivoli Directory Server features to install including the Web Adminsitration Tool 6.0, and click on Next as shown in Figure 8.7.

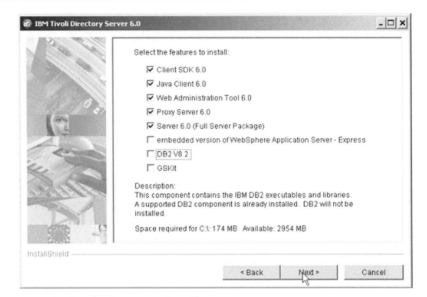

Fig. 8.7 Selecting the Features to Install

The installation settings get listed. Click on Next to install the Tivoli Directory Server 6.0. The Tivoli Directory Server 6.0 gets installed. Click on Finish. A configuration tool gets started. Click on Create to create a directory server instance as shown in Figure 8.8.

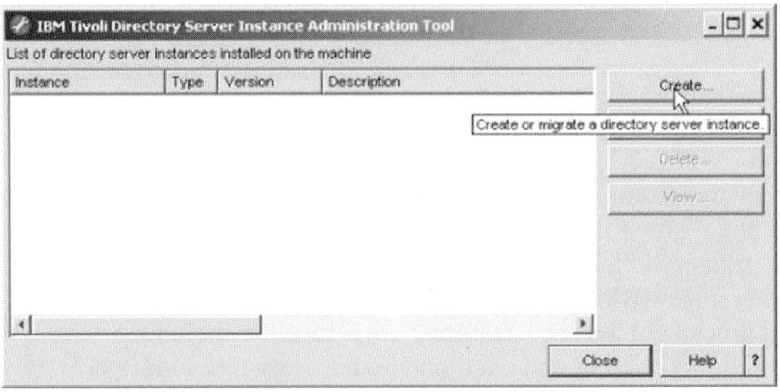

Fig. 8.8 Creating a Tivoli Directory Server Instance

Select "Create a new directory server instance" and click on Next. Specify a username, db2admin for example. Specify an encryption seed string (0123456789abc for example), which is a string of characters that contains only printable ISO-8859-1 ASCII characters with values in the range of 33 to 126, such as a-z, A-Z, and 0-9, and is from 12 to 1016 characters in length. Click on Next. Select DB2 instance that is to be associated with the directory server instance. Select DB2 instance name, DB2, and click on Next as shown in Figure 8.9.

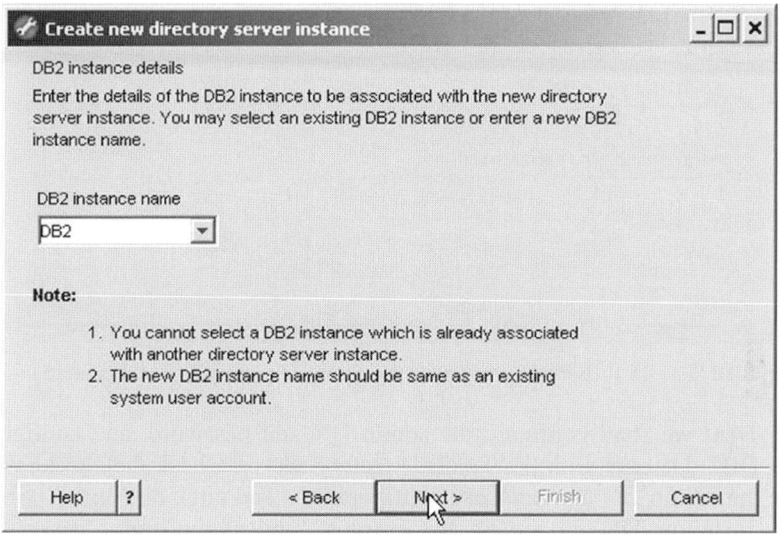

Fig. 8.9 Setting the Database for the Tivoli Directory Server Instance

In the TCP/IP settings frame check the "Listen on all configured IP addresses" checkbox and click on Next. Select the default TCP/IP port settings, Server port number being 389, and click on Next as shown in Figure 8.10.

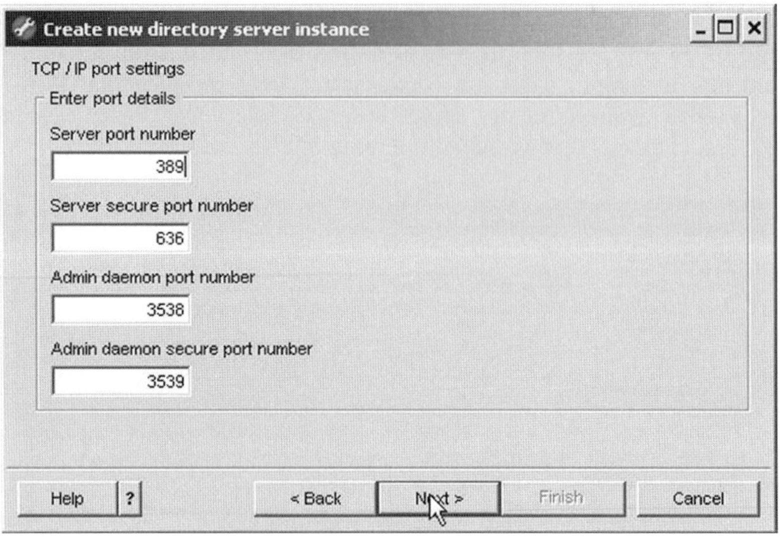

Fig. 8.10 The TCP/IP Port Settings for the Tivoli Directory Server Instance

Next we shall configure the admin DN and password, and configure the DB2 database with the Tivoli Directory server. Check the checkboxes for the admin DN and database configurations and click on Next. Specify administrator DN, `cn=root` for example, and administrator password, `tivoli` for example. Click on Next as shown in Figure 8.11.

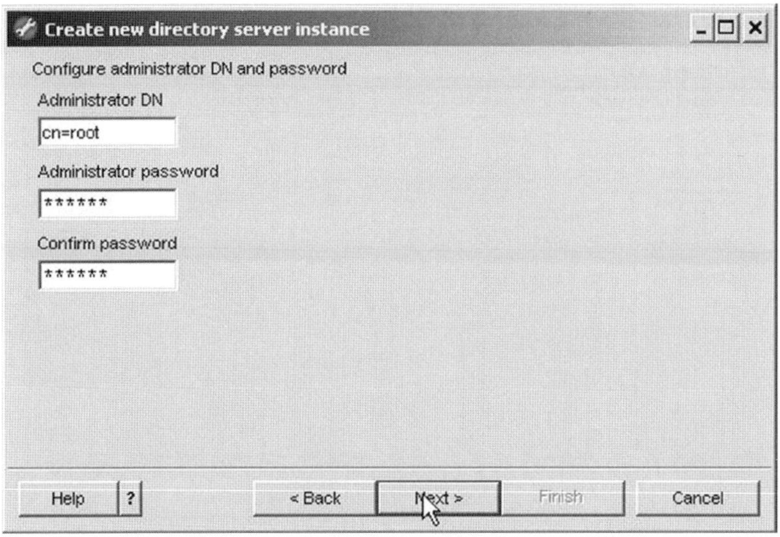

Fig. 8.11 Specifying the Administrator DN and Password

In the Configure database frame, specify the database username, db2, and password, db2admin, that were specified when installing the DB2 database. Specify database name as SAMPLE, which was created earlier. Click on Next as shown in Figure 8.12.

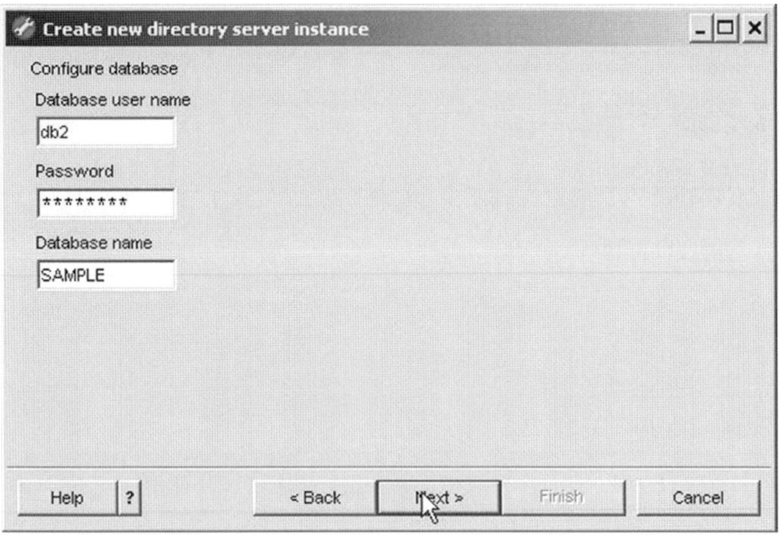

Fig. 8.12 Configuring the Directory Server Instance with the DB2 Database

The directory server instance settings get listed. Click on Finish as shown in Figure 8.13.

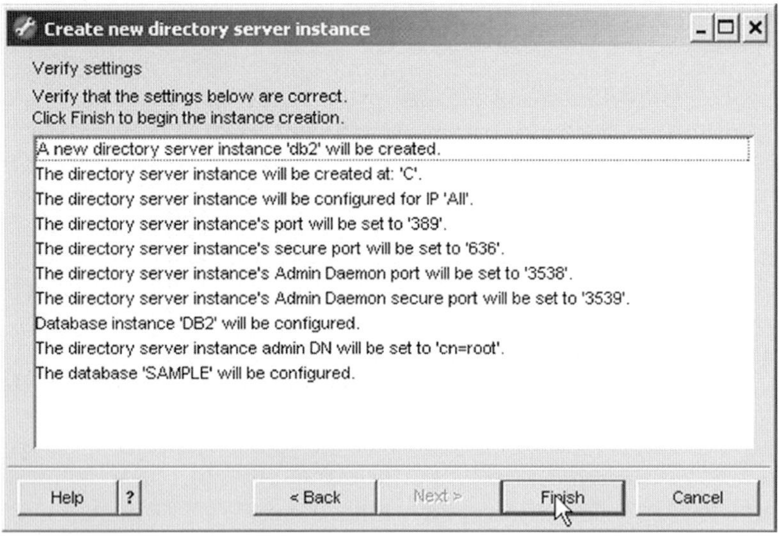

Fig. 8.13 Settings for the Directory Server Instance

A directory server instance gets created. Click on Close. Click on Close in the instance administration tool as shown in Figure 8.14.

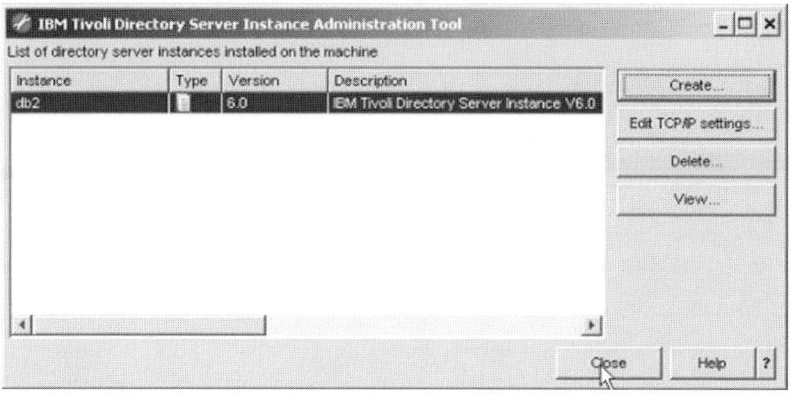

Fig. 8.14 New Directory Server Instance

Tivoli Directory Server 6.0 provides a Web Administration Tool to administer the directory server. Before we may use the Web Administration Tool we need to install the WebSphere Application server and install the Web Administration Tool application in the WebSphere application server. Download WebSphere Application Server 6.1 and extract the zip file to a directory. Double-click on the launchpad application. Start the installation wizard for WebSphere Application Server. Click on Next in the WebSphere application server installation wizard. Accept the license agreement and click on Next. Click on Next in the System Prerequisites check frame. Check the Install the Sample Applications checkbox and click on Next. Specify the installation folder, C:\Program Files\IBM\WebSphere\AppServer by default, and click on Next. Specify administrative username and password and click on Next. In the Installation Summary frame click on Next to install the WebSphere application server. WebSphere application server gets installed. Click on Finish.

Next, we shall deploy the Web Administration Tool to the WebSphere Application Server. Copy the C:\Program Files\IBM\LDAP\V6.0\idstools\IDSWebApp WAR file to the C:\Program Files\IBM\WebSphere\AppServer6\installableApps directory. Start the WebSphere Application Server from the WebSphere Application Server-First Steps. Start the Administrative Console. In the Administrative console, select Applications>Install New Application to install the Web Administration Tool application. Specify the directory path the Web

Administration   Tool   application,   C:\Program
Files\IBM\WebSphere\AppServer6\installableApps\IDSWebApp,   and
specify context root as IDSWebApp, and click on Next as shown in Figure
8.15.

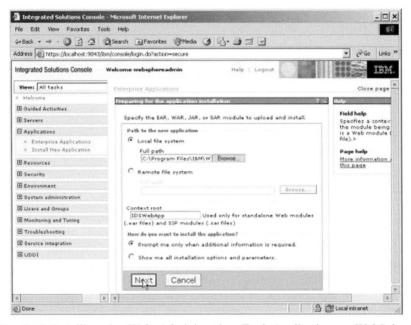

Fig. 8.15 Installing the Web Administration Tool Application to WebSphere
Application Server

Select the default installation options and click on Next. Map the IBM
Tivoli Directory Server application to the WebSphere application server
and click on Next. Select the default_host as the virtual host to deploy the
directory server web application and click on Next. In the installation
summary page click on Finish. The Web Administration Tool application
gets deployed to the WebSphere application server. Click on Save to save
the install configuration to master configuration. The Web Administration
Tool application gets installed and started as shown in Figure 8.16. If the
IDSWebApp application is not started click on Start.

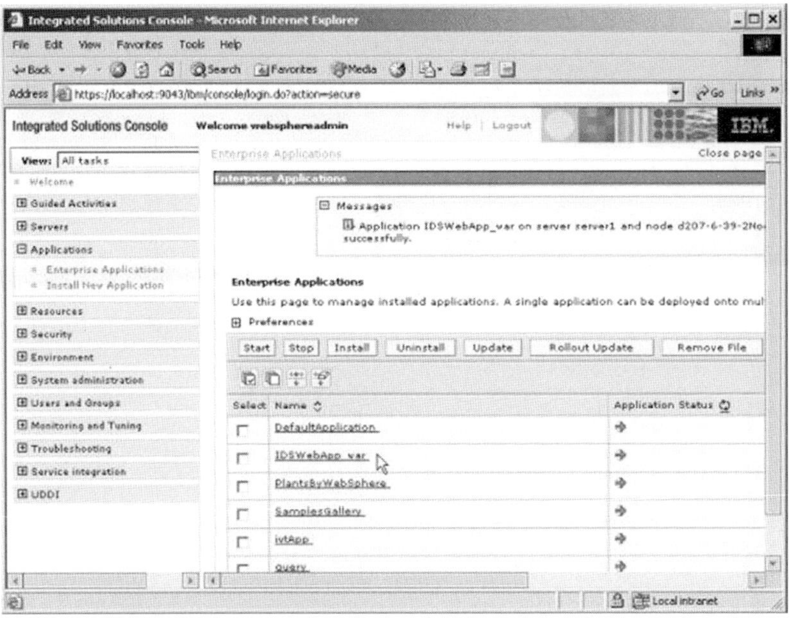

Fig. 8.16 Web Administration Tool Application

Next, we shall login to the Web Administration Tool and create a server configuration for the Tivoli Directory Server instance. Login to the Web Administration Tool console with the URL http://localhost:9080/IDSWebApp/IDSjsp/Login.jsp. Console Admin as LDAP Hostname. Specify the default username, "superadmin", and the default password, "secret", and click on Login as shown in Figure 8.17.

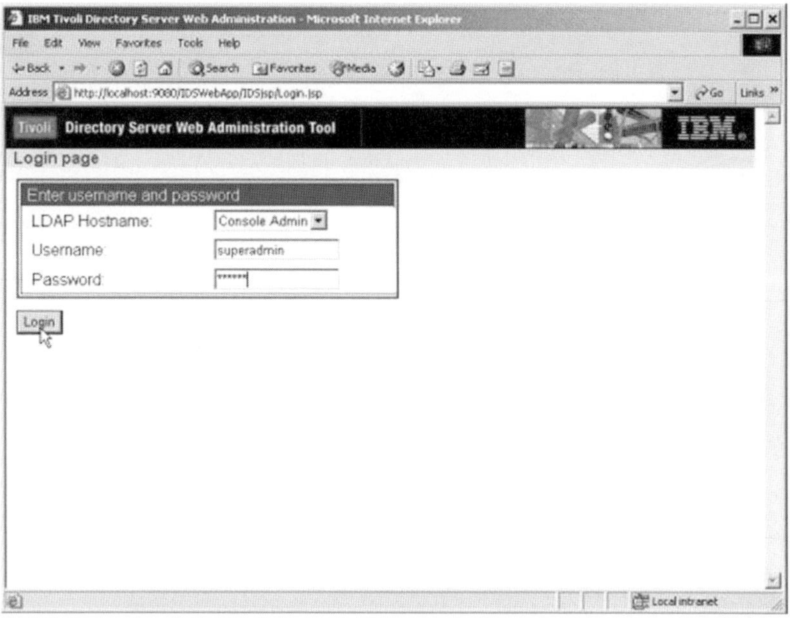

Fig. 8.17 Logging in to Web Administration Console as Console Adminstrator

In the Web Administration Tool console the console administrator username may be modified with the "Change console administrator login" link. The password may be modified with the "Change console administrator password" link. Click on "Manage console servers" to create a server configuration for the Tivoli directory server as shown in Figure 8.18.

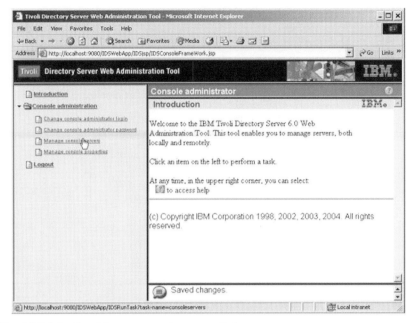

Fig. 8.18 Selecting Manage console servers link

In Manage Console Servers click on Add as shown in Figure 8.19.

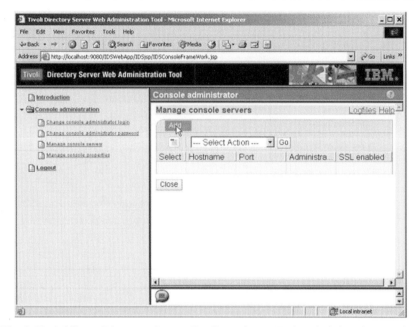

Fig. 8.19 Adding a Directory Server Configuration to Web Administration Tool

Specify Hostname as `localhost` and select the default port settings. Click on OK as shown in Figure 8.20.

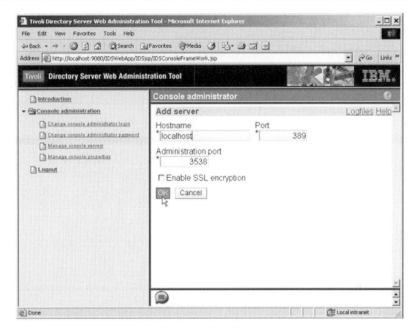

Fig. 8.20 Specifying the Host and Port settings for the Directory Server

The directory server configuration gets added to the Web Administration Tool. Click on OK. The directory server configuration gets listed in Manage console servers as shown in Figure 8.21.

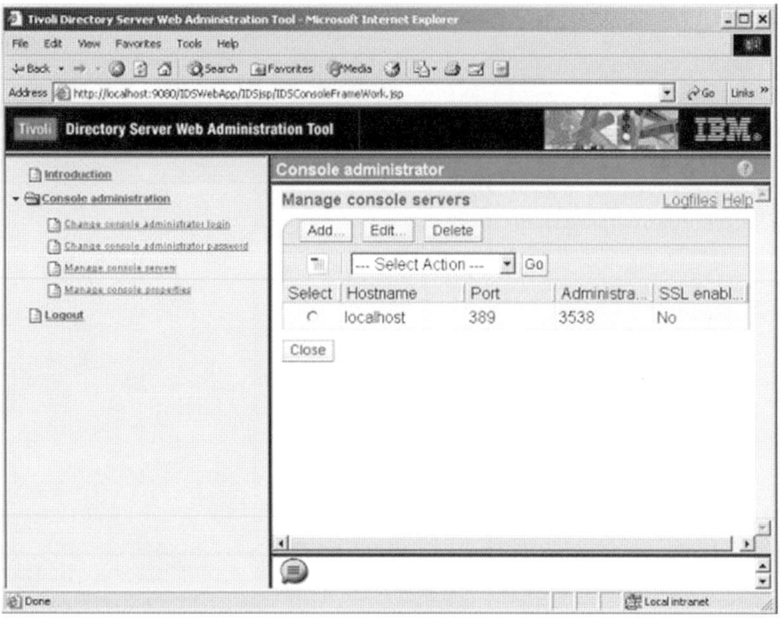

Fig. 8.21 Directory Server Configuration Added

Logout from the Console Admin. Re-login with http://localhost:9080/IDSWebApp/IDSjsp/Login.jsp URL. Select LDAP Hostname as `localhost:389`. Specify Username as `cn=root`, and Password as `tivoli`, which we configured when creating a directory server instance. Click on Login as shown in Figure 8.22.

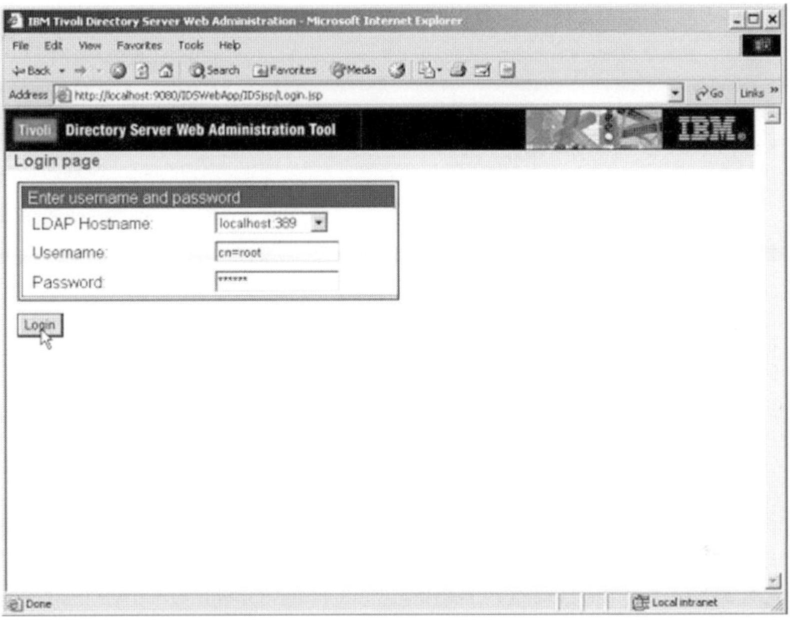

Fig. 8.22 Logging in to Web Administration Tool

The Web Administration Tool console gets displayed. Start the Tivoli Directory Server instance if not already started. Click on Directory Management>Manage Entries to display the directory entries in the directory server instance a shown in Figure 8.23. A directory entry may be created in the cn=localhost directory entry using Ruby on Rails.

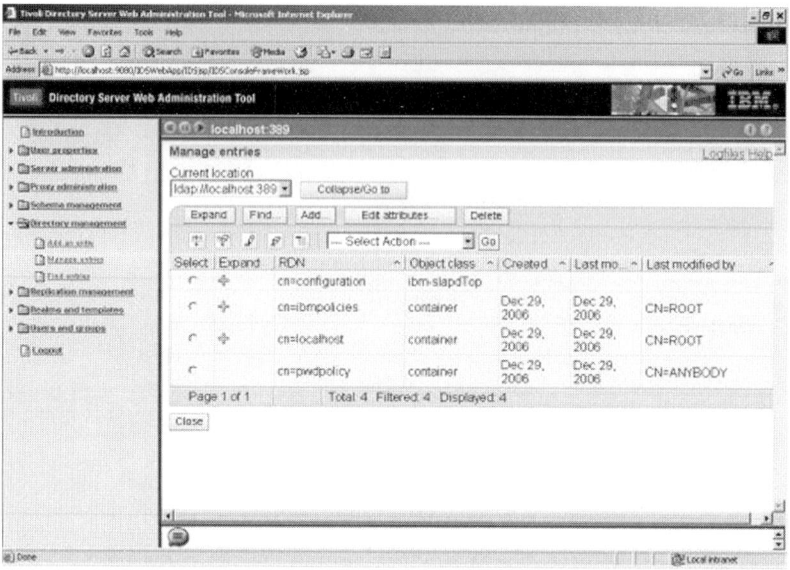

Fig. 8.23 Listing the Directory Entries in the Tivoli Directory Server Instance

8.4 Installing Oracle Internet Directory

Oracle Internet Directory provides a user repository for Oracle Identity Management and is included in the Oracle Identity Management Infrastructure and Oracle Identity Federation download. Download Disk1 and Disk2 of the Oracle Identity Management Infrastructure and Oracle Identity Federation zip files. Extract disk1 to a directory. Extract disk2 zip file to the same directory as disk 1. To install Oracle Internet Directory click on the \install\setup application. The Oracle Universal Installer gets started. Click on Next. Specify the installation directory in the Specify File Locations frame and click on Next as shown in Figure 8.24.

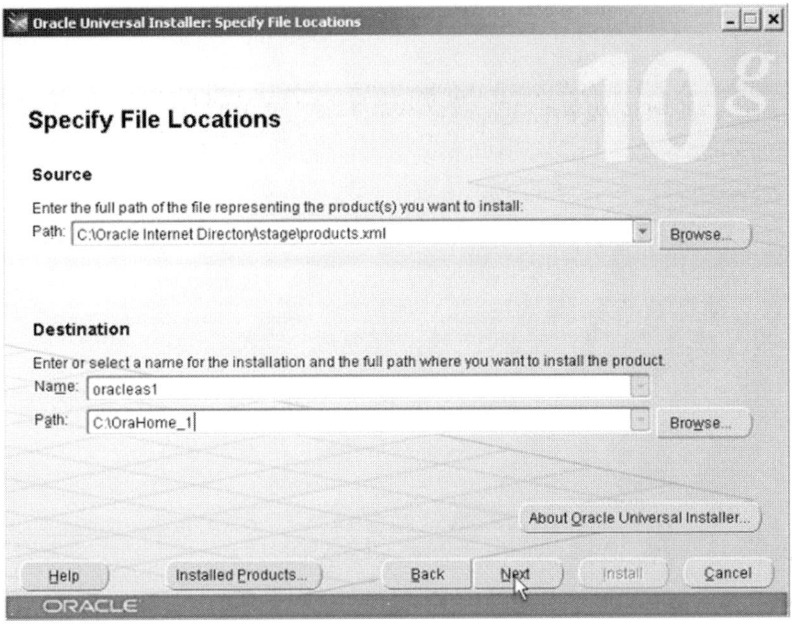

Fig. 8.24 Installing Oracle Internet Directory

Select Oracle Application Server Infrastructure 10g and click on Next as shown in Figure 8.25. The Oracle Application Server Infrastructure 10g includes the Oracle Internet Directory and the Oracle database.

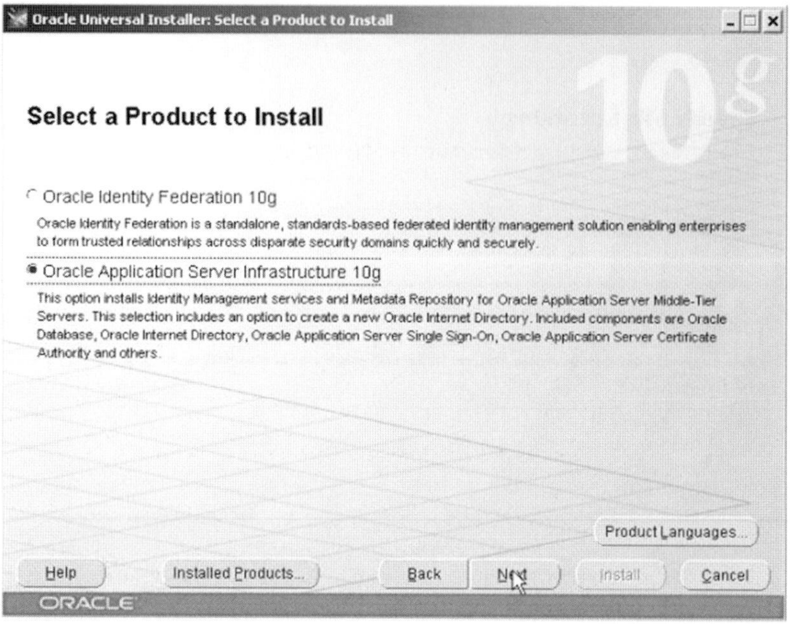

Fig. 8.25 Selecting Oracle Application Server Infrastructure

In the Select Installation Type frame select Identity Management and Metadata Repository, which installs the Oracle Internet Directory, and the Oracle 10g database 10g including the Metadata repository. Click on Next as shown in Figure 8.26.

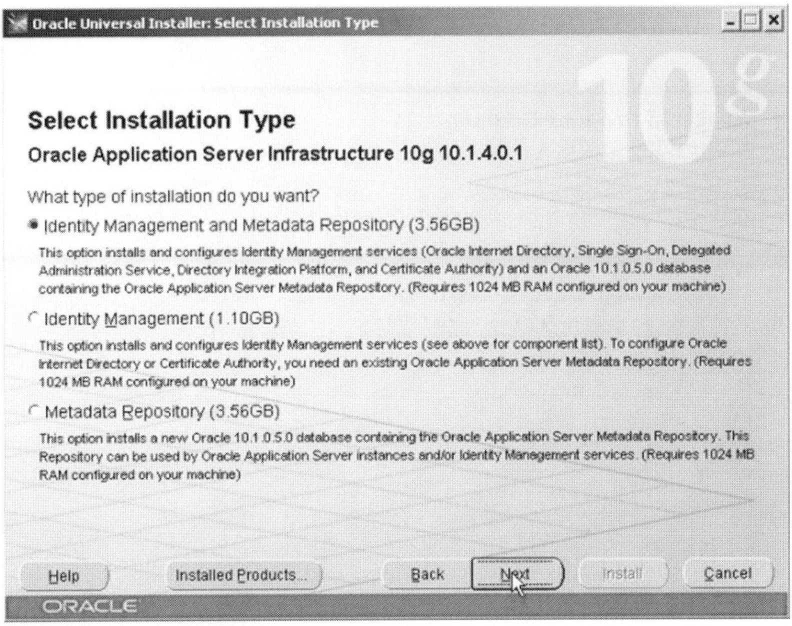

Fig. 8.26 Selecting Installation Type

Select the default Oracle Application Server Infrastructure 10g components to install and click on Next as shown in Figure 8.27.

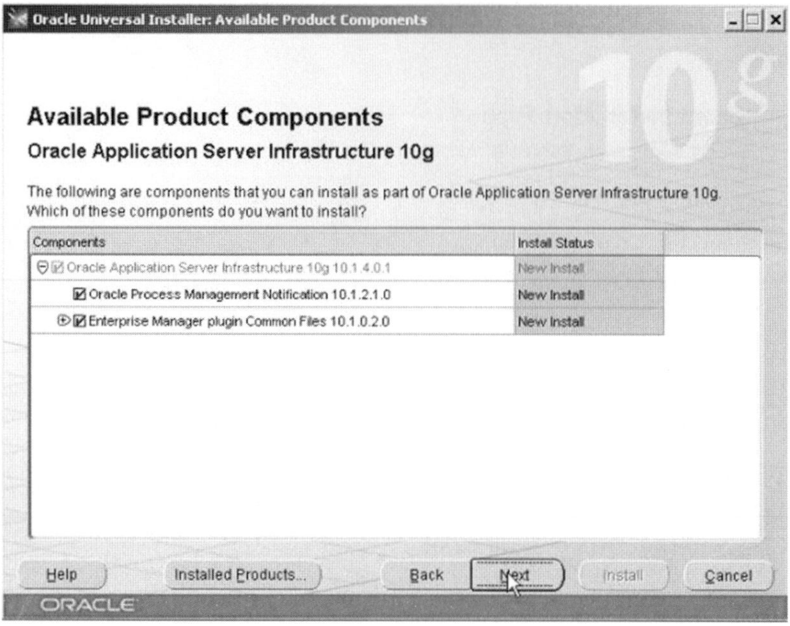

Fig. 8.27 Selecting Oracle Application Server Infrastructure Components

Check the pre-installation requirements and click on Next. Select the default configuration options and click on Next as shown in Figure 8.28.

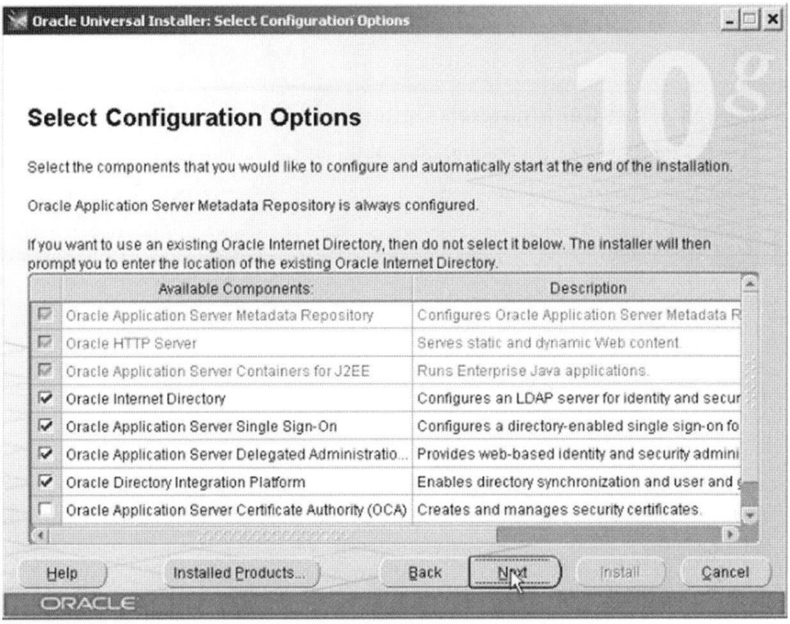

Fig. 8.28 Selecting Configuration Options

Select the default port configuration options and click on Next as shown in Figure 8.29.

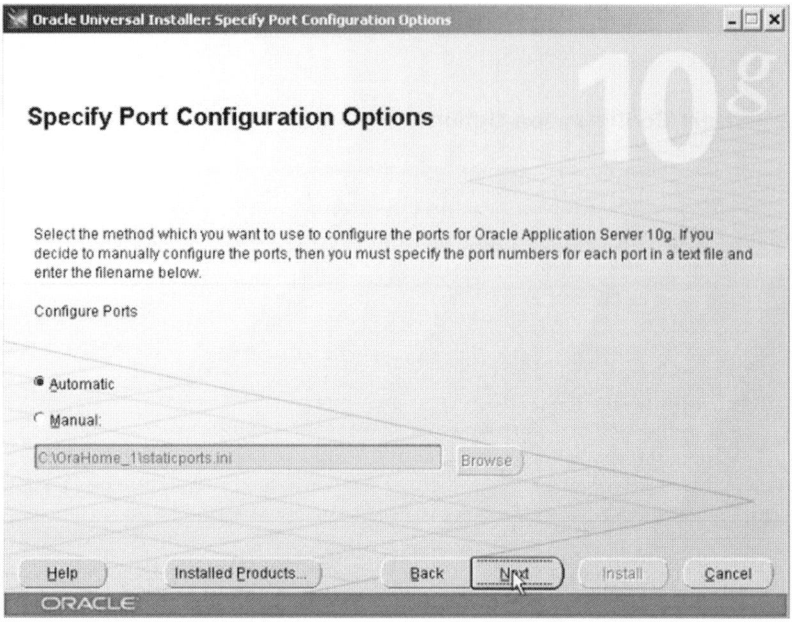

Fig. 8.29 Selecting Port Configuration Options

Specify a namespace in the Oracle Internet Directory to create new users. For example specify `dc=example,dc=com` and click on Next as shown in Figure 8.30.

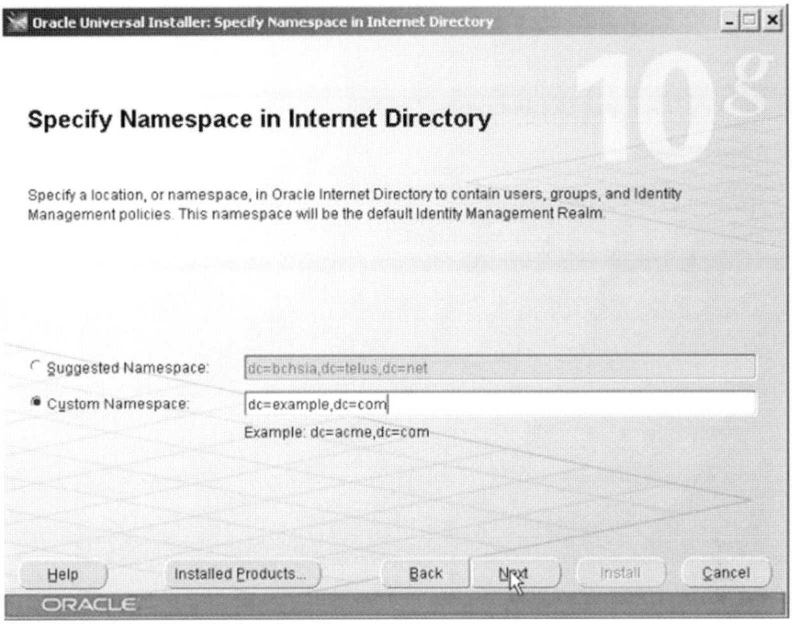

Fig. 8.30 Specifying Root DN

Specify database configuration options, or select the default database configuration options, and click on Next as shown in Figure 8.31.

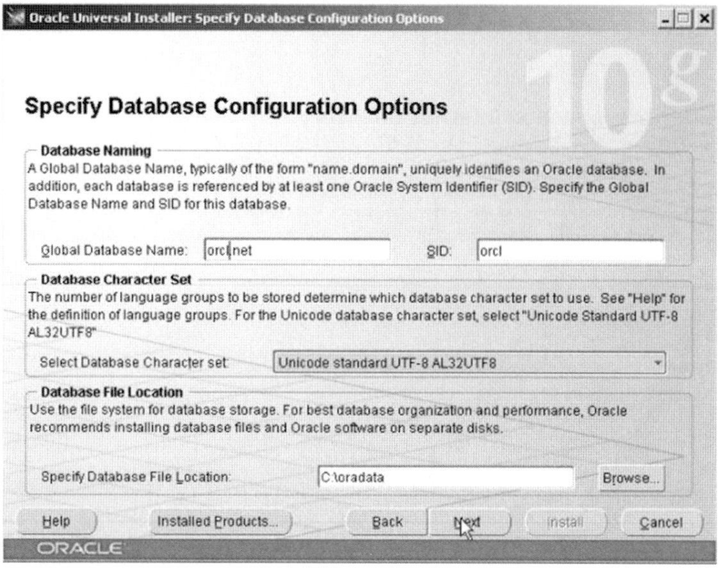

Fig. 8.31 Specifying Database Configuration Options

Specify database schema password and click on Next as shown in Figure 8.32.

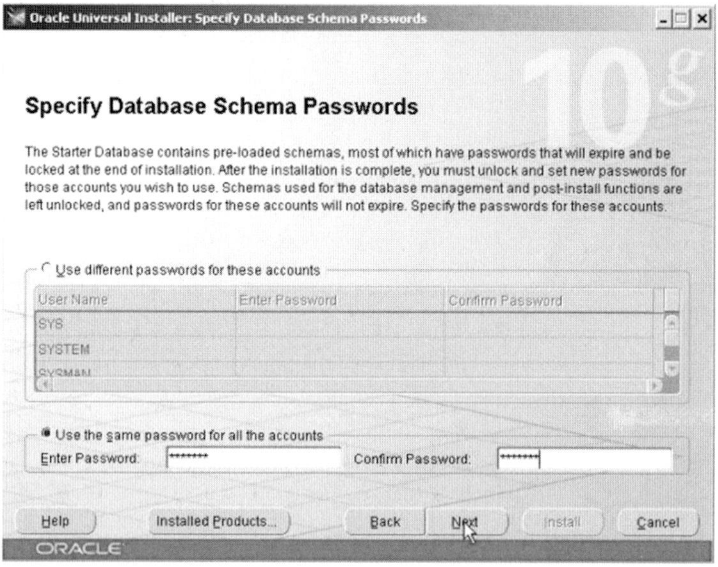

Fig. 8.32 Specifying Database Schema Passwords

Specify an Oracle Application Server Infrastructure instance name. Specify a password for ias_admin administrator username and click on Next as shown in Figure 8.33.

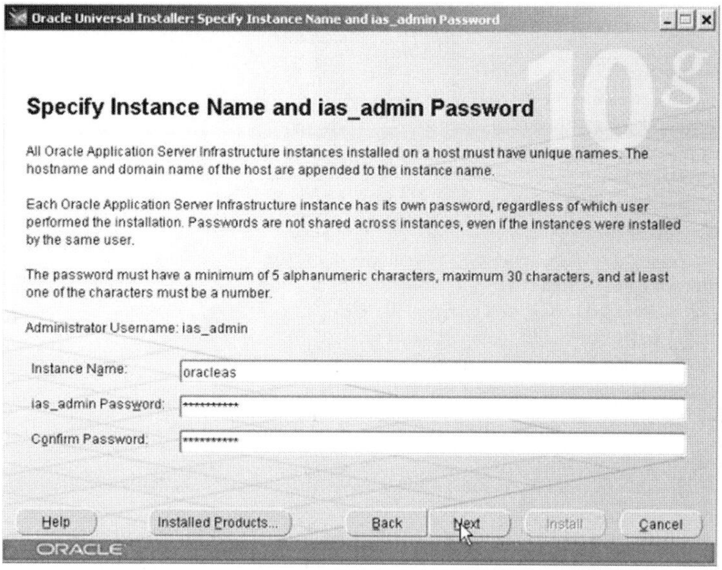

Fig. 8.33 Specifying Oracle Application Server Infrastructure Instance Name and Password

Click on Install to install the Oracle Application Server Infrastructure as shown in Figure 8.34.

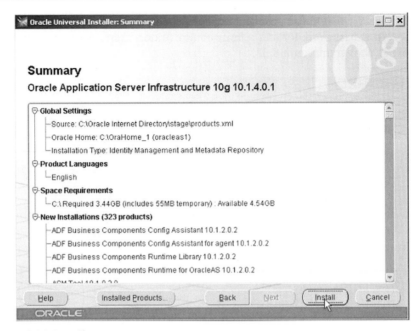

Fig. 8.34 Install

The installation starts as shown in Figure 8.35. A dialog shall prompt for the Oracle Application Server 10g disk 2. Specify the stage directory of disk2.

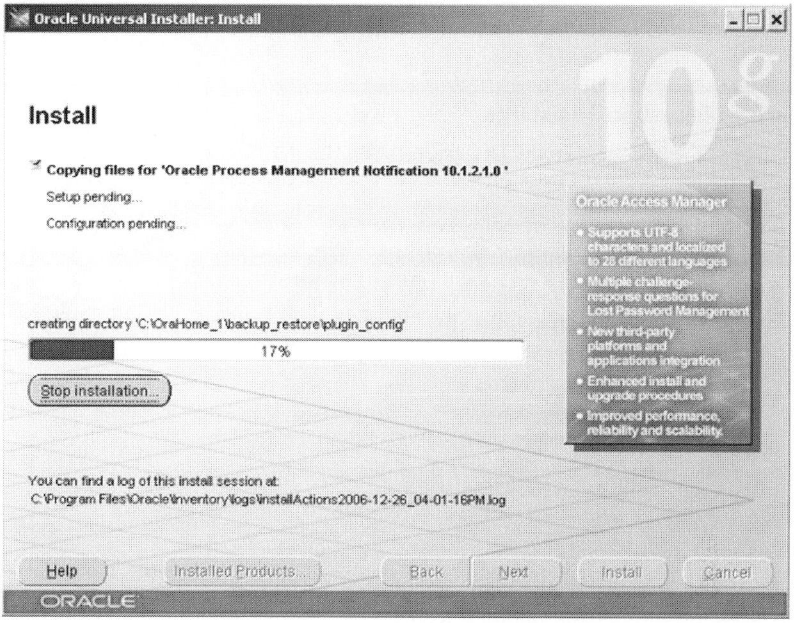

Fig. 8.35 Installing Oracle Application Server Infrastructure

Next, the configuration assistants get installed as shown in Figure 8.36.

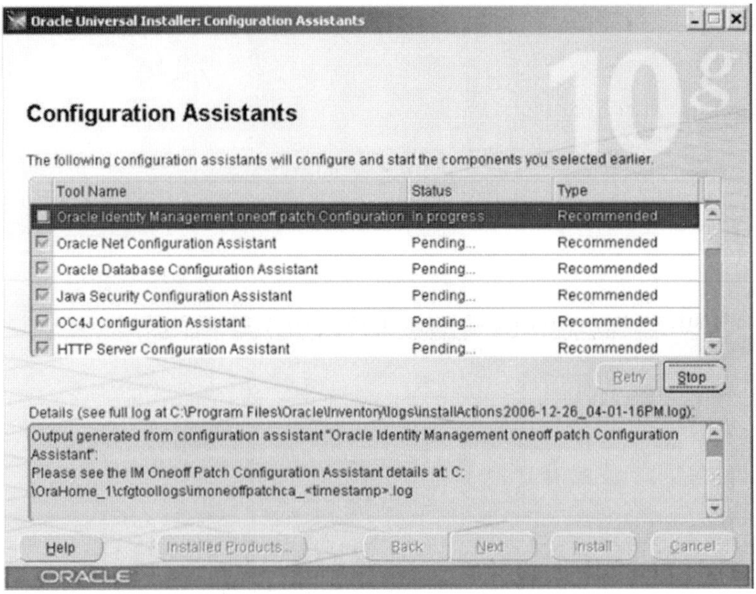

Fig. 8.36 Installing Configuration Assistants

Click on Next after all the Configuration Assistants have installed as shown in Figure 8.37.

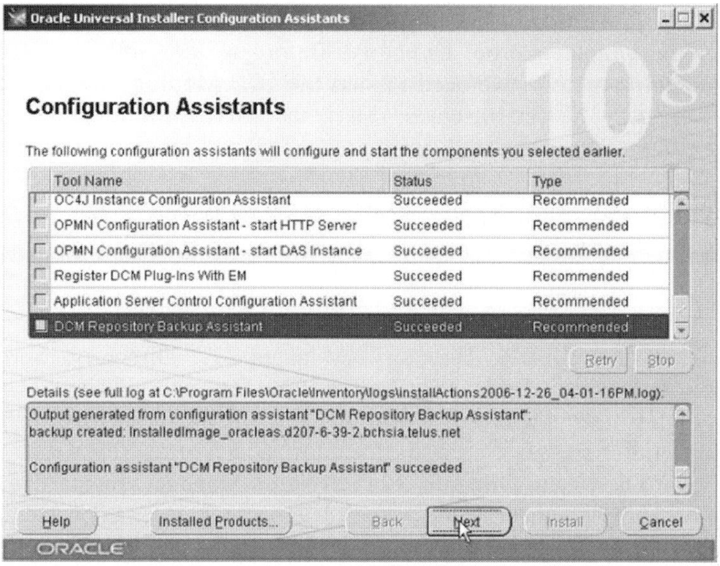

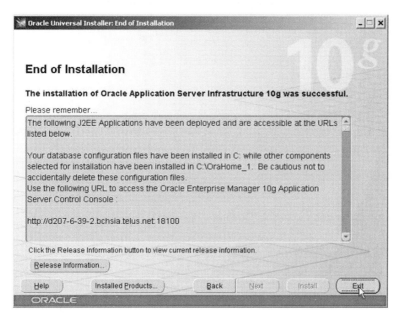

Fig. 8.37 Installation of Configuration Assistants Completed

Click on Exit to complete the installation as shown in Figure 8.38.

Fig. 8.38 Installation of Oracle Application Server Infrastructure Completed

Next, we shall start the Oracle Directory Manager, which is used to administer the Oracle Internet Directory. Before we are able to use the Oracle Internet Directory we need to start the OID Monitor and a Oracle Internet Directory server instance. Start the OID Monitor with the following command.

```
C:\>oidmon start
```

Start an Oracle Directory Server Instance with the following command.

```
C:\>oidctl  server=oidldapd instance=2 start
```

Next, start the Oracle Directory Manager. A Directory Server Connection dialog gets displayed. Click on OK. Directory Server Name Manager dialog gets displayed. Click on Add. In the Directory Server Connection dialog specify Server as localhost and port as 389. Click on OK. Click on OK in the Directory Server Name Manager. In the Oracle Directory Manager Connect frame specify username as User as orcladmin, which is the superuser and specify the password as the password specified for the Oracle Application Server Infrastructure 10g instance. Specify Server as localhost and Port as 389, the default port. Click on Login as shown in Figure 8.39.

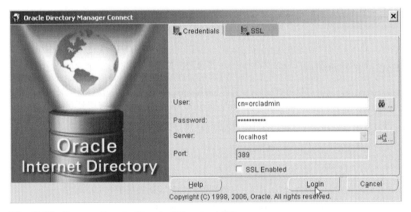

Fig. 8.39 Connecting to Oracle Directory Manager

The Oracle Directory Manager gets started as shown in Figure 8.40.

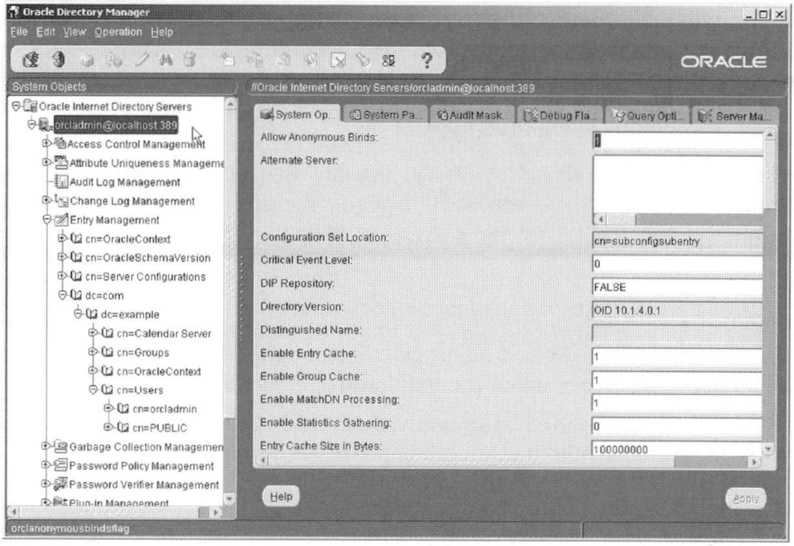

Fig. 8.40 Oracle Directory Manager

8.5 LDAP with PHP

In PHP a LDAP directory service is created with the PHP LDAP extension. A connection is created with the LDAP server using the ldap_connect() function.

```
$ldapconn = ldap_connect($ldaphost, $ldapport);
```

Bind to the LDAP server with the ldap_bind() function.

```
$r=ldap_bind($ldapconn,"userdn","password");
```

To add a directory an entry, create an entry consisting of an array of attributes. For example, the 'cn' attribute is specified as follows.

```
$directory_entry["cn"]="JohnSmith";
```

Specify the dn of the directory entry to be added and add the directory entry to the LDAP directory using the ldap_add() method.

```
$dn="cn=JohnSmith,dc=example,dc=com";
$r=ldap_add($ldapconn, $dn, $directory_entry);
```

To modify a directory entry, create an array of directory entry attributes with the modified values. Modify the directory entry with the ldap_modify() function.

```
$r=ldap_modify($ldapconn,$dn, $directory_entry);
```

To search for a directory entry, specify an attribute array for which attribute values are to be retrieved. Specify the dn of the directory entry to search. Specify a filter for the search.

```
$attribute_array=array("cn", "sn", "title");
$dn="JohnSmith,dc=example,dc=com";
$filter = "(objectclass=*)";
```

Search the directory using the ldap_search() method.

```
$sr=ldap_search($ldapconn,$dn, $filter,
$attribute_array);
```

8.6 LDAP with Java

The Java Naming and Directory Interface (JNDI) API provides the directory service functionality in the javax.naming.directory package. Using the JNDI API a directory entry's attributes may be created, added, updated and removed. First, we would create an initial directory context. Create a Hashtable and set the INITIAL_CONTEXT_FACTORY and PROVIDER_URL properties. The PROVIDER_URL property specifies the LDAP server url to access a directory service.

```
Hashtable env = new Hashtable();
env.put(Context.INITIAL_CONTEXT_FACTORY,
          "com.sun.jndi.ldap.LdapCtxFactory");
env.put(Context.PROVIDER_URL,
"ldap://localhost:389/cn=localhost");
```

Create a DirContext object using the Hashtable of environment properties.

```
DirContext ctx = new InitialDirContext(env);
```

For example, retrieve the attributes of the directry entry with dn "cn=John Smith,cn=localhost".

```
Attributes attr=ctx.getAttributes("cn=John
Smith,cn=localhost");
```

Obtain the enumeration of attributes. Iterate over the attributes to output attribute id and attribute values.

```
for(NamingEnumeration
enum=attrs.getAll();enum.hasMore();){
    Attribute attr=enum.next();
  System.out.println("Attribute ID:
  "+attr.getID());
  for(NamingEnumeration
  attrVals=attr.getAll();attrVals.hasMore();)
  {
  System.out.println("Attribute value:
  "+attrVals.next();
  }
  }
```

The DirContext interface provides various search() methods to search for a directory entry. Specify the attributes to match using an Attributes object.

```
Attributes attrs = new BasicAttributes();
  attrs.put(new BasicAttribute("sn",
  "Smith"));
```

Search a directory service using a search() method.

```
NamingEnumeration
enum=ctx.search("cn=localhost",attrs);
```

The search() methods return an enumeration of SearchResult objects. Iterate over the enumeration to output attributes for the directory entries retrieved with the search.

```
while(enum.hasMore()){
    SearchResult
    result=(SearchResult)enum.next();
  Attributes attrs=result.getAttributes();
    }
```

The DirContext interface provides the modifyAttributes() methods to modify attributes in a directory entry. The ModificationItem class represents an object to modify. A ModificationItem object may be created using one of the modifications: DirContext.ADD_ATTRIBUTE, DirContext.REPLACE_ATTRIBUTE and DirContext.REMOVE_ATTRIBUTE. For example, create an array of ModificationItem objects.

```
ModificationItem[] mods = new
ModificationItem[3];
```

Initialize the array to replace the title attribute, add the telephonenumber attribute and remove the facsimileTelephoneNumber attribute.

```
mods[0] = new
ModificationItem(DirContext.REPLACE_ATTRIBUTE,
          new BasicAttribute("title", "J2EE
    Developer"));

mods[1] = new
ModificationItem(DirContext.ADD_ATTRIBUTE,
          new
    BasicAttribute("telephonenumber", "1 555
    555 1234"));

    mods[2] = new
    ModificationItem(DirContext.REMOVE_ATTRI
    BUTE,
          new
    BasicAttribute("facsimileTelephoneNumber
    "));
```

Specify the dn to modify.

```
String dn="cn=John Smith,cn=localhost";
```

Modify the attributes.

```
ctx.modifyAttributes(dn, mods);
```

8.7 Installing NET::LDAP

Install the ruby-net-ldap gem with the following command while connected to the Internet.

```
C:/ruby>gem install ruby-net-ldap
```

The Net::LDAP class provides a Ruby implementation of the LDAP client protocol. The Net::LDAP class is used for bind, search, add, modify, delete, and rename operations. The Net::LDAP class methods are discussed in Table 8.4.

Table 8.4 Net::LDAP Class Methods

Method	Description
add(args)	Adds a new directory entry. Arguments are as follows: :dn-DN of the new entry. :attrs-Attributes of the new entry specified as a Hash.
add_attribute(dn, attribute, value)	Adds a value to an attribute. If the specified attribute is not already defined, creates a new attribute.
authenticate(username, password)	Specifies the authentication credentials to the LDAP server.
bind(auth=@auth)	Connects to the LDAP server and requests authentication based on the the authentication credentials specified in the open or new method. Returns true if a connection with the LDAP server is established.
bind_as(args={})	Binds as a specified user
delete(args)	Deletes a directory entry for a specified DN, which is the only supported argument.
delete_attribute(dn, attribute)	Deletes an attribute and all its values. The dn parameter specifies the directory entry and the attribute specifies the attribute to delete.
new(args = {})	Creates an object of type Net::LDAP, but does not open a connection with the server. The arguments may be as follows: :host-LDAP server host, defaults to localhost. :port-LDAP server port, defaults to 389. :auth-A hash containing authorization parameters.

Table 8.4 (continued)

Method	Description
get_operation_result()	Returns a operation result code and message for the bind, search, add, modify, rename, and delete operations.
modify(args)	Modifies the attribute values for a specified directory entry. Takes the following arguments as a Hash: :dn-The DN of the directory entry to modify. :operations-The modifications, each of which is specified as an array consisting of the following elements: Operator-May be :add, :replace, or :delete. Attribute name-The attribute to be modified. Attribute value-The value of attribute.

8.8 Creating a Rails Application

We need to create a Rails application to create a directory service with the Net::LDAP Ruby library. Use the rails command to create a rails application, oidldap.

```
c:/ruby>rails oidldap
```

A rails application with the complete directory structure of the rails application gets created. We shall run the Net::LDAP Ruby on Rails application as a controller script with controller actions for creating a directory entry, modifying a directory entry, searching a directory entry and deleting a directory entry. We shall also create RHTML view templates corresponding to each of these controller actions to input data for the directory entries. Create a controller script, directory, which consists of controller actions index, add_entry, modify_entry, search_entry, and delete_entry.

```
C:/ruby/netldap>ruby script/generate controller
directory index add_entry modify_entry search_entry
delete_entry
```

A controller script *directory_controller.rb* gets created in the controllers directory. The controller script consists of controller actions index, add_entry, modify_entry, search_entry, and delete_entry. View templates index.rhtml, add_entry.rhtml, modify_entry.rhtml, search_entry.rhtml, and delete_entry.rhtml get created in the views/directory folder. In the following sections we shall modify the controller actions and view templates to add a directory entry, modify a directory entry, search a directory entry and delete a directory entry. Next, modify the config/routes.rb to add routes for the .rhtml templates.

```
map.connect '/directory/add_entry.rhtml',
:controller => 'directory', :url =>
'/directory/add_entry.rhtml'

map.connect '/directory/modify_entry.rhtml',
:controller => 'directory', :url =>
'/directory/modify_entry.rhtml'

map.connect '/directory/search_entry.rhtml',
:controller => 'directory', :url =>
'/directory/search_entry.rhtml'

map.connect '/directory/delete_entry.rhtml',
:controller => 'directory', :url=>
'/directory/delete_entry.rhtml'
```

We also need to configure the rendering of the files corresponding to file URLs specified in *routes.rb*. In the directory controller index action, render the file specified in the URL in a map.connect in routes.rb.

```
def index
            render
:file=>"C:/ruby/oidldap/app/views"+params[:url]
            return
   end
```

8.9 Creating a Directory Entry

Next, we shall create a directory entry in the Oracle Internet Directory server. First, install Oracle Internet Directory. A directory entry consists of attributes and attribute values. Dn of a directory entry represents the distinguished name for the directory entry. A Dn consists of the relative distinguished name and the base dn. We shall create a directory entry in the "cn= PUBLIC,cn=Users,dc=example,dc=com" root/base DN. Start the OID Monitor with the following command.

```
C:\>oidmon start
```

Start an Oracle Directory Server Instance with the following command.

```
C:\>oidctl  server=oidldapd instance=2 start
```

Next, start the Oracle Directory Manager. The Oracle Directory Manager lists the directory entries in the Entry Management node as shown in Figure 8.41.

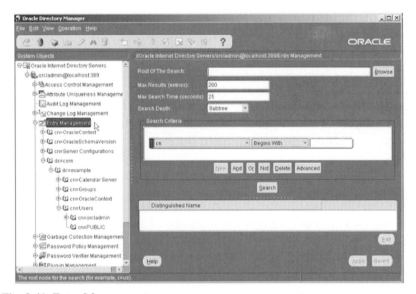

Fig. 8.41 Entry Management

Each directory entry is identified with a dn attribute. The objectClass attributes specify the type of data, and required and optional attributes in an entry. Object classes form a class hierarchy and some of the commonly used object classes are top, organization, and organizationalPerson. All object classes are sub classes of the object class top. We shall create a directory service with the top, person, and organizationalPerson object classes. The "top" object class does not have any required attributes. "Person" object class required attributes are "cn" and "sn". "OrganizationalPerson" object class does not have any required attributes. Some of the attributes that may specified in a directory entry of object class type organizationalPerson are "title" and "telephoneNumber".

First, modify the add_entry.rhtml view template to input data for the directory entry. Define a form with the form_tag method of the FormTagHelper class. Define a field in the form with the text_field(object_name, method, options = {}) method, which returns an input tag of type "text". Method parameter object_name represents an object for the form template. The method parameter represents a form field as an attribute of the form object. For example, the following text field:

```
text_field("directory_entry", "title", "size" => 20)
```

converts to HTML form text field:

```
<input type="text" id="directory_entry_title"
name="directory_entry[title]" size="20"
value="#{@directory_entry.title}" />
```

To the add_entry.rhtml, add text fields for first name, last name, title, telephone number, department, and fax number. A directory entry's attribute for first name is "gn", attribute for last name is "sn", attribute for title is "title", attribute for telephone number is "telephoneNumber", attribute for department is "physicalDeliveryOfficeName", and attribute for FAX number is "facsimileTelephoneNumber". The add_entry.rhtml is listed below.

```
<html>
<body>

<div>
    <table border='0' cellspacing='0'
cellpadding='5'>
        <tr>
          <caption>
            Add Directory Entry
          </caption>
        </tr>
            <!-- start_form_tag -->
      <%= form_tag :action => "add_entry" %>
        <tr>
           <td>First Name*</td>
           <td><%= text_field(:add_entry, :gn)
%></td>
        </tr><tr>
           <td>Last Name*</td>
```

```
              <td><%= text_field(:add_entry, :sn)
%></td>
        </tr>

        <tr>
            <td>Title</td>
             <td><%= text_field(:add_entry, :title)
        %></td>
        </tr><tr>
            <td>Telephone Number</td>
              <td><%= text_field(:add_entry,
              :telephoneNumber) %></td>
        </tr>

        <tr>
            <td>Department</td>
            <td><%= text_field(:add_entry,
:physicalDeliveryOfficeName) %></td>
        </tr>


        <tr>
            <td>Fax Number</td>
            <td><%= text_field(:add_entry,
:facsimileTelephoneNumber) %></td>
        </tr>


        <tr>
            <td><input type="submit"
value="Submit"></td>
        </tr>
      <%= end_form_tag %>
      </table>
         </div>
 * indicates a required field.
</body>
</html>
```

Next, modify the controller action add_entry. Retrieve the parameter values. Retrieve the first name (:gn) and the last name (:sn) and define a variable cn.

```
values = params[:add_entry]
    gn=values[:gn]
    sn= values[:sn]
    cn=gn+sn
```

Define the distinguished name for the directory entry, dn, which consists of the rdn and the base dn.

```
dn="cn="+cn+",cn=PUBLIC,cn=Users,dc=example,dc=com"
```

Retrieve values for the other form fields.

```
title=values[:title]
telephoneNumber=values[:telephoneNumber]
physicalDeliveryOfficeName=values[:physicalDeliveryOf
ficeName]
facsimileTelephoneNumber=values[:facsimileTelephoneNu
mber]
```

Define a variable, *attr*, which consists of the different attributes of the directory entry.

```
attr = {
    :cn => cn,
    :objectclass => ['top', 'person',
'organizationalPerson'],
    :sn => sn,
    :title => title,
    :telephoneNumber => telephoneNumber,
    :physicalDeliveryOfficeName =>
physicalDeliveryOfficeName,
    :facsimileTelephoneNumber =>
facsimileTelephoneNumber
    }
```

Open a connection to the Oracle Internet Directory server and add the directory entry to the server using the add() method.

```
Net::LDAP.open( :host => 'localhost', :port =>
389,:base =>
'cn=PUBLIC,cn=Users,dc=example,dc=com', :auth => {
:method => :simple, :username => 'cn=orcladmin',
:password => 'oidadmin10' } ) do |ldap|
    ldap.add( :dn => dn, :attributes => attr )
end
```

Start the WEBrick server with the following command.

```
C:/ruby/oidldap>ruby script/server
```

Invoke the add_entry.rhtml view template with the URL http://localhost:3000/directory/add_entry.rhtml. Specify the values for the different attributes and click on the Submit button as shown in Figure 8.42.

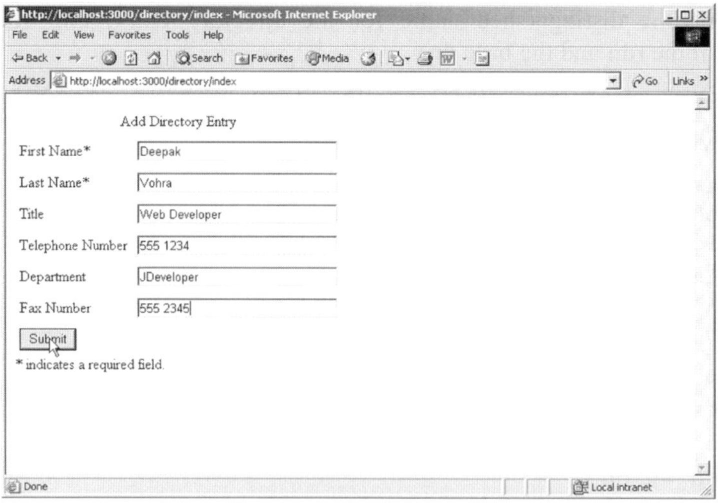

Fig. 8.42 Creating a New Directory Entry

A directory entry gets created in the "cn=PUBLIC,cn=Users,dc=example,dc=com" directory entry in the Oracle Internet Directory server instance. Select the cn=PUBLIC,cn=Users,dc=example,dc=com directory entry in the Oracle Directory Manager.The directory that was added using Ruby on Rails is listed in the cn=PUBLIC directory entry as shown in Figure 8.43.

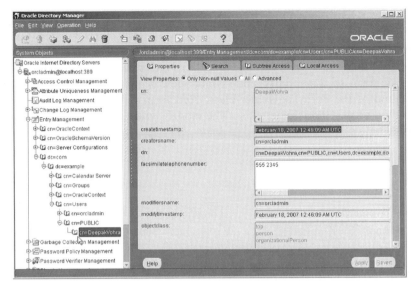

Fig. 8.43 Directory Entry Added with Ruby on Rails

The attributes of the directory entry also get added as shown in Figure 8.44.

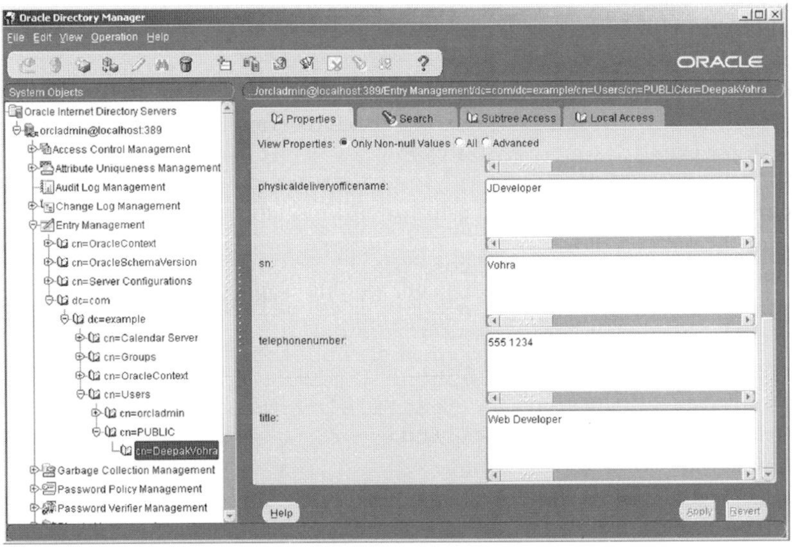

Fig. 8.44 Directory Entry Attributes

8.10 Modifying a Directory Entry

In this section we shall modify a directory entry. The data to be modified is input in the modify_entry.rhtml. Similar to the section on adding an entry, add a form to the modify_entry.rhtml view template with the form_tag method of the FormTagHelper class. Add form fields with the text_field method of the FormHelper class. The modify_entry.rhtml view template is listed below.

```
<html>
<body>

<div>
    <table border='0' cellspacing='0'
cellpadding='5'>
        <tr>
          <caption>
             Modify Directory Entry
          </caption>
        </tr>
      <!-- start_form_tag -->
       <%= form_tag :action => "modify_entry" %>
        <tr>
            <td>First Name*</td>
            <td><%= text_field(:modify_entry, :gn)
%></td>
        </tr><tr>
            <td>Last Name*</td>
            <td><%= text_field(:modify_entry, :sn)
%></td>
        </tr>

        <tr>
            <td>Title</td>
            <td><%= text_field(:modify_entry,
:title) %></td>
        </tr><tr>
            <td>Telephone Number</td>
            <td><%= text_field(:modify_entry,
:telephoneNumber) %></td>
        </tr>

        <tr>
            <td>Department</td>
            <td><%= text_field(:modify_entry,
:physicalDeliveryOfficeName) %></td>
```

```
        </tr>


        <tr>
                <td>Fax Number</td>
                <td><%= text_field(:modify_entry,
 :facsimileTelephoneNumber) %></td>
        </tr>


        <tr>
                <td><input type="submit"
 value="Submit"></td>
        </tr>
    <%= end_form_tag %>
    </table>
            </div>
 * indicates a required field.
 </body>
    </html>
```

When the modify_entry.rhtml template is submitted the modify_entry controller action of the controller directory gets invoked. Modify the modify_entry controller action. Retrieve the values for the form fields, :gn and :sn, and define a variable cn.

```
values = params[:modify_entry]
    gn=values[:gn]
    sn= values[:sn]
      cn=gn+sn
```

A directory entry is identified with a distinguished name. Define the dn of the directory entry to modify.

```
dn="cn="+cn+",cn=PUBLIC,cn=Users,dc=example,dc=com"
```

Retrieve the values of the other form fields.

```
title=values[:title]
telephoneNumber=values[:telephoneNumber]
physicalDeliveryOfficeName=values[:physicalDeliveryOf
ficeName]
   facsimileTelephoneNumber=values[:facsimileTelephone
Number]
```

Open a connection with the Oracle Internet Directory server and replace the attribute values with the replace_attribute method. For example, the :title attribute is replaced as follows.

```
Net::LDAP.open( :host => 'localhost', :port =>
389,:base =>
'cn=PUBLIC,cn=Users,dc=example,dc=com', :auth => {
:method => :simple, :username => 'cn=orcladmin',
:password => 'oidadmin10' } ) do |ldap|

    ldap.replace_attribute dn, :title, title
end
```

Start the WEBrick web server and invoke the modify_entry.rhtml view template with the URL http://localhost:3000/directory/modify_entry.rhtml. Specify the directory entry to be modified and the modified attributes. Click on the Submit button as shown in Figure 8.45.

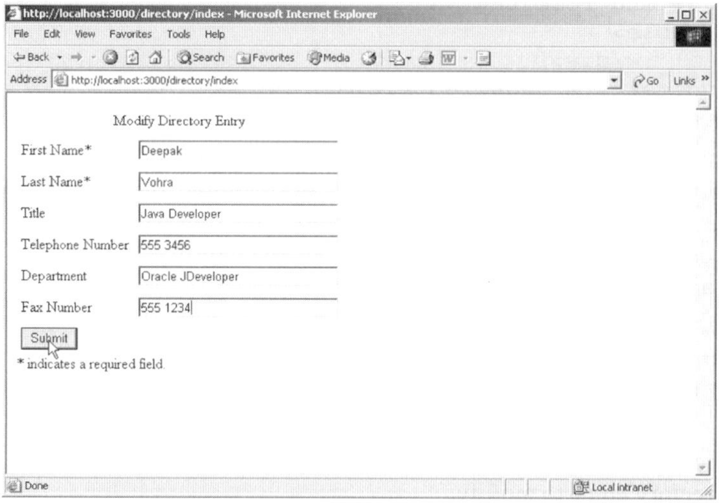

Fig. 8.45 Modifying Directory Entry

The directory entry gets modified as shown in the Oracle Directory Manager in Figure 8.46.

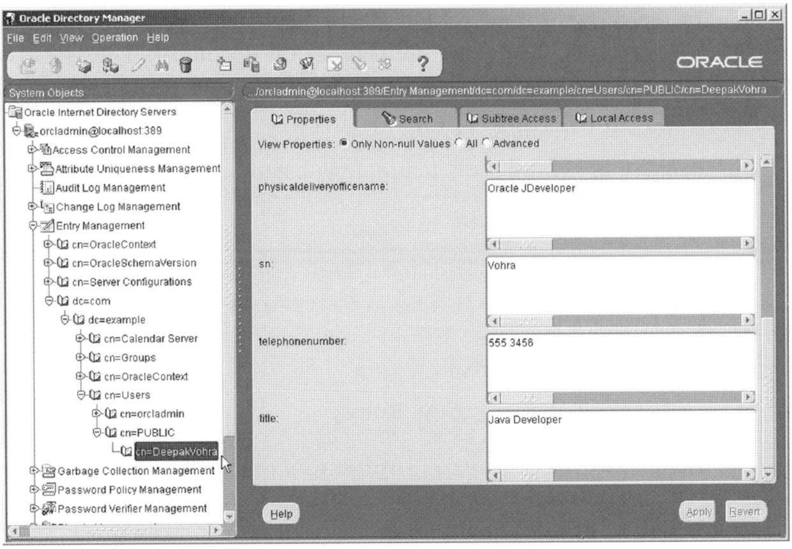

Fig. 8.46 Modified Directory Entry

8.11 Searching a Directory

In this section we shall search for a directory entry. We shall display the result of the directory search on the same page as the directory entry data is input using the Ajax web technique. The Ajax web technique is implemented by the Prototype library. The prototype library includes a class, PrototypeHelper to create a form that may be updated asynchronously using Ajax. Include the prototype library in the search_entry.rhtml view template.

```
<%= javascript_include_tag "prototype" %>
```

Add a form that is submitted using Ajax with the form_remote_tag method of the PrototypeHelper class. The :update option of the form_remote_tag specifies the form element to be updated with the server response. The :url option specifies the URL to which the form is submitted, the controller action is specified with the :action parameter.

```
<%=form_remote_tag(:update=>"directory_entry",
:url=>{:action=>:search_entry}) %>
  <% end form_tag %>
```

Specify the directory entry input fields, with the text_field_tag of the FormTagHelper class. The form element to be updated is specified as a div.

```
<div id="directory_entry"></div>
```

The search_entry.rhtml view template is listed below.

```
<html><head>
   <title></title>
   <%= javascript_include_tag "prototype" %>
  </head>

<body>
   <caption>
    Search  Directory Entry
   </caption>
   <%=form_remote_tag(:update=>"directory_entry",
          :url=>{:action=>:search_entry}) %>
   <table>
        <tr>
   <label>First Name*</label>
   <%=text_field_tag:firstName %></tr>
     <tr><label>Last Name*</label>
   <%=text_field_tag:lastName %></tr>
     <%=submit_tag "Search" %>
   </table>
    <caption>
       <b> Directory Entry Table</b>
    </caption>

  <div id="directory_entry"></div>
  <% end_form_tag %>
      * indicates a required field.
</body>

  </html>
```

When the search_entry.rhtml form is submitted the search_entry controller action of the directory controller gets invoked. Modify the search_entry action. Retrieve the values of the :gn and :sn fields and define the base dn of the directory entry to search.

```
gn=values[:gn]
 sn= values[:sn]
cn=gn+sn
```

Specify the attributes of the directory entry to retrieve.

```
attrs = ["cn", "sn","title",
"telephoneNumber","physicalDeliveryOfficeName","facs
imileTelephoneNumber"]
```

Open a connection with the Oracle Internet Directory Server and search for the specified directory entry using the search() method of the Net::LDAP class.

```
Net::LDAP.open( :host => 'localhost', :port =>
389,:base =>
'cn=PUBLIC,cn=Users,dc=example,dc=com', :auth => {
:method => :simple, :username =>
'cn=orcladmin', :password => 'oidadmin10' } ) do
|ldap|
   ldap.search( :base => treebase,   :attributes =>
attrs,
:return_result => true ) do |directory|
end
```

The search() method returns a result set. Iterate over the result set and create a HTML table to send as a response to the view template. For example a row for the cn attribute is added to the table as follows.

```
directoryEntry+="<tr>"
directoryEntry+="<td>cn</td>"
directoryEntry+="<td>"+"#{directory.cn}"+"</td>"
directoryEntry+="</tr>"
```

Invoke the search_entry.rhtml view template with the URL http://localhost:3000/directory/search_entry.rhtml to search for a directory entry. Specify the :gn and :sn attributes, which form the rdn of a directory entry, and click on the Search button as shown in Figure 8.47.

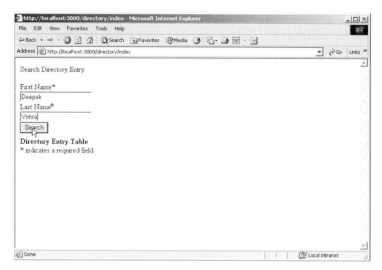

Fig. 8.47 Searching for a Directory Entry

The directory entry attributes get listed as shown in Figure 8.48.

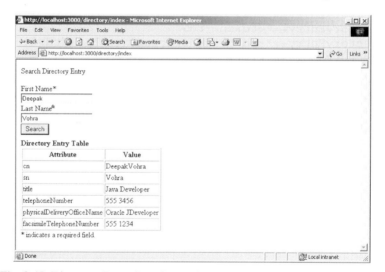

Fig. 8.48 Directory Entry Search Result

8.12 Deleting a Directory Entry

In this section, we shall delete a directory entry. A directory entry is
identified by a dn, which is comprised of the rdn and the base dn. The rdn
of the directory entry to be deleted is specified in the delete_entry.rhtml
view template. The form_tag method is used to create a form and the
text_field tag is used to create a form text field. The delete_entry.rhtml
view template consists of input fields for first name and last name. The
delete_entry.rhtml form is listed below.

```
<html>
<body>

<div>
     <table border='0' cellspacing='0'
cellpadding='5'>
            <tr>
                <caption>
                    Delete Entry
                </caption>
            </tr>
             <!-- start_form_tag -->
             <%= form_tag :action => "delete_entry" %>
            <tr>
                <td>First Name*</td>
                <td><%= text_field(:delete_entry, :gn)
%></td>
            </tr><tr>
                <td>Last Name*</td>
                <td><%= text_field(:delete_entry, :sn)
%></td>
            </tr><tr>
                <td><input type="submit"
value="Submit"></td>
            </tr>
        <%= end_form_tag %>
        </table>
        </div>
 * indicates a required field.
</body>
    </html>
```

When the delete_entry.rhtml form is submitted the delete_entry
controller action of the directory controller gets invoked. In the
delete_entry controller action retrieve the values of the form fields and
create a dn of the directory entry to delete.

```
values = params[:delete_entry]
    gn=values[:gn]
    sn= values[:sn]
    cn=gn+sn
```

```
dn="cn="+cn+",cn=PUBLIC,cn=Users,dc=example,dc=com"
```

Open a connection with the Oracle Internet Directory server and delete the directory entry with the delete method of the Net::LDAP class.

```
Net::LDAP.open( :host => 'localhost', :port => 389,
:base => 'cn=PUBLIC,cn=Users,dc=example,dc=com',
:auth => { :method => :simple, :username =>
'cn=orcladmin', :password => 'oidadmin10' } ) do
|ldap|
     ldap.delete :dn => dn

end
```

To delete a directory entry invoke the delete_entry.rhtml view template with the URL http://localhost:3000/directory/delete_entry.rhtml. Specify the :gn (first name) and :sn (last name) attributes of the directory entry to delete and click on the Submit button as shown in Figure 8.49.

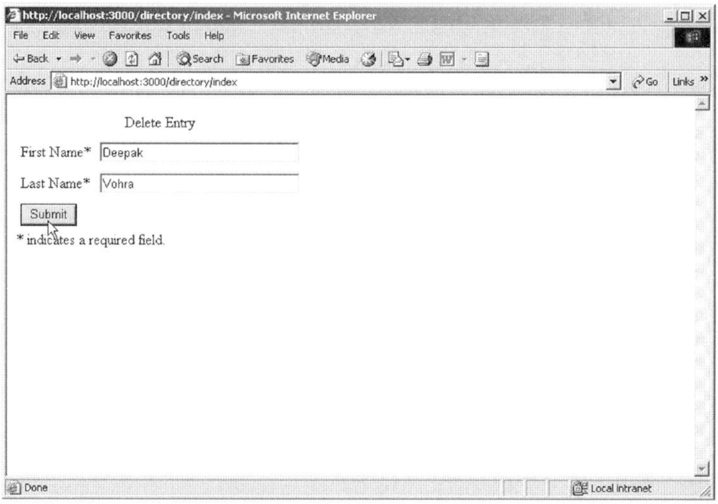

Fig. 8.49 Deleting a Directory Entry

The directory entry gets deleted as shown in the Oracle Directory Manager as shown in Figure 8.50.

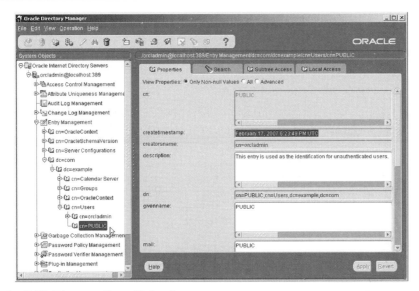

Fig. 8.50 Directory Entry Deleted

The directory_controller.rb controller script is listed below.

```
require 'net/ldap'

class DirectoryController < ApplicationController

def add_entry

values = params[:add_entry]
gn=values[:gn]
sn= values[:sn]
 cn=gn+sn

dn="cn="+cn+",cn=PUBLIC,cn=Users,dc=example,dc=com"
title=values[:title]
telephoneNumber=values[:telephoneNumber]
physicalDeliveryOfficeName=values[:physicalDeliveryO
fficeName]
facsimileTelephoneNumber=values[:facsimileTelephoneN
umber]

attr = {   :cn => cn,
:objectclass => ['top', 'person',
'organizationalPerson'],
 :sn => sn,
```

```ruby
:title => title,
:telephoneNumber => telephoneNumber,
:physicalDeliveryOfficeName =>
physicalDeliveryOfficeName,
 :facsimileTelephoneNumber =>
facsimileTelephoneNumber
  }

Net::LDAP.open( :host => 'localhost', :port =>
389,:base => 'cn=PUBLIC,cn=Users,dc=example,dc=com',
:auth => { :method =>

:simple, :username => 'cn=orcladmin', :password =>
'oidadmin10' } ) do |ldap|    ldap.add( :dn => dn,
:attributes => attr )

end
 end

def modify_entry

values = params[:modify_entry]
  gn=values[:gn]
 sn= values[:sn]
cn=gn+sn
dn="cn="+cn+",cn=PUBLIC,cn=Users,dc=example,dc=com"
title=values[:title]
telephoneNumber=values[:telephoneNumber]
physicalDeliveryOfficeName=values[:physicalDeliveryO
fficeName]
facsimileTelephoneNumber=values[:facsimileTelephoneN
umber]

Net::LDAP.open( :host => 'localhost', :port =>
389,:base => 'cn=PUBLIC,cn=Users,dc=example,dc=com',
:auth => { :method =>

:simple, :username => 'cn=orcladmin', :password =>
'oidadmin10' } ) do |ldap|
ldap.replace_attribute dn, :title, title
ldap.replace_attribute dn, :telephoneNumber,
telephoneNumber
ldap.replace_attribute dn,
:physicalDeliveryOfficeName,
physicalDeliveryOfficeName
ldap.replace_attribute dn,
:facsimileTelephoneNumber, facsimileTelephoneNumber
```

```
end
end

def search_entry

gn=params[:firstName]
 sn= params[:lastName]
  cn=gn+sn
treebase=
"cn="+cn+",cn=PUBLIC,cn=Users,dc=example,dc=com"
attrs = ["cn", "sn","title",
"telephoneNumber","physicalDeliveryOfficeName","facs
imileTelephoneNumber"]
directoryEntry="<table
border><tr><th>Attribute</th><th>Value</th></tr>"

Net::LDAP.open( :host => 'localhost', :port =>
389,:base => 'cn=PUBLIC,cn=Users,dc=example,dc=com',
:auth => { :method =>

:simple, :username =>'cn=orcladmin', :password =>
'oidadmin10' } ) do |ldap|
ldap.search(:base => treebase,   :attributes =>
attrs, :return_result => true ) do |directory|
directoryEntry+="<tr>"
directoryEntry+="<td>cn</td>"
directoryEntry+="<td>"+"#{directory.cn}"+"</td>"
directoryEntry+="</tr>"
directoryEntry+="<tr>"
directoryEntry+="<td>sn</td>"
directoryEntry+="<td>"+"#{directory.sn}"+"</td>"
directoryEntry+="</tr>"
directoryEntry+="<tr>"
directoryEntry+="<td>title</td>"
directoryEntry+="<td>"+"#{directory.title}"+"</td>"
directoryEntry+="</tr>"
directoryEntry+="<tr>"
directoryEntry+="<td>telephoneNumber</td>"
directoryEntry+="<td>"+"#{directory.telephoneNumber}
"+"</td>"
directoryEntry+="</tr>"
directoryEntry+="<tr>"
directoryEntry+="<td>physicalDeliveryOfficeName</td>
"
directoryEntry+="<td>"+"#{directory.physicalDelivery
OfficeName}"+"</td>"
```

```
directoryEntry+="</tr>"
directoryEntry+="<tr>"
directoryEntry+="<td>facsimileTelephoneNumber</td>"
directoryEntry+="<td>"+"#{directory.facsimileTelepho
neNumber}"+"</td>"
directoryEntry+="</tr>"
end
directoryEntry+="</table>"

render:text=> directoryEntry


end
end


def delete_entry

values = params[:delete_entry]
 gn=values[:gn]
sn= values[:sn]
cn=gn+sn
dn="cn="+cn+",cn=PUBLIC,cn=Users,dc=example,dc=com"
Net::LDAP.open( :host => 'localhost', :port =>
389,:base => 'cn=PUBLIC,cn=Users,dc=example,dc=com',
:auth => { :method =>

:simple, :username => 'cn=orcladmin', :password =>
'oidadmin10' } ) do |ldap|    ldap.delete :dn => dn
end

 end

def index
     render
:file=>"C:/ruby/oidldap/app/views"+params[:url]
     return

end
  end
```

8.13 Summary

In this chapter we installed some of the commonly used directory servers such as OpenLDAP, Tivoli Directory Server, and Oracle Internet Directory and created a directory service with RubyGems ruby-net-ldap gem. We used the Oracle Internet Directory to create a directory service. The procedure is the same for the other directory servers. Only the root/base DN would be different for the other directory servers.

9 Web Services On Rails

9.1 Introduction

A web service is a software system designed for interoperable interaction over a network. A webservice is defined with a WSDL(Web Services Description Language) document and other systems interact with the Web service using SOAP messages, transferred using HTTP with an XML serialization. A web service is an abstract resource that provides a set of functions, and is implemented by an agent, which sends and receives messages. A provider entity provides the functionality of a web service with a provider agent and a requester entity uses the web service functionality with a requester agent. Web services implement various technologies, some of which are XML, SOAP and WSDL. XML is a standard format for data exchange. Web service requests and responses are sent as XML messages. The elements and attributes that may be specified in an XML document are specified in an XML Schema. SOAP provides a standard framework for packaging and exchanging XML messages. WSDL is an XML document in the "http://schemas.xmlsoap.org/wsdl/" namespace for describing a web service as a set of endpoints operating on messages. A WSDL document specifies the operations (methods) provided by a web service and the format of the XML messages.

The `ActionWebService` module implements the web services functionality in Ruby on Rails. Action Web Service implements server side support for SOAP and XML-RPC web service protocols. Using the Action Web Services you may declare and publish APIs(application programming interfaces).

9.2 Web Services with PHP

PHP 5 provides the SOAP and XML-RPC extensions to create a Web Service. To create a SOAP Web Service, first create a SOAP server.

```
$server = new SoapServer("document.wsdl");
```

Add functions to the SOAP server with the addFunction() method. Handle a SOAP request with the handle() function. A SOAP client is created with the SoapClient constructor.

```
$client = new SoapClient("document.wsdl");
```

Invoke methods of the SOAP web service. For an XML-RPC web service, create an XML-RPC server using the xmlrpc_server_create() method.

```
$xmlrpc_server=xmlrpc_server_create();
```

Register functions with the server using the xmlrpc_server_register_method method. The second argument is the method provided by the web service. The third argument is the PHP function that is registered.

```
$registered=xmlrpc_server_register_method
($xmlrpc_server, "webservice_method", "php_function"
);
```

In the XML-RPC client, to send a request to the XML-RPC server specify the XML string to be sent in the request.

```
$request_xml = <<< END
<?xml version="1.0"?>
<methodCall>
...
<methodCall>
END;
```

Invoke the web service method using the xmlrpc_server_call_method function. The first argument to the xmlrpc_server_call_method function is the server resource. The second argument is the string containing the XML-RPC request. The third argument is the application data that is sent to the third parameter of the method handler function.

```
$response=xmlrpc_server_call_method(  $xmlrpc_server,
$request_xml, '', array(output_type => "xml"));
```

9.3 Web Services with Java

Java EE 5 provides the Java API for XML Web Services (JAX-WS) to create web services and web service clients. To create a web service create an Service Endpoint Implementation class. The implementation class is annotated with javax.jws.WebService or javax.jws.WebServiceProvider annotation. The implementation class is required to be not abstract or final, and is required to contain a default public constructor. Add business methods, which are annotated with the javax.jws.WebMethod annotation, and which are made available to web service clients to the implementation class. The business methods are public and not static or final. The example Web Service implementation class, Hello, in following listing has a public method msg(String name) annotated with the @WebMethod annotation.

```
import javax.jws.WebService;


@WebService
public class Hello {
   private String message = new String("Hello");

   public void Hello() {}

   @WebMethod
   public String msg(String name) {
      return message+ "   "+name +".";
   }
}
```

Compile the Service Endpoint Implementation class. Next, we need to generate the JAX-WS portable artifacts used in a JAX-WS web service deployment and invocation using the wsgen tool. Specify the protocol, servicename, HelloService for example, and portname in the wsgen options.

```
wsgen [options] Hello
```

Package the Web Service files into a WAR file, helloservice.war. Deploy the WAR file to an application server that supports Java EE 5. When the web application is deployed the application server and the JAX-WS runtime generate the WSDL file and any additional artifacts required to invoke the web service from a client. The WSDL may be accessed with URL http://localhost:port/helloservice/hello?WSDL.

Variable port is the application server port number. helloservice is the web application war file. Next, create a web service client class. Declare a reference to a Web Service using the javax.xml.ws.WebServiceRef annotation. Obtain a proxy to the service.

```
Hello port = service.getHelloPort();
```

Invoke the msg(String) method of the web service.

```
String response = port.msg("Dave");
System.out.println(response);
```

The example client class is listed below.

```
import javax.xml.ws.WebServiceRef;
public class HelloClient {
```

```
@WebServiceRef(wsdlLocation="http://localhost:8080/hell
oservice/hello?WSDL")
    static HelloService service;

    public static void main(String[] args) {
      try {

        Hello port = service.getHelloPort();
        String response = port.msg("Dave");
        System.out.println(response);
      } catch(Exception e) {
        System.out.println(e.getMessage());
      }
    }
}
```

Use the wsimport tool to generate the web service artifacts required to connect to the Web service including the Service Endpoint Interface (SEI) . Specify the WSDL file location with the -wsdllocation option.

```
wsimport [options] wsldfile.wsdl
```

Compile and run the client class to invoke the web service and generate an output. The output from the web service invocation is "Hello Dave".

9.4 Creating a Web Service with Ruby on Rails

Before discussing the Web services support in Ruby on Rails in detail, we shall create a simple web service using the Action Web Service module.

Install the `actionwebservice` Ruby gem if not already installed. Run the following gem install command while connected to the Internet.

```
C:/ruby>gem install actionwebservice
```

Ruby gem `actionwebservice-1.2.2` gets installed. Create a Rails application for the Web service.

```
C:/ruby>rails webservice
```

Create a directory, *apis*, in the `app` directory. Create a web service API class, *HelloMessageApi* that extends the `ActionWebService::API::Base` class. Store the following Ruby script to hello_message_api.rb in the app/apis directory.

```
class HelloMessageApi < ActionWebService::API::Base
  api_method :hello_message, :expects =>
[{:firstname=>:string}, {:lastname=>:string}],
:returns => [:string]

  end
```

Create a controller script, which defines a controller class, *HelloMessageController*. Copy the following Ruby code to the controller script and save the controller script, hello_message_controller.rb, in the app/controllers directory.

```
class HelloMessageController < ApplicationController

web_service_api HelloMessageApi
 web_service_dispatching_mode :direct
  wsdl_service_name 'hello_message'
  web_service_scaffold :invoke

  def hello_message(firstname, lastname)
    return "Hello "+ firstname +" "+lastname
  end
  end
```

Start the WEBrick web server.

```
C:/ruby/webservice>ruby script/server
```

Display the WSDL file for the web service with the URL http://localhost:3000/hello_message/wsdl as shown in Figure 9.1.

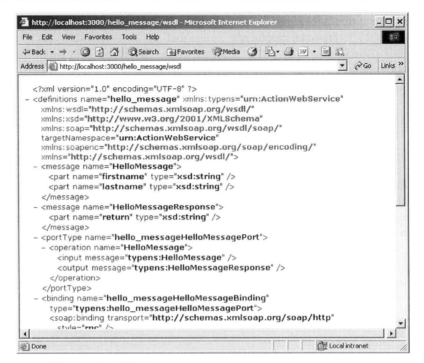

Fig. 9.1 Web Service WSDL

Invoke the web service with the URL http://localhost:3000/hello_message/invoke. The API methods for the web service get displayed as shown in Figure 9.2. Select the *HelloMessage* method.

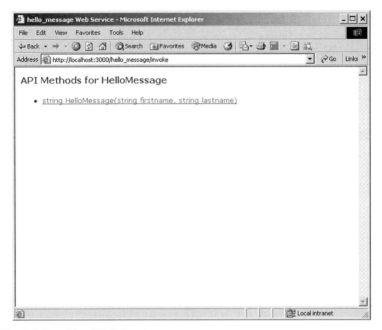

Fig. 9.2 Invoking Web Service

To test the web service specify a first name , and a last name and click on the Invoke button as shown in Figure 9.3.

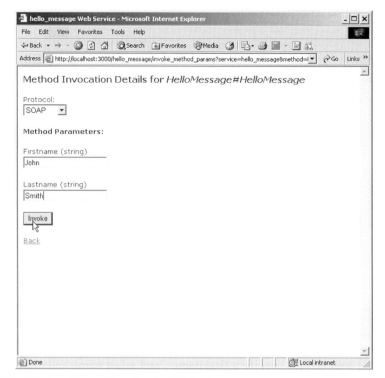

Fig. 9.3 Invoking a Web Service Method

Return value gets output. Also the request XML and response XML gets displayed as shown in Figure 9.4.

Fig. 9.4 Output from Web Service

Let's discuss the web service we created in some detail. The web service API class defines the methods that the web service provides. The example API class defines the *hello_message* method, which takes two parameters of type string and returns a string value. An API method is defined with the `api_method` method of the `ActionWebService::API::Base` class. The WSDL for the web service is created from the API class. The web service API class extends the ActionWebService::API::Base class. The controller class contains the code that the web service makes available to a client. The `web_service_api` option specifies the API definition class. The `web_service_dispatching_mode` option specifies the dispatching method; where remote callers send their invocation methods, the endpoint URLs, and how the method invocation is routed to the object that implements the method. With the 'direct' dispatching mode method invocations are made directly to the controller. The API method implementations are defined in the controller class as public instance methods. The 'direct' mode is the default mode. The `wsdl_service_name` option specifies the web service name. The `web_service_scaffold` option generates a web service scaffolding for method invocations. The web service scaffolding is similar to the Active Record's scaffolding. The 'invoke' method specified in the example web service lists all the methods in all the APIs attached to the controller. The *hello_message* action in the controller class is available to clients for method invocation.

9.5 Web Service API Class

In the previous example the web service API class is *HelloMessageApi*. The web service API class extends the ActionWebService::API::Base class and specifies the methods that are to be made available for an API in a web service. Some of the methods of the class are discussed in Table 9.1.

Table 9.1 ActionWebService::API::Base Methods

Method	Description
api_method(name, options={})	Specifies an API method. The options are as follows: :expects-Signature for method input parameters. :returns-Signature for return value. :expects_and_returns-Signature for input parameters and return values.
api_method_name(public_name)	Specifies a service method name for a public method name.
api_methods()	Specifies a Hash of service methods on this API.
soap_client(endpoint_uri, options={})	Specifies a SOAP client.
xmlrpc_client(endpoint_uri, options={})	Specifies an XML RPC client

Table 9.1 (continued)

Method	Description
has_public_api_method?(public_name)	Specifies whether a public method has a corresponding service method on this API.

The procedure to define a API class is as follows.

1. Determine which methods are to be made available on the API.
2. Create a class that extends the `ActionWebService::API::Base` class.
3. Define the methods using the `api_method` option including the method signature.

9.6 Dispatching

Dispatching is the dispatching of method invocations on a web service. A dispatching approach refers to where remote callers send their invocation messages and how the method invocations are routed to the method implementation object. An API is implemented based on the dispatching approach. Three dispatching approaches are available.

1. Direct
2. Delegated
3. Layered

We shall discuss each of these dispatching approaches.

9.6.1 Direct Dispatching

With the Direct dispatching approach, the API definition class is attached to the controller class and the API methods are implemented in the controller class as public instance methods. As in the example application discussed earlier, the direct dispatching is specified as follows.

```
web_service_dispatching_mode :direct
```

The direct dispatching approach is the default approach. With the direct dispatching approach a controller class may implement only one API. The endpoint URL for a web service with direct dispatching is of the following format.

```
http://SERVER/CONTROLLER_NAME/api
```

The endpoint URL for the example web service discussed earlier is http://localhost:3000/hello_message/api as specified in the service element of the WSDL document.

```
<service name="hello_messageService">
 <port name="hello_messageHelloMessagePort"
binding="typens:hello_messageHelloMessageBinding">
  <soap:address
location="http://localhost:3000/hello_message/api" />
  </port>
</service>
```

In the direct dispatching mode the `web_service_api` option may be omitted if the API definition class is of the same name as the controller class and is stored in the app/apis directory in a Ruby file of the format apiclass_api.rb. In the example application discussed earlier the web_service_api option is not required in the controller class as the API class is stored in the hello_message_api.rb. The procedure to develop an Action Web Service web service using the 'direct' dispatching approach is as follows.

1. Define an API class, a class that extends the ActionWebService::Base class, and define the API methods.
2. Attach the API web service class to a controller class using the web_service_api option.
3. Set   the   dispatching   mode   to   'direct'   with `web_service_dispatching_mode :direct`
4. Implement the API methods in the controller class as public instance methods.
5. Test the web service by adding scaffolding to the controller class.

9.6.2 Delegated Dispatching

A limitation of the `direct` dispatching approach is that a controller class may implement only one API. In the `delegated` dispatching approach, a controller class may implement more than one APIs. We shall discuss delegated dispatching with an example.

Define two different API classes, *HelloMessageApi* and *DeveloperApi*. Store the HelloMessageApi class in hello_message_api.rb Ruby script in the app/apis directory. The HelloMessageApi class defines an API method *hello_message* that takes two string parameters, firstname and lastname, and returns a string value. The hello_message_api.rb script is listed below.

```
class HelloMessageApi < ActionWebService::API::Base
  api_method :hello_message, :expects =>
[{:firstname=>:string}, {:lastname=>:string}],
:returns => [:string]

  end
```

Store the DeveloperApi class in the developer_api.rb Ruby script in the app/apis directory. The DeveloperApi class defines a method `developer` that also takes two string parameters and returns a string value. The developer_api.rb script is listed below.

```
class DeveloperApi < ActionWebService::API::Base
  api_method :developer, :expects =>
[{:firstname=>:string}, {:lastname=>:string}],
:returns => [:string]

  end
```

Create a service class for each of the API classes. A service class extends the ActionWebService::Base class. The service class implements the methods defined in the API class. The API class is attached with the service class using the web_service_api option. The HelloMessageService class implements the HelloMessageApi API class. Store the service class HelloMessageService in the app/models directory as Ruby script hello_message_service.rb. The hello_message_service.rb script is listed below.

```
class HelloMessageService < ActionWebService::Base
  web_service_api HelloMessageApi

def hello_message(firstname, lastname)
    return "Hello "+ firstname +" "+lastname
  end
  end
```

Similarly create a service class, DeveloperService, for the API class DeveloperApi. The Ruby script for the DeveloperService class is stored in the app/models directory as developer_service.rb. The developer_service.rb script is listed below.

```
class DeveloperService < ActionWebService::Base
  web_service_api DeveloperApi

def developer(firstname, lastname)
```

```
   return "This web service is developed by "+
firstname +" "+lastname
  end
  end
```

Create a controller class for the service classes. Set the dispatching mode to 'delegated' with the following option setting.

```
web_service_dispatching_mode :delegated
```

Attach the service classes to the controller class using the web_service option. For example, the HelloMessageService class is attached to the controller class with the following declaration.

```
web_service :hello_message, HelloMessageService.new
```

hello_message is a web service that represents the HelloMessageService class. To test the web service add scaffolding to the controller class with the web_service_scaffold option.

```
web_service_scaffold :invoke
```

Store the controller class in the app/controllers directory. The controller script, delegated_controller.rb is listed below.

```
class DelegatedController < ApplicationController
 web_service_dispatching_mode :delegated

 web_service :hello_message, HelloMessageService.new
 web_service :developer, DeveloperService.new
 web_service_scaffold :invoke
  end
```

The controller class does not have to be named DelegatedController. Next, we shall test the web service. Start the WEBrick web server if not already started.

```
C:/ruby/helloservice>ruby script/server
```

Invoke the web service listing of methods with the URL http://localhost:3000/delegated/invoke. API methods for all the API service classes specified in the controller class get listed as shown in Figure 9.5.

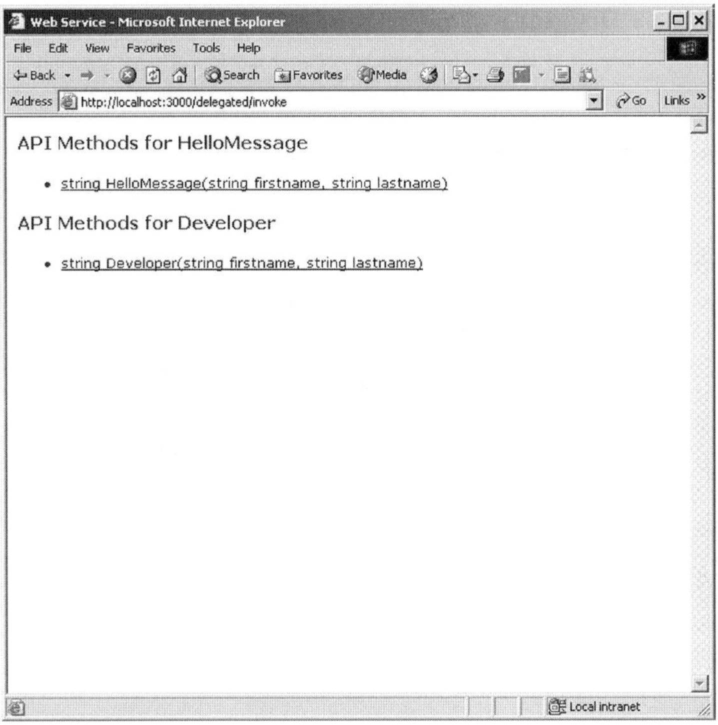

Fig. 9.5 Invoking Delegated Web Service

In contrast to the 'direct' dispatching approach more than one API classes may be attached to the controller class using the service classes. The procedure to develop a Action Web Service web service using the delegated approach is as follows.

1. Define API classes that are to be implemented by the web service.
2. Create a service class, a class that extends the `ActionWebService::Base` class, for each of the API classes. Attach the API class to the service class with the `web_service_api` option.
3. Implement the API methods in the service class as public instance methods.
4. Create a controller class and set the dispatching mode to 'delegated'.
5. Attach the service classes to the controller class with the `web_service` option.
6. Test the web service by generating a scaffolding for the web service using the `web_service_scaffold` option.

9.6.3 Layered Dispatching

The `layered` dispatching approach procedure is similar to the delegated dispatching approach procedure except the following declaration.

```
web_service_dispatching_mode :layered
```

Each method invocation is prefixed with the service name in the format *servicename.methodname*. A `layered` dispatching approach web service may also be tested using scaffolding, generated with the web_service_scaffold option.

9.7 Protocol Clients

Action Web Services provides some client classes for accessing remote web services. A remote web service may be accessed from inside a controller using the `web_client_api` helper function or directly using an instance of the `ActionWebService::Client::Soap` or `ActionWebService::Client::XmlRpc` class. In this section, we shall create a Action Web Services web service and access the web service using using the `web_client_api` function and the `direct` instance method invocation. We need to create two separate rails applications, one for the web service and the other for the client. First, create a Rails application for the web service.

```
C:/ruby>rails helloservice
```

Create a web service, *Hello*, with an API class *HelloApi* and an API method *getMsg* using the `web_service` script generator.

```
C:/ruby/helloservice>ruby                    script/generate
web_service Hello getMsg
```

An API class HelloApi gets created in the *apis* directory as Ruby script hello_api.rb. A controller script hello_controller.rb gets created in the controllers directory. The controller class HelloController includes a controller action getMsg. The controller class also specifies the wsdl_service_name, the web service name. The WSDL for a web service is available when the web service is run. Modify the controller script to specify the web_service_api option and also specify the scaffolding with the web_service_scaffold option. The web_service_api option maps the controller to the API class. Modify the getMsg controller action to take a string parameter and return a string value. The getMsg method implements the getMsg method in the API class. The modified controller script is listed below.

```
class HelloController < ApplicationController
      wsdl_service_name 'Hello'

      web_service_api HelloApi
      web_service_scaffold :invoke
   def getMsg(name)
      "Hello "+ name
   end
end
```

Modify the API class HelloApi to add a parameter and a return value to the getMsg method signature. The HelloApi class is listed below.

```
class HelloApi < ActionWebService::API::Base
   api_method :getMsg, :expects => [:name=>:string],
 :returns => [:string]
   end
```

Next, we shall test the web service. Start the web service with the following command from the web service directory.

```
C:/ruby>webservice>ruby script/server
```

Invoke the web service using the URL http://localhost:3000/hello/invoke The API methods for the web service get listed. Click on the GetMsg method as shown in Figure 9.6.

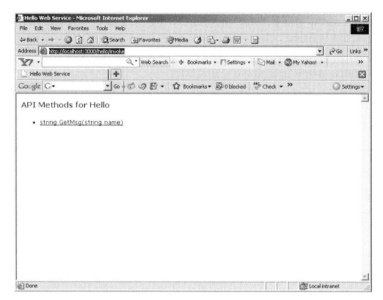

Fig. 9.6 Invoking a Web Service Scaffolding

An input field for name gets displayed. You may also select the protocol: SOAP or XML RPC. Specify a value in the Name field and click on the Invoke button as shown in Figure 9.7.

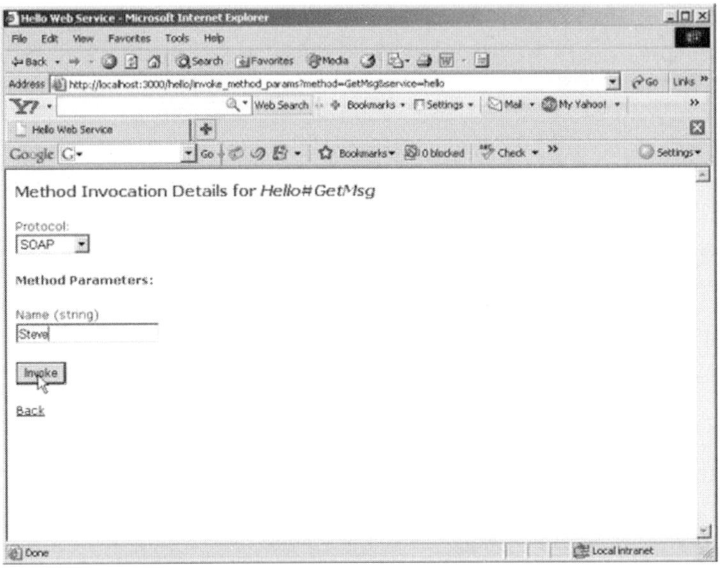

Fig. 9.7 Invoking a Web Service Method

The web service method getMsg gets invoked with name parameter value as "Steve" and the return value gets output. Also the request XML and response XML messages get displayed as shown in Figure 9.8.

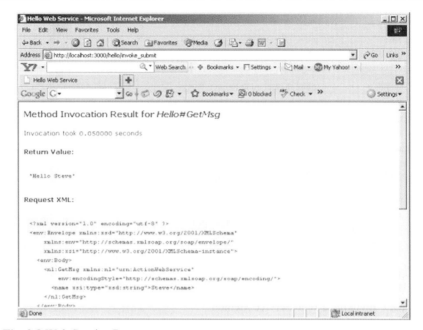

Fig. 9.8 Web Service Response

Next, we shall create a rails application for the client. Create a rails application with the following command.

```
C:/ruby>rails helloadmin
```

Create an *apis* directory in the app directory of the *helloadmin* rails application and copy the hello_api.rb script from the *helloservice* rails application to the apis directory. Create a controller script for the web service client.

```
C:/ruby/helloadmin>ruby    script/generate    controller
helloadmin getMsg
```

A controller class *HelloadminController* consisting of a controller action *getMsg* gets created. Access the web service API from the controller class using the web_client_api function.

```
web_client_api              :hello,              :xmlrpc,
http://localhost:3001/hello/api
```

The web_client_api(name, protocol, endpoint_uri, options={}) method creates a protected method specified with 'name' parameter using the specified protocol to communicate with the specified endpoint URI. We have created a method 'hello' using the xmlrpc protocol to connect with the endpoint uri http://localhost:3001/hello/api. We shall run the Hello web service on port 3001 and access the web service with a client on port 3000. Modify the getMsg controller action to create a variable for the output of the web service method invocation. Using the 'hello' method created with web_client_api invoke the getMsg method of the Hello web service with a 'name' parameter as input to the method. We shall define the 'name' parameter value in an index.rhtml view template. The controller script helloadmin_controller.rb is listed below.

```
class HelloadminController < ApplicationController
web_client_api :hello, :xmlrpc,
"http://localhost:3001/hello/api"
    def getMsg
        @service_output= hello.getMsg(params[:name])
    end
end
```

The web service Hello may also be accessed directly using an instance of the ActionWebService::Client::Soap or ActionWebService::Client::XmlRpc class. The helloadmin_controller.rb script may also be represented using an instance of the ActionWebService::Client::Soap class as shown below.

```
class HelloadminController < ApplicationController
    def getMsg
hello_client =
ActionWebService::Client::Soap.new(HelloApi,
"http://localhost:3001/hello/api")
        @service_output=
hello_client.getMsg(params[:name])

    end
  end
```

Create an index.rhtml view template in the views/helloadmin directory and add a form with an input field, 'name', in the RHTML template. When the form is submitted the getMsg method of the Helloadmin controller is invoked. View template index.rhtml is listed below.

```
<html>
   <head>
      <title>Hello Web Service</title>
   </head>
   <body>
      <h1>Hello Web Service</h1>
      <p>
      This rails application tests a web service.
      </p>
      <%= start_form_tag :action=> 'getMsg' %>
      <p><label>Name</label><br/>
      <%= text_field 'name', '' %></p>
      <%= submit_tag "Get Message" %>
      <%= end_form_tag %>
   </body>
</html>
```

Modify the getMsg.rhtml view template to output the value of the variable @service_output, which is defined in the Helloadmin controller class's getMsg method. The getMsg.rhtml view template is listed below.

```
<html>
   <head>
      <title>Hello Web Service</title>
   </head>
   <body>
      <h1>Hello Web Service </h1>
      <p>

      </p>
      <p>
      <%= @service_output %>
      </p>
   </body>
</html>
```

Next, we shall test the web service, Hello, using the client rails application. Start the web service on port 3001 with the following command from the helloservice directory.

```
C:/ruby/helloservice>ruby script/server --port=3001
```

Start the client rails application on the default port 3000 from the helloadmin directory.

```
C:/ruby/helloadmin>ruby script/server
```

The example application is to demonstrate accessing a web service from a protocol client. Invoke the index controller action of the Helloadmin controller with the URL http://localhost:3000/helloadmin/index. The index.rhtml view template gets displayed. Specify a name value and click on the Get Message button as shown in Figure 9.9.

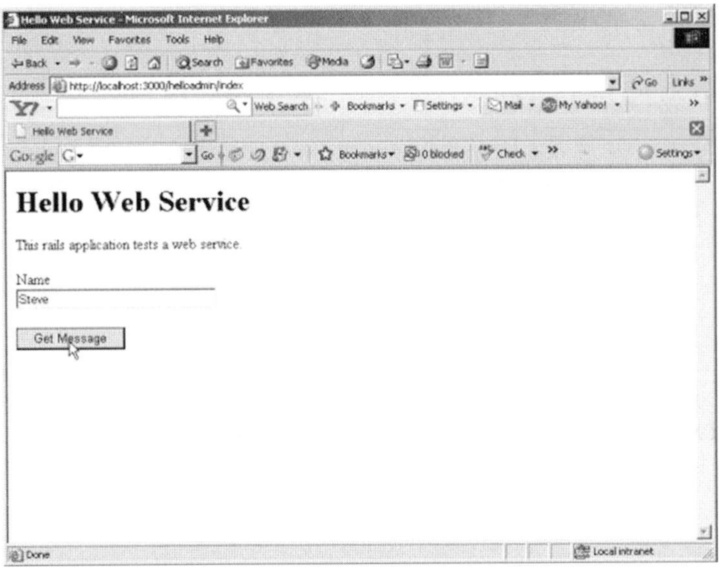

Fig. 9.9 Testing a Web Service with a Protocol Client

The getMsg method of the Helloadmin controller gets invoked. Using the 'hello' method, which is defined using the web_client_api option, the web service Hello is accessed and the getMsg method of the web service is invoked. The output from the web service is displayed in the getMsg.rhtml view template as shown in Figure 9.10.

Fig. 9.10 Output from Web Service

The procedure to access a web service using a protocol client is as follows.

1. Create a rails application for a web service.
2. Create a web service.
3. Define the API method/s and implement the method/s in the controller class.
4. Create a rails application for the protocol client.
5. Define the API class and the API method/s.
6. Access the web service from the client application controller using either the `web_client_api` option or an instance of the ActionWebService::Client::Soap   or ActionWebService::Client::XmlRpc.
7. Implement the API method/s in the client controller class.
8. Start the web service on port 3001.
9. Start the client application on port 3000.
10. Invoke the API method/s from a RHTML view template and output the web service output to another RHTML view template.

9.8 Summary

In this chapter we discussed the procedure to create a Web Service with Ruby on Rails. We discussed the different dispatching approaches. We also discussed the procedure to access a Web Service with a protocol client.

10 Ruby on Rails in Eclipse

10.1 Introduction

Eclipse is the most commonly used Java IDE. Ruby on Rails provides some plugins to use Ruby on Rails in Eclipse. Two such plugins are Ruby Development Tools and RadRails. Ruby Development Tools (RDT) and RadRails are open source Ruby IDEs for the Eclipse platform. Some of the features of RDT are syntax highlighting, syntax validation, error markers, code completion, code formatting, and Ruby unit testing framework integration. RadRails features include code assist on Ruby and RHTML files, debugging support, integrated server views, generators, dynamic testing and integrated deployment. In this chapter we shall develop a Ruby on Rails Create-Read-Update-Delete (CRUD) application in Eclipse. If you haven't already installed Eclipse, download and install Eclipse 3.2[1]. Also install the MySQL database if not already installed. First, install Ruby on Rails.

10.2 PHP in Eclipse

Various PHP extensions for Eclipse are available. PHP IDE is an open source project in the Eclipse Tools Project. Dev-PHP IDE is a SourceForge.net project. PHP Eclipse-Plugin is another SourceForge.net project. The Eclipse plugins for PHP may be used to create and run PHP scripts.

Eclipse being a Java IDE, no plugins are needed to develop Java applications in Eclipse.

---

[1] Eclipse 3.2- http://www.eclipse.org/downloads/

10.3 Installing RDT

To install Ruby Development Tools, select Help>Software Updates>Find and Install in Eclipse IDE. In the Features Updates frame, select Search for new features to install and click on Next. In the Install frame click on the New Remote Site button. In the New Update Site frame, specify a Name (RDT for example) and in the URL field specify http://updatesite.rubypeople.org/release. Click on OK button. In the Update sites to visit frame select RDT and click on Finish. Select the features to install, select the checkbox "Select the latest version of a feature only", and click on Next as shown in Figure 10.1.

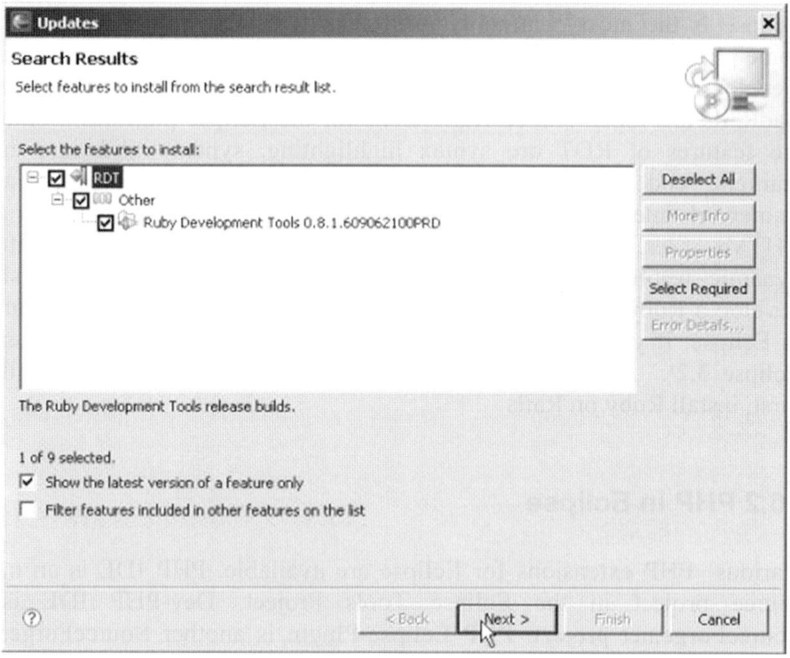

Fig. 10.1 Installing Ruby Development Tools

Accept the feature license agreement and click on Next. In the Installation frame select the Ruby Development Tools feature and click on Finish. In the Feature Verification frame click on Install All. Ruby Development Tools plugin gets installed. Restart Eclipse for the configuration changes to take effect. Next, we need to configure the Ruby preferences. Select Window>Preferences. In the Preferences frame select Ruby>Installed Interpreters. In the Add RubyVM frame specify a

RubyVM name, Ruby for example, and in the RubyVM home directory field specify the location of rubyw.exe application. If Ruby on Rails is installed in the c:/ruby directory, rubyw is in the c:/ruby/bin directory. Click on the OK button in the Add RubyVM frame. . Click on the OK button in the Preferences frame.

10.4 Creating a Rails Project in RDT

Next, we create a new Ruby project in Eclipse. Select File>New>Project. In the New frame select the Ruby Project wizard and click on Next as shown in Figure 10.2.

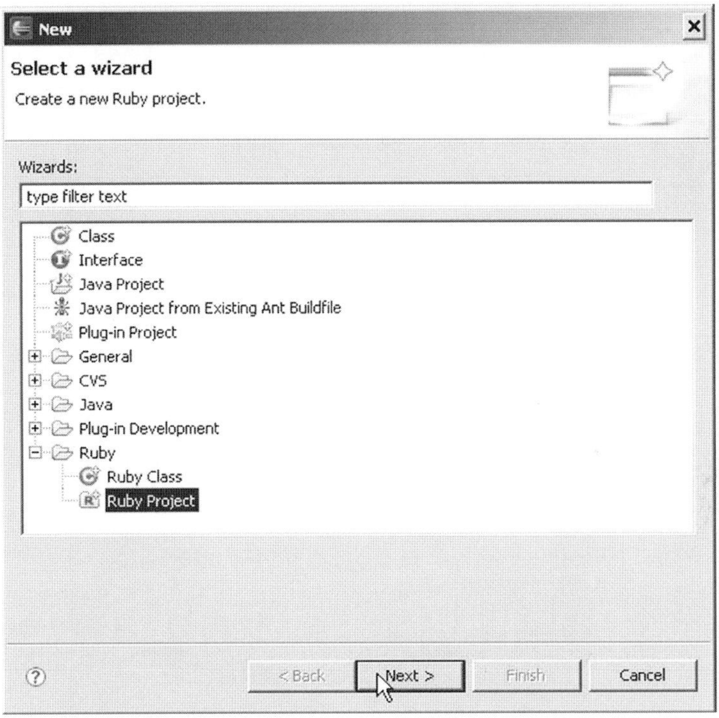

Fig. 10.2 Creating a Ruby Project

In the Ruby Project frame specify a Project Name and click on Finish. Open the Ruby perspective if not already open. A new Ruby project gets added to the Eclipse IDE. Next we need to configure external tools for various tasks such as creating a Rails application, creating a Model, creating a Controller, creating a scaffold, and starting the WEBrick server. Select Run>External Tools>External Tools to create an external tools configuration. In the External Tools frame, create configurations for various tasks. To create a configuration, right-click on the Program node and select New. Create a configuration, "Create Rails Application", to create a Rails application. In the Location field specify the rails.cmd file. In the Working Directory field select the variable ${project_loc}. To create an application by the same name as the rails project, specify ../${project_name} in the Arguments text area using the Variables button to select the project_name variable. Click on the Apply button to apply the configuration as shown in Figure 10.3.

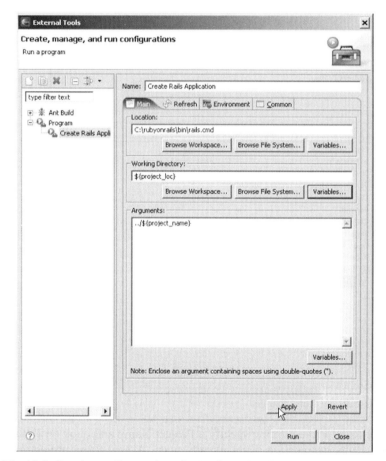

Fig. 10.3 Creating an External Tools Configuration for a Rails Application

As the rails application generates some directories and classes, we would need to refresh the project resources. Select the Refresh tab. In the Refresh frame select the checkbox "Refresh resources upon completion.". Click on the Apply button. To add the configuration to favorites, select the Common tab and select the External Tools checkbox in the Display in favorites menu. Click on the Apply button. Next, create a configuration to start the WEBrick server. In the Location field specify the ruby.exe application, in the Working directory frame specify ${project_loc} using the Variables button to select the variable, and in the Arguments text area specify script/server. Click on the Apply button to apply the configuration as shown in Figure 10.4.

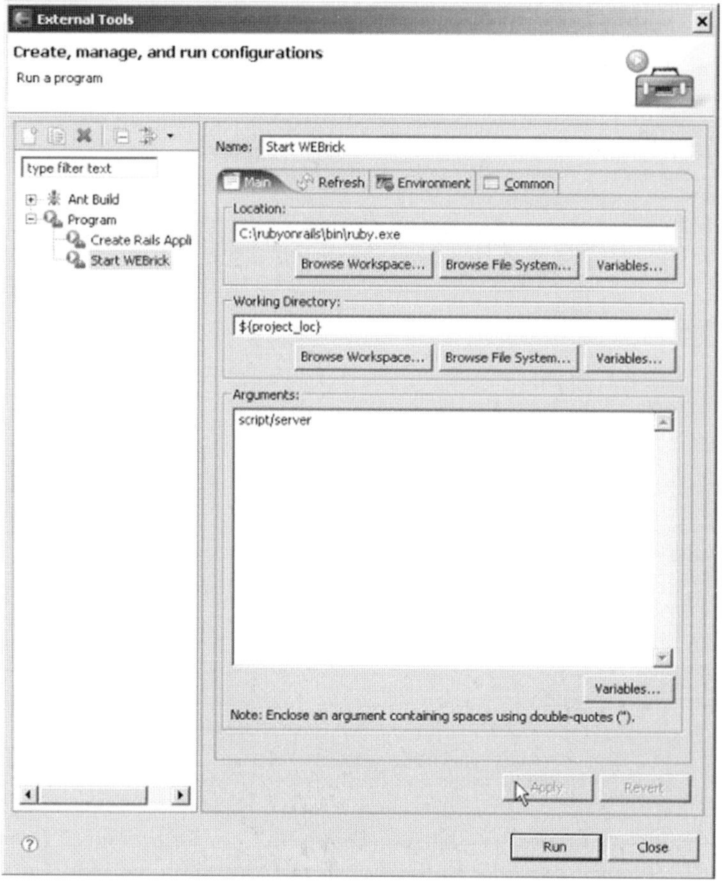

Fig. 10.4 Creating an External Tools Configuration to start WEBrick Server

Similarly, create configurations to create a ruby model script, create a controller script, create a scaffolding and run the rake command. To create a model script, specify ruby.exe in the Location field, specify ${project_loc} in the Working Directory field, and script/generate model ${string_prompt: Model name} -f in the Arguments text area using the Variables buttons to select variables. Click on Apply as shown in Figure 10.5.

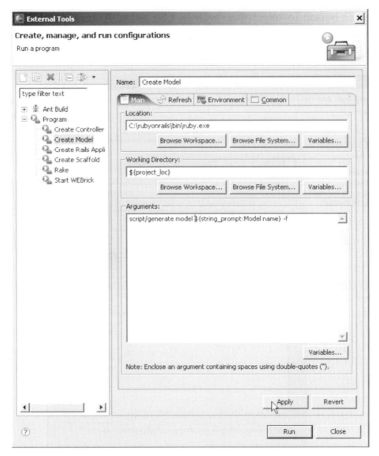

Fig. 10.5 Creating an External Tools Configuration for a Model

To create a controller script create a configuration, "Create Controller". Specify ruby.exe in the Location field, ${project_loc} in the Working Directory field, and script/generate controller ${string_prompt:Controller name} –f in the Arguments text area using the

Variables buttons to select variables. Click on Apply as shown in Figure 10.6.

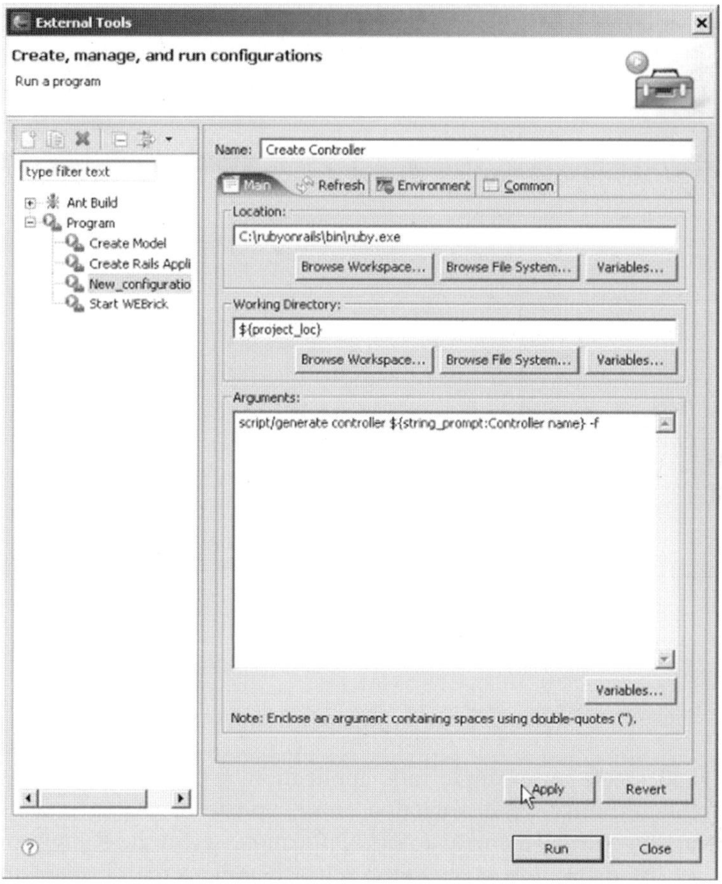

Fig. 10.6 Creating an External Tools Configuration for a Controller

We also need to create a configuration, "Create Scaffold", for creating scaffolding classes. Specify ruby.exe in Location field, ${project_loc} in the Working Directory field and script/generate scaffold ${string_prompt:Model name} ${:string_prompt:Controller name} –f in Arguments using the Variables buttons to select variables as shown in Figure 10.7.

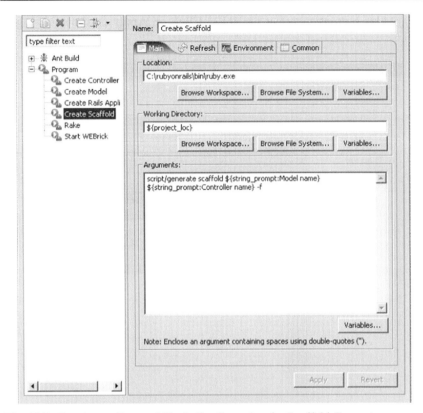

Fig. 10.7 Creating an External Tools Configuration for Scaffold Generator

We shall create an example rails application, a CRUD application to create a catalog entry, read a catalog entry, update a catalog entry and delete a catalog entry. To create a rails application, select the Ruby project 'catalog' in the Ruby Resources view, select Run>External Tools>Create Rails Application. A rails application, catalog, gets created with the directory structure shown in Figure 10.8.

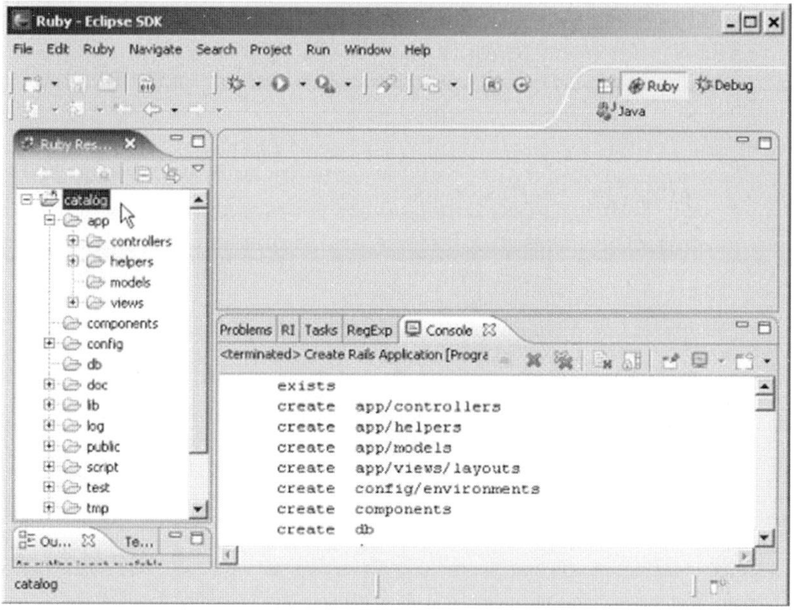

Fig. 10.8 Creating a Rails Application

In the next section we shall create a MySQL database table using Rails migrations.

10.5 Creating a Database Table with RDT

First, we need to modify the database.yml file for the MySQL database. Modify the development configuration with the following settings as shown in Figure 10.9.

```
development:
  adapter: mysql
  database: test
  username: root
  password:
  host: localhost
```

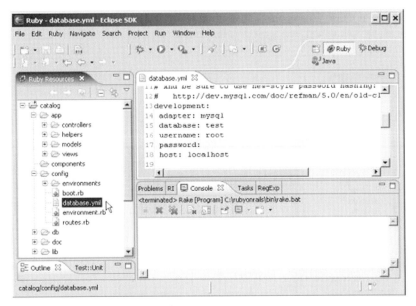

Fig. 10.9 Modifying database.yml

Next, we shall create a database table in the MySQL database using migrations for which we need to create an external tools configuration for the rake command. Rake is similar to Java's ant command and is used to run the migrate target. Specify rake.bat in the Location field of the Rake configuration. Specify ${project_loc} in the Working Directory field using the Variables button and migrate in Arguments. Click on Apply as shown in Figure 10.10.

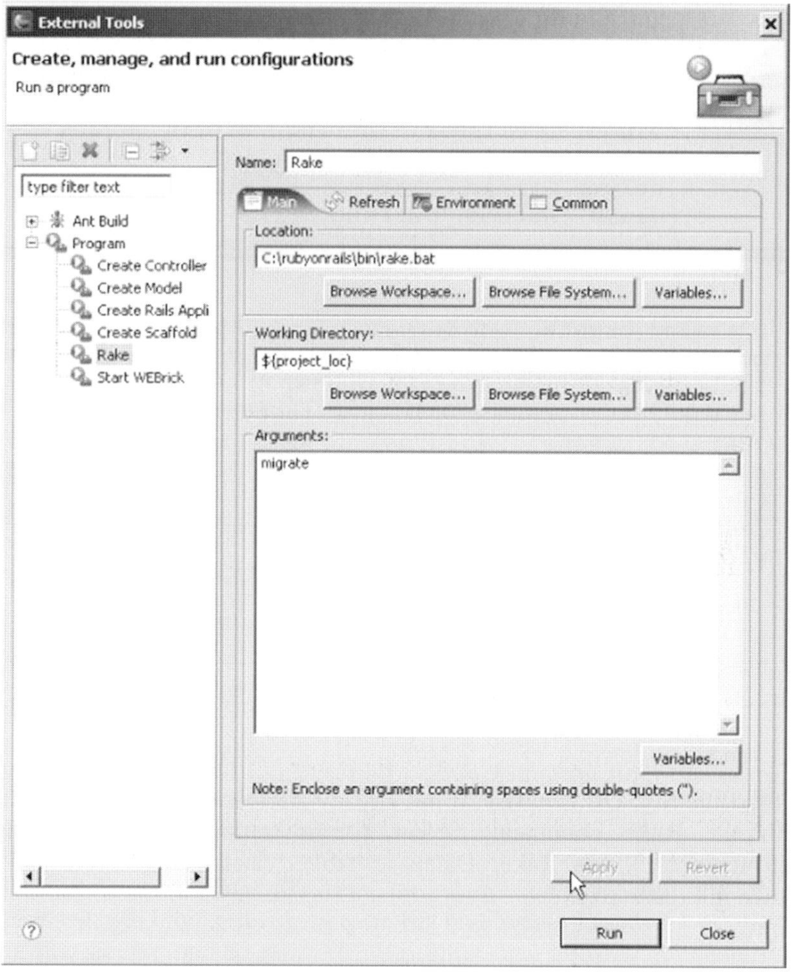

Fig. 10.10 Creating an External Tools Configuration for Rake

We shall create a migration script by creating a model script, which also creates a migration script. Select Run>External Tools>Create Model to create a model script. In the Variable Input frame specify catalog as the model name and click on OK. A model script, catalog.rb, and a migration script,001_create_catalogs.rb, get added to the rails project catalog. Modify the migration script to create a database table 'catalogs'. Migration script 001_create_catalogs.rb is listed below.

```
class CreateCatalogs < ActiveRecord::Migration
  def self.up
    create_table :catalogs do |t|
    t.column :journal, :string, :limit => 255
    t.column :publisher, :string, :limit => 255
    t.column :edition, :string, :limit => 255
     t.column :title, :string, :limit => 255
    t.column :author, :string, :limit => 255

end

  Catalog.create   :journal   =>   "developerWorks",
:publisher => "IBM", :edition => "September 2006",
:title=> "A PHP V5 migration
  guide",:author=>"Jack D. Herrington"
  Catalog.create   :journal   =>   "developerWorks",
:publisher => "IBM", :edition => "September 2006",
:title=> "Make Ruby on Rails
  easy  with  RadRails  and  Eclipse",:author=>"Pat
Eyler"

    end

  def self.down
    drop_table :catalogs
  end
end
```

Start the MySQL database, if not already started, and run the migration with the Rake command. Select the migration script and select Run>External Tools>Rake. Database table 'catalogs' gets created as shown in Figure 10.11.

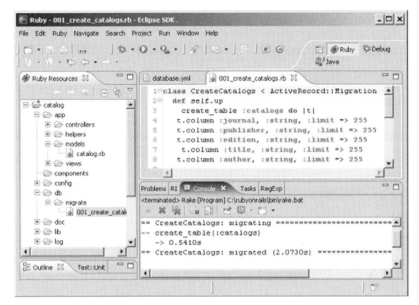

Fig. 10.11 Creating a Database Table

10.6 Creating a CRUD Application with RDT

Next, we shall create a CRUD application with the scaffold generator. The scaffold generator generates all the required model and controller scripts and the RHTML view templates for an interface to data in a database table. Select Run>External Tools>Create Scaffold to create a scaffolding for the database table catalogs. A Variable input dialog prompts for a value for the Model name. Specify a model name, 'catalog' for example. A Variable input dialog prompts for a Controller name. Specify a controller name, 'catalog'. A scaffolding, which consists of a model class, catalog.rb, a controller class, catalog_controller.rb, and view templates, _form.rhtml, edit.rhtml, show.rhtml, list.rhtml, and new.rhtml gets created in the rails application. Start the WEBrick server with Run>External Tools>Start WEBrick server as shown in Figure 10.12.

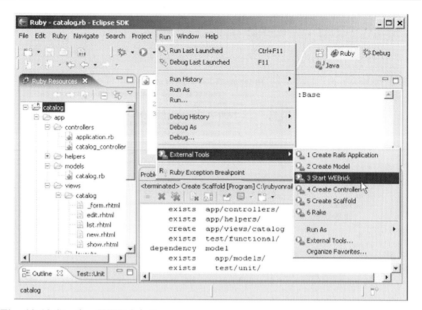

Fig. 10.12 Starting WEBrick Server

Access the WEBrick server with the URL http://localhost:3000 as shown in Figure 10.13.

Fig. 10.13 WEBrick Server Console

The catalog entries listing may be displayed with the list.rhtml template. Invoke the controller action list with the URL http://localhost:3000/catalog/list as shown in Figure 10.14.

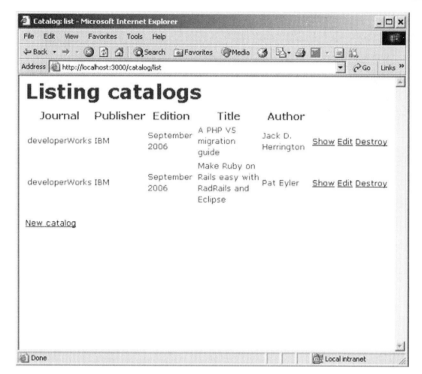

Fig. 10.14 Listing Catalog Entries

Next, we shall discuss the RadRails plugin.

10.7 Installing RadRails

The RadRails plugin requires the RDT plugin to be installed prior to being installed. Therefore, if you have not installed the RDT plugin, as explained in the previous section, install the RDT plugin. To install the RadRails plugin select Help>Software Updates>Find and Install. Select "Search for new features to install" in the Feature Updates frame and click on Next. Click on New Remote Site button in the "Update sites to visit" frame. Specify an update site name, RadRails for example, and specify URL http://radrails.sourceforge.net/update in the URL field. Click on the OK button. Select the RadRails update site configuration and click on Finish. Select the features to install and click on Next. Accept the feature license and click on Next. In the Installation frame click on the Finish button. Select Install All in the Feature Verification frame. Restart Eclipse for the plugin configuration to take effect. In the Eclipse IDE open the RadRails perspective. Select Window>Open Perspective>Other>Rails as shown in Figure 10.15.

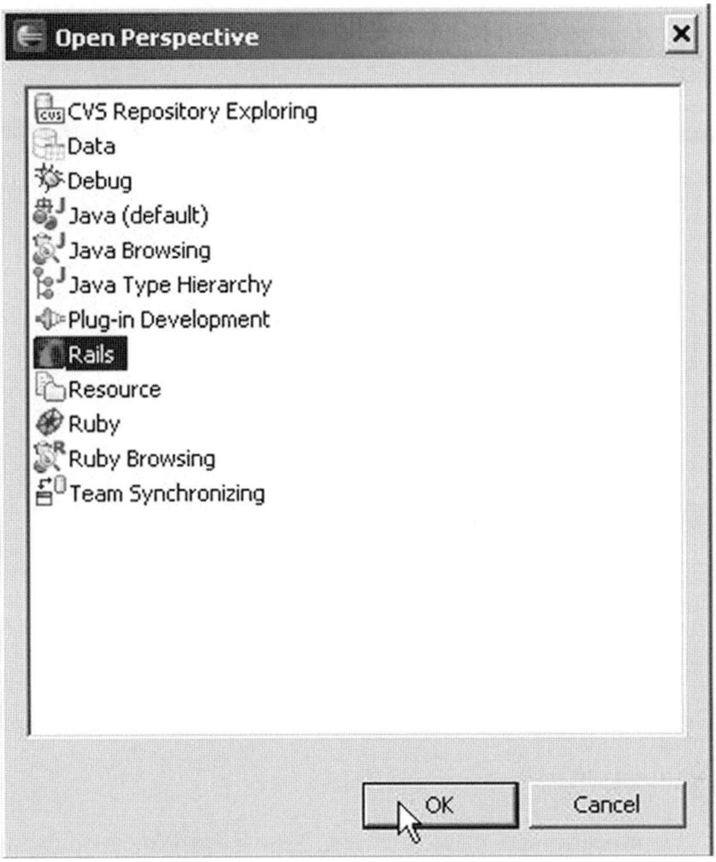

Fig. 10.15 Opening Rails Perspective

The RadRails perspective includes the following views: Servers, Generators, Rake Tasks, Console, RI, and Rails Plugins. The Servers view consists of WEBrick server configurations for the rails applications. The Generators view consists generators for model, controller, scaffold, and migration scripts. The Rake Tasks view is still in development and consists of rake tasks such as migrate.

10.8 Creating a Rails Application with RadRails

Next, we create a rails project with File>New>Project. In the New gallery select the Rails Project wizard and click on Next as shown in Figure 10.16.

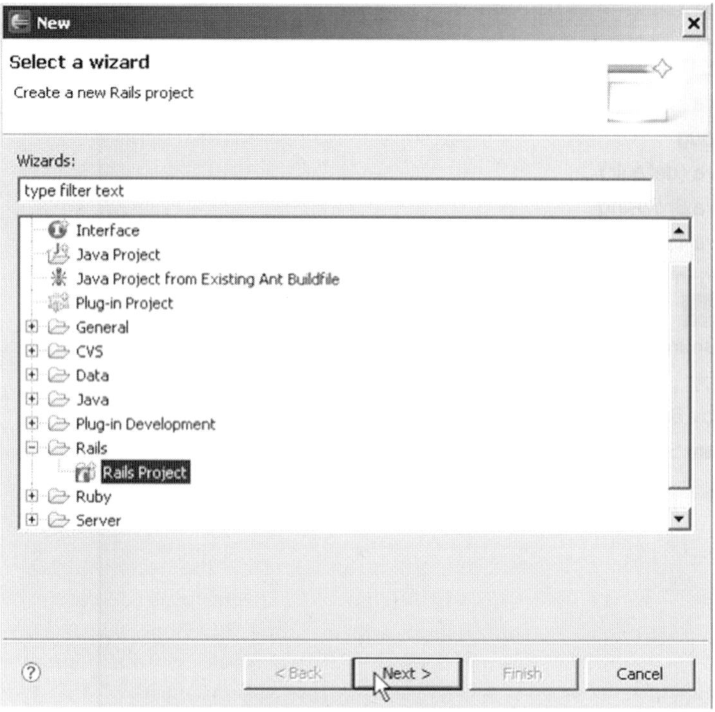

Fig. 10.16 Creating a Rails Project in RadRails

Specify a project name, catalog, in the New Rails Project frame and select the options "Generate Rails Application skelton" and "Create a WEBrick Server". Click on Finish. A rails application gets created as shown in the Rails Navigator view in Figure 10.17.

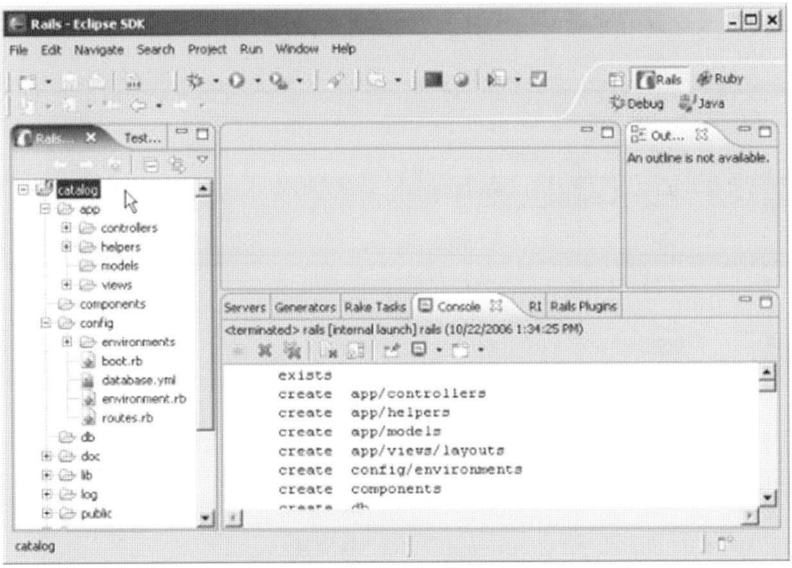

Fig. 10.17 Rails Project in RadRails

We need to modify the development environment settings in database.yml file for the MySQL database to as listed below and as shown in Figure 10.18.

```
development:
  adapter: mysql
  database: test
  username: root
  password:
  host: localhost
```

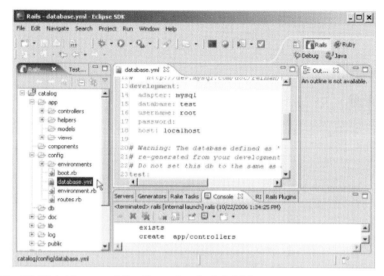

Fig. 10.18 database.yml Configuration for MySQL

Create a database table catalogs in the MySQL database using SQL script listed below.

```
CREATE    TABLE    catalogs(Journal    VARCHAR(255),
Publisher VARCHAR(255),
   Edition VARCHAR(255), Title Varchar(255), Author
Varchar(255));

INSERT    INTO    catalogs    VALUES('developerWorks',
'IBM', 'September 2006', 'A PHP V5 migration  guide',
'Jack D. Herrington');

INSERT    INTO    catalogs    VALUES('developerWorks',
'IBM',  'September  2006',  'Make  Ruby  on  Rails  easy
with RadRails and Eclipse
   ', 'Pat Eyler');
```

10.9 Creating a CRUD Application with RadRails

Next, we create the scaffolding for the database table catalogs. ActiveRecord uses pluralization; the database table name is the plural of the model class name with the first letter of the table name as lowercase. The scaffolding consists of model and controller scripts and RHTML view templates. Create the scaffolding with the scaffold generator. Select the

Generators view and select the scaffold generator. Specify a model name, catalog, and click on Go button as shown in Figure 10.19. A controller name is optional in the scaffold generator and defaults to the plural of the model name.

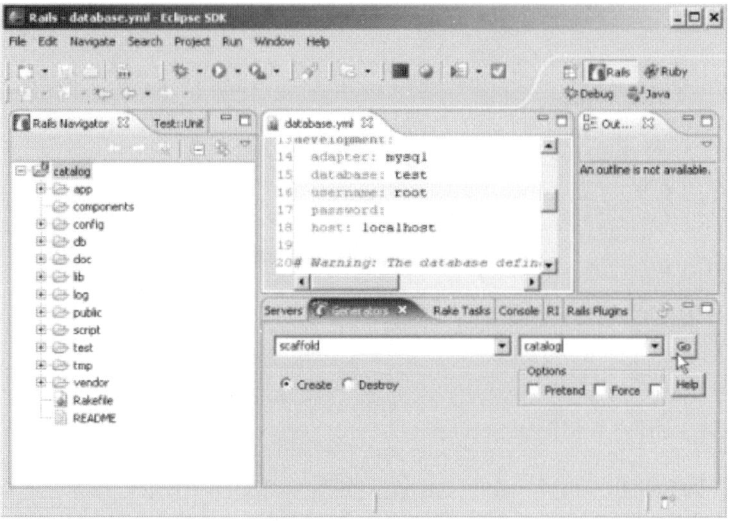

Fig. 10.19 Scaffold Generator

The scaffolding for the catalogs table gets created. The scaffolding consists of model class Catalog, which extends the ActiveRecord::Base class, and a controller class CatalogsController, which extends the ApplicationController   class   which   further   extends   the ActionController::Base class. The model script is generated in the app/models directory and the controller script is generated in the app/controllers directory. The view templates, _form.rhtml, show.rhtml, list.rhtml, edit.rhtml, and new.rhtml get created in the app/views/catalogs directory as shown in Figure 10.20. Next, we start the WEBrick server configuration for the rails application catalog as shown in Figure 10.20.

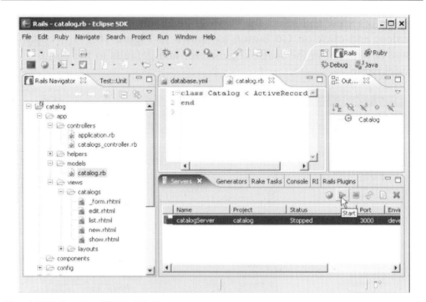

Fig. 10.20 Starting WEBrick Server

The WEBrick server gets started. Display the WEBrick console with the URL http://localhost:3000. Display the list the catalog entries with the controller action list. Invoke the list action with the URL http://localhost:3000/catalogs/list as shown in Figure 10.21.

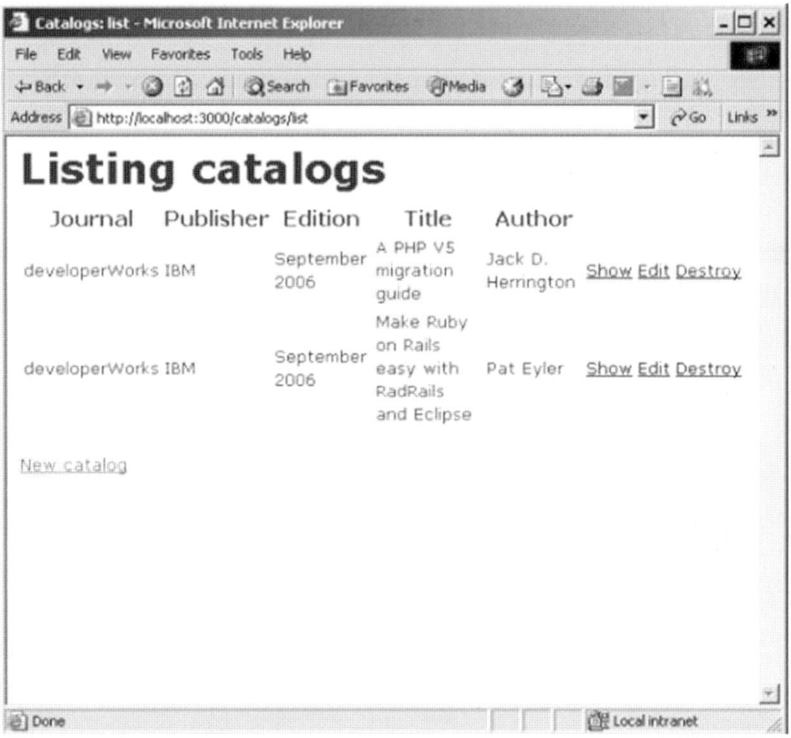

Fig. 10.21 Listing Catalog Entries

10.10 Summary

In this chapter we installed the Ruby Development Tools (RDT) and RadRails plugins in Eclipse. We created a Rails project in the RDT and RadRails plugins. We created a database tool using the rake tool with RDT. We created scaffolding for a CRUD application with RDT and RadRails.

11 Rails Testing and Fixtures

11.1 Introduction

Tests are test applications that produce consistent result and prove that a
Rails application does what it is expected to do. Tests are developed
concurrently with the actual application. Alternatively, in a Test Driven
Development (TDD) tests are run before the actual application is created.
Tests are run to minimize errors in the actual Rails application. Tests also
provide information about what is likely to cause an application to fail.

11.2 Unit Testing in PHP and Java

Various open source testing tools are available for unit testing in Java.
JUnit is a regression testing framework for implementing unit tests in
Java. Some of the other unit testing tools in Java are Abbot, JUnitPerf,
Jameleon, DbUnit, XMLUnit for Java, jfcUnit, JTestCase, StrutsTestCase,
SQLUnit, JTR (Java Test Runner). With JUnit a test method is annotated
with @Test. An example JUnit test to test the equality of two strings is as
follows.

```
package junittest;

    import org.junit.*;
    import static org.junit.Assert.*;
    import java.util.*;

    public class JUnitTest {

      @Test
      public void testStringCompare() {
          String str1="Example JUnit Test";
          String str2="Example JUNIT TEST";
          assertTrue(str1.equals(str2));
```

```
    }

    public static void main(String args[]) {
      org.junit.runner.JUnitCore.main("junittest.JUnitTe
  st");
      }
    }
```

PhpUnit is the unit testing framework for PHP based on the JUnit framework for Java. Some of the other PHP unit testing frameworks are Simple Test for PHP, PHP Assertion Unit Framework and Spike PHPCheckstyle. Unit testing in Ruby on Rails is similar to PHP and Java unit testing in that we use test case classes and test methods.

11.3 Rails Example Test

How are tests run in Ruby on Rails? Tests are run by creating a sub-class of `Test::Unit::TestCase` class. To the TestCase sub-class add test methods. When the tests are run the results are collected in a `Test::Unit::TestResult` object. Tests are run using *fixtures*, which are sample data against which a test is run. A test may be run on the command-line. Create a Ruby script, example_test.rb, to run a test. The testing API is provided in the test/unit gem, therefore, import the test/unit gem.

```
require 'test/unit'
```

Create a class, ExampleTestCase that extends the Test::Unit::TestCase class. To the class add a test method test_example that contains a single line "assert true". All test methods are required to start with "test". The test method contains an assert statement that specifies an assertion. An assertion is a line of code that evaluates an object or expression for the expected result. If the output of the assert statement is true the assertion has passed. If the output of the assert statement is false, the assertion has failed.

```
require 'test/unit'
class ExampleTestCase < Test::Unit::TestCase
  def test_example
    assert true
  end
end
```

Run the ruby script on command-line. The output from the test indicates that the test has passed as shown in Figure 11.1. The '.' in the line after Started denotes the test has passed. An 'F' indicates the test has failed and an 'E' indicates that an error has occurred.

Fig. 11.1 Running a Rails Test

Test cases are grouped into a suite. Thus, Rails testing follows a hierarchy shown in Figure 11.2.

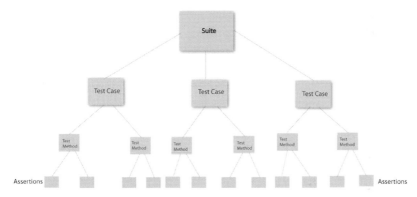
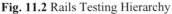

Fig. 11.2 Rails Testing Hierarchy

Next, we shall discuss how tests may be used to test different class objects. For example, if a Login class represents a user a test may be developed to validate a user name. First, create a class Login with a accessor username. In the class define a test method that determines if a username is valid based on some conditions as shown in Login.rb listing below.

```
class Login

    # Accessor
    attr_accessor :username
```

```
# Constructor
def initialize(username)
  @username = username
end

# Test to determine if username is valid
def is_username_valid?
  return false if @username.nil?
  return false if @username.empty?
  return false if @username.size < 5
  return false if @username 'ruby'
  true
end
end
```

Next, create a test case to test different usernames. The test case
LoginTestCase has a test method test_usernames, which has 6 assert
statements. The login_test.rb Ruby scipt is shown below.

```
require 'test/unit'
require 'login'

class LoginTestCase < Test::Unit::TestCase

  def test_example
  assert true
  end

  def test_usernames

    assert !Login.new(nil).is_username_valid?
    assert !Login.new("").is_username_valid?
    assert
    !Login.new("rubyonrails").is_username_valid?
    assert !Login.new("ruby").is_username_valid?
    assert !Login.new("john").is_username_valid?
    assert !Login.new("johnsmith").is_username_valid?


  end
end
```

Run the test case in Ruby command line. The output indicates that the
first test passes and the second test (test_usernames) fails. Out of 7
assertions 6 assertions pass and 1 assertion fails as shown in Figure 11.3.

Fig. 11.3 Login Test Case

The assertion that fails is the last assertion in the test method test_usernames. If the assertion that failed were before some of the other assertions the assertions after the failed assertion won't run and the test case would stop the execution of the test method. For example specify the assertion that failed as the 3rd assertion.

```
def test_usernames

      assert !Login.new(nil).is_username_valid?
      assert !Login.new("").is_username_valid?
      assert !Login.new("johnsmith").is_username_valid?
      assert
!Login.new("rubyonrails").is_username_valid?
      assert !Login.new("ruby").is_username_valid?
      assert !Login.new("john").is_username_valid?

   End
```

Run the test case again. The output indicates that only 4 assertions were run and 1 assertion failed as shown in Figure 11.4. The assertion after the failed assertion are not run.

```
Command Prompt                                            _ |□| x|
C:\ruby>ruby login_test.rb
Loaded suite login_test
Started
.F
Finished in 0.05 seconds.

  1) Failure:
test_usernames<LoginTestCase> [login_test.rb:14]:
<false> is not true.

2 tests, 4 assertions, 1 failures, 0 errors
C:\ruby>
```

Fig. 11.4 Assertions After a Failed Assertion are not run

The Rails testing framework provides 2 methods setup and teardown that if included in a test case are run with each test. The "setup" method is run before each test method and the "teardown" method is run after each test method. The "setup" method is used to setup objects to be used in a test method. Modify the test case LoginTestCase to add a setup method and a teardown method. In the setup method set @username to "JohnSmith" and in the teardown method set the @username to an empty string. Modified login_test.rb is listed below.

```
require 'test/unit'
require 'login'

class LoginTestCase < Test::Unit::TestCase
  def setup
    @username="JohnSmith"
  end

  def teardown
    @username=""
  end

  def test_usernames

    assert Login.new(@username).is_username_valid?
    assert !Login.new("").is_username_valid?

  end

  def test_username
    assert Login.new(@username).is_username_valid?
  end
end
```

Run the modified test case. The output indicates that 2 tests are run and 3 assertions are tested as shown in Figure 11.5. All 3 assertions pass.

Fig. 11.5 Running a test with setup and teardown

11.4 Assertion Types

The test/unit gem provides different types of assertions, which we shall discuss in this section. The assertion type that we have already used is shown below.

```
assert ( boolean, [msg] )
```

The msg is an optional string that specifies the test failure message. Create a test case to test different types of assertions. Add a test method and an assertion as shown below.

```
require 'test/unit'
class AssertionTestCase < Test::Unit::TestCase
  def test_assertion
    assert(false, "Assertion has failed")
  end
end
```

The output from the test case indicates that the test has failed as shown in Figure 11.6. The test failure message is the string specified in the msg argument.

Fig. 11.6 Assertion Type assert

Another type of assertion type tests if two ruby objects are equal.

```
assert_equal ( obj1, obj2, [msg] )
```

In a test method test if two ruby objects are equal as shown below.

```
require 'test/unit'
class AssertionTestCase < Test::Unit::TestCase
  def test_assertion
    obj1="ruby"
    obj2="ruby"
    assert_equal ( obj1, obj2, "Objects not Equal" )
  end
end
```

The output from the test case indicates that the objects are equal as shown in Figure 11.7.

Fig. 11.7 Assertion type assert_equal

Make the objects in the previous test case not equal and test again.

```
require 'test/unit'

class AssertionTestCase < Test::Unit::TestCase
  def test_assertion
    obj1="ruby"
    obj2="rails"

    assert_equal(obj1, obj2, "Objects not Equal" )
  end
end
```

The output from the test case indicates that the objects are not equal and test has failed as shown in Figure 11.8. The string specified in the msg argument is output as the test failure message.

Fig. 11.8 Objects not Equal

The following assertion type asserts that two objects are not equal.

```
assert_not_equal( obj1, obj2, [msg] )
```

The assertion type assert_same(obj1, obj2,[msg]) tests if two objects are the same. Two objects are the same if they have the same id. In the following test case two ruby objects, both of which are strings "ruby" are tested for sameness.

```ruby
require 'test/unit'

class AssertionTestCase < Test::Unit::TestCase
  def test_assertion
    obj1="ruby"
    obj2="ruby"

    assert_same(obj1, obj2, "Objects not Same" )
  end
end
```

The output indicates that the objects are not the same as shown in Figure 11.9.

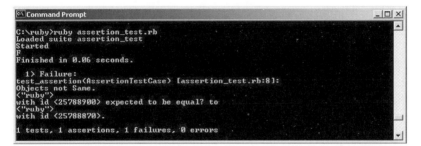

Fig. 11.9 Assertion type assert_same

Assertion type assert_not_same (obj1, obj2, [msg]) asserts that two objects are not the same. The other assertion types are discussed in Table 11.1.

Table 11.1 Assertion Types

Assertion Type	Description
assert_nil(obj, [msg])	Asserts that on object is nil.
assert_not_nil(obj, [msg])	Asserts that object is not nil.
assert_match(regexp, string, [msg])	Asserts that a string matches a regular expression.
assert_no_match(regexp, string, [msg])	Asserts that a string does not match a regular expression.
assert_in_delta(expecting, actual, delta, [msg])	Asserts that a expected value and a actual value do not differ by more than delta.
assert_throws(symbol, [msg]){ block }	Asserts that a block has a throw statement for the catch block with label specified in symbol.
assert_raises(exceptions){ block }	Asserts that a block raises one of the exceptions.
assert_nothing_raised(exceptions){ block }	Asserts that none of the exceptions are raised in the block.
assert_instance_of(class, obj, [msg])	Asserts that an object is an instance of a class.
assert_respond_to(obj, symbol, [msg])	Asserts that obj has a method called symbol.
assert_operator(obj1, operator, obj2, [msg])	Asserts that obj1.operator(obj2)
assert_send(array, [msg])	Asserts that invoking method in array[0] on object in array[1] with parameters specified in array[2], array[3]… returns true.
flunk([msg])	Causes failure

11.5 Rails Testing

We have discussed what are test cases, test methods, and assertions. In this section we shall discuss how testing is used in the Rails framework. Create an example Rails application as shown below.

```
C:/ruby>rails catalog
```

A Rails application with models in the app/models directory, controllers in the app/controllers directory, helpers in the app/helpers directory and view templates in the app/views/catalog directory gets created. Also a test directory gets created. The test directory includes 4 sub-directories: unit, functional, fixtures and mock. The unit directory contains the model tests, the functional directory contains the controller tests, the fixtures directory contains the sample data files and the mock directory contains the mock objects. Initially the unit, functional and fixtures directories are empty. We shall add test and sample data to these directories. To run unit tests run the following command.

```
C:/ruby/catalog> rake test:units
```

To run controller tests run the following command.

```
C:/ruby/catalog>rake   test:functionals
```

The config/database.yml configuration file has 3 different database setups: development, production and test. The test mode is for running Rails tests. The test database should be different from the development database. The configuration for the test mode is as follows.

```
test:
  adapter: mysql
  database: catalog_test
  username: root
  password:
  host: localhost
```

Using the test database configuration the database gets loaded with sample data from the fixtures. The sample data loaded into the database becomes available to the tests. Create a catalog_test database with the following mysql command.

```
CREATE DATABASE catalog_test
DEFAULT CHARACTER SET utf8
```

Also create a catalog_development database with the following mysql command.

```
CREATE DATABASE catalog_development
DEFAULT CHARACTER SET utf8
```

11.6 Fixtures

Fixtures are sample data and are of two type: YAML fixtures and CSV fixtures. YAML are the default types of fixtures. YAML fixtures are stored in a YAML fixture file in the test/fixtures directory. YAML fixtures are stored in a single file per mode and the YAML fixture file has the .yml extension. For the Rails application catalog create a database table catalogs in the catalog_test database using migrations or with the following mysql command.

```
CREATE TABLE catalogs(id VARCHAR(25)
PRIMARY KEY, journal VARCHAR(25), publisher
VARCHAR(25),
 edition VARCHAR(25), title Varchar(255), author
Varchar(25));
```

Create a YAML fixture file catalogs.yml with 3 fixtures as listed below.

```
catalog1:
  id: 1
  journal: Oracle Magazine
  publisher: Oracle Magazine
  edition: July-August 2005
  title: Tuning Undo Tablespace
  author: Kimberly Floss

catalog2:
  id: 2
  journal: Oracle Magazine
  publisher: Oracle Magazine
  edition: May-June 2006
  title: Tuning Your View Objects
  author: Steve Muench

catalog3:
  id: 3
  journal: Oracle Magazine
  publisher: Oracle Magazine
  edition: July-August 2006
  title: Evolving Grid Management
  author: David Baum
```

If the CSV fixtures are used the same sample data is specified in a catalogs.csv file as follows.

```
id,journal,publisher,edition,title,author
1,Oracle     Magazine,Oracle     Magazine,July-August
2005,Tuning Undo Tablespace,Kimberly Floss
2,Oracle     Magazine,Oracle     Magazine,May-June
2006,Tuning Your View Objects,Steve Muench
3,Oracle     Magazine,Oracle     Magazine,July-August
2006,Evolving Grid Management,David Baum
```

The first line in CSV format is the header and each fixture is specified on a separate line. Null values may be specified with two consecutive commas without any value. In the YAML format each fixture has a name specified in the fixture file, but in the CSV format each fixture has a name of the format model_counter. For example, the first fixture in the catalogs.csv file has the name catalog_1. If a field value has a comma specify the field value with a double-quote. If a field value has a double quote, escape the double quote with another double-quote.

11.7 Unit Testing

Unit tests are tests run on models. To run a unit test using the fixtures first, create a model catalog with the following command.

```
C:/ruby/catalog>ruby script/generate model catalog
```

A model script catalog.rb gets created in the models directory. A unit test script catalog_test.rb gets created in the test/unit directory. A fixtures file catalogs.yml gets created in the test/fixtures directory. Copy the catalogs.yml file from the Fixtures section to the catalogs.yml file in the fixtures directory. Next, we shall run the unit test, which is model test, using the fixtures in the catalog.yml file. The default unit test consists of a test case CatalogTest, which extends the Test::Unit::TestCase class. The catalog_test.rb unit test script is listed below.

```ruby
require File.dirname(__FILE__) + '/../test_helper'

class CatalogTest < Test::Unit::TestCase
  fixtures :catalogs
  # Replace this with your real tests.
  def test_truth
    assert true
  end
end
```

The unit test class has a fixtures method, which specifies a comma separated list of symbols representing fixtures.

```
fixtures :catalogs
```

When the test case is run the testing environment automatically loads the specified fixtures into the database. Modify the unit test class to add a test method test_catalogs_count, which counts the catalogs in the sample data. The modified unit test case class is shown below.

```
require File.dirname(__FILE__) + '/../test_helper'

  class CatalogTest < Test::Unit::TestCase

    fixtures :catalogs

    def test_catalogs_count
      assert_equal 3, Catalog.count
    end
  end
```

Next, run the model test using from the test/unit directory.

```
C:/ruby/catalog/test/unit>ruby catalog_test.rb
```

The output from the unit test indicates that the test has passed as shown in Figure 11.10.

Fig. 11.10 Running a Unit Test

Fixtures are available as hash objects by the same name as the fixture. The :catalogs symbol fixtures are available as local variable *catalogs*, which is a hash object, in the test case class. If instantiated fixtures, which we shall discuss later, are enabled the fixtures are available as an instance variable @catalogs, which is a hash object with the same name as the symbol specified in the fixtures method. And each of the fixtures in the fixtures file is also available as a instance variable, for example catalog1 fixture is available as instance variable @catalog1. Instantiated fixtures should be used sparingly as they reduce performance. Assertions may be tested using the hash object, either the default local variable hash or the instance variable hash enabled with instantiated objects. For example, test the value of the title for the fixture catalog1 using the local variable "catalogs".

```
require File.dirname(__FILE__) + '/../test_helper'

class CatalogTest < Test::Unit::TestCase
  fixtures :catalogs
   def test_find
     assert_equal  catalogs(:catalog1).title,   "Tuning
     Undo Tablespace"
     end
end
```

The output from the test, shown in Figure 11.11, indicates that the assertion about the title is true.

```
C:\ruby\catalog\test\unit>ruby catalog_test.rb
Loaded suite catalog_test
Started
.
Finished in 1.022 seconds.

1 tests, 1 assertions, 0 failures, 0 errors
C:\ruby\catalog\test\unit>
```

Fig. 11.11 Using Local Variables

Using instantiated fixtures the fixtures are loaded into hash object, an instance variable by the same name as the symbol. Each of the fixtures is available as a hash object, an instance variable by the same name as the fixture. To enable instantiated fixtures set use_instantiated_fixtures in the test/test_helper.rb to true.

```
self.use_instantiated_fixtures  = true
```

In the CatalogTest test case use instance variables @catalogs, for the database table catalogs, and @catalog1, for a fixture in the catalogs.yml fixture file, to test an assertion.

```
require File.dirname(__FILE__) + '/../test_helper'
class CatalogTest < Test::Unit::TestCase
  fixtures :catalogs
   def test_find
      assert_equal      @catalogs["catalog1"]["title"],
  @catalog1.title
     end
end
```

The output from the test, shown in Figure 11.12, case indicates that the assertion is true.

Fig. 11.12 Using Instantiated Fixtures

The model class method `find` may be used to find a fixture. For example, find the model class object for id 2 and test the values of the different columns using accessors.

```
require File.dirname(__FILE__) + '/../test_helper'

class CatalogTest < Test::Unit::TestCase
  fixtures :catalogs
   def test_find
     catalog2=Catalog.find(2)
     assert_equal catalog2.edition, "May-June 2006"
        assert_equal  catalog2.title,  "Tuning  Your
     View Objects"
     assert_equal catalog2.author, "Steve Muench"
     end
end
```

The output indicates that 3 assertions have passed. Test assertions may be used to create update or delete (CRUD) column values. To use the create, save, delete update methods of the model class set use_transactional_fixtures to false in test/test_helper.rb file.

```
self.use_transactional_fixtures = false
```

As an example, update the edition, title and author columns of database row with id 2. Test the assertion that the database row has been updated.

```
require File.dirname(__FILE__) + '/../test_helper'
class CatalogTest < Test::Unit::TestCase
  fixtures :catalogs
   def test_find
     catalog2=Catalog.find(2)

     catalog2.edition="MayJune2006"
     catalog2.title="Tuning Your ADF View Objects"
     catalog2.author="Muench, Steve"
```

```
    assert catalog2.save
      end
end
```

Run the test case; the output indicates that test has passed. The database row gets updated. Transactional fixtures are used by default. With transactional fixtures every test case rolls back its changes. If the test database is pre-loaded with all the fixture data and you are using transactional fixtures, the fixtures declarations may be omitted as the fixtures data is already loaded and the test cases roll back their changes. For example, the following test case may run without the fixtures declaration if the fixture data has been pre-loaded and transactional fixtures are being used.

```
require File.dirname(__FILE__) + '/..//test_helper'

class CatalogTest < Test::Unit::TestCase

  def test_find
    catalog2=Catalog.find(2)
    assert_equal catalog2.edition, "May-June 2006"
    assert_equal catalog2.title, "Tuning Your View
    Objects"
    assert_equal catalog2.author, "Steve Muench"
  end

end
```

Transactional fixtures should not be used to test transactions and if a database does not support transactions.

Both the YAML fixtures and CSV fixtures have the provision to embed Ruby in the fixture file to create dynamic fixtures. The following example creates dynamic fixtures fixture_1, fixture_2…fixture_10 with fields id an edition that are also generated dynamically.

```
<% for i in 1..10 %> fixture_<%= i %>:
id: <%= i %>
edition: edition_<%= i %>

<% end %>
```

11.8 Testing Controllers

Controller testing is also known as functional testing. Functional testing tests the functionality of the controller such as was the response redirected as expected, was the expected template rendered, was the routing as expected, and does the response contain the expected tags. The Rails framework provides the ActionController::TestRequest class to simulate a request and the ActionController::TestResponse class to simulate a response.

We shall run some controller tests using a rails application hello. Create a Rails application hello.

```
C:/ruby>rails hello
```

Create MySQL databases hello_development and hello_test with SQL commands as shown earlier. Create a controller "hello" with controller actions "hello" and "index".

```
C:/ruby/hello>ruby  script/generate  controller  hello
hello index
```

A default controller test script hello_controller_test.rb gets created in the test/functional directory as listed below.

```
require File.dirname(__FILE__) + '/../test_helper'
require 'hello_controller'

# Re-raise errors caught by the controller.
class HelloController; def rescue_action(e)  raise  e
end; end

class HelloControllerTest < Test::Unit::TestCase
  def setup
    @controller = HelloController.new
    @request    = ActionController::TestRequest.new
    @response   = ActionController::TestResponse.new
  end
  # Replace this with your real tests.
  def test_truth
    assert true
  end
end
```

The controller test consists of a setup method in which a controller object, a TestRequest object and a TestResponse object are created. The controller test case also consists of the default test method test_truth. The controller class, hello_controller.rb, consists of actions hello and index and is listed below.

```
class HelloController < ApplicationController

    def hello
    end

    def index
    end
end
```

View templates hello.rhtml and index.rhtml get created in the views/hello directory. Run the default controller test with the following command.

```
C:/ruby/hello>rake test:functionals
```

The output generated, shown in Figure 11.13, indicates that the test passed.

```
C:\ruby\hello>rake test:functionals
(in C:/ruby/hello)
c:/ruby/bin/ruby -Ilib;test "c:/ruby/lib/ruby/gems/1.8/gems/rake-0.7.1/lib/rake/
rake_test_loader.rb" "test/functional/hello_controller_test.rb"
Loaded suite c:/ruby/lib/ruby/gems/1.8/gems/rake-0.7.1/lib/rake/rake_test_loader

Started

Finished in 1.042 seconds.

1 tests, 1 assertions, 0 failures, 0 errors

C:\ruby\hello>_
```

Fig. 11.13 Running a Controller Test

Rails framework supports 5 types of requests: get, post,put,head, and delete. Request type "get" and "post" are the most commonly used in controller testing. Add a controller test to the test case HelloControllerTest to send a request to the index action with the GET HTTP method. Use the assert_response assertion to test is the request was successful.

```
def test_index
    get :index
    assert_response :success
    end
```

Run the controller test. The test passes. The assert_response(type, message = nil) method is one of the methods in the

ActionController::Assertions::ResponseAssertions module to test controller response. The optional message parameter specifies the message to display if the controller test fails. Response may be one of the following types.

```
:success (status code 200)
:redirect (status code in the range of 300-399)
:missing (status code 404)
:error (status code in the range of 500-599)
```

The status code or the symbolic equivalent may be used to invoke the assert_response method. The assert_redirected_to(options = {}, message=nil) method asserts that the action has been redirected as specified in the method options. The assert_template(expected = nil, message=nil) method asserts that a template was rendered. Add assert_template and assert_redirected_to assertions to the HelloControllerTest test case as shown below.

```
require File.dirname(__FILE__) + '/../test_helper'
require 'hello_controller'

# Re-raise errors caught by the controller.
class HelloController; def rescue_action(e) raise e
end; end

class HelloControllerTest < Test::Unit::TestCase
  def setup
    @controller = HelloController.new
    @request    = ActionController::TestRequest.new
    @response   = ActionController::TestResponse.new
  end
  def test_index
    get :index
    assert_response :success
    assert_template "hello/index"
    assert_redirected_to  :controller  =>  'hello',
    :action => 'hello'
  end
end
```

Run the modified controller test case. The output, shown in Figure 11.14, indicates that 2 of the assertions passed and 1 of the assertion (the assert_redirected_to assertion) failed.

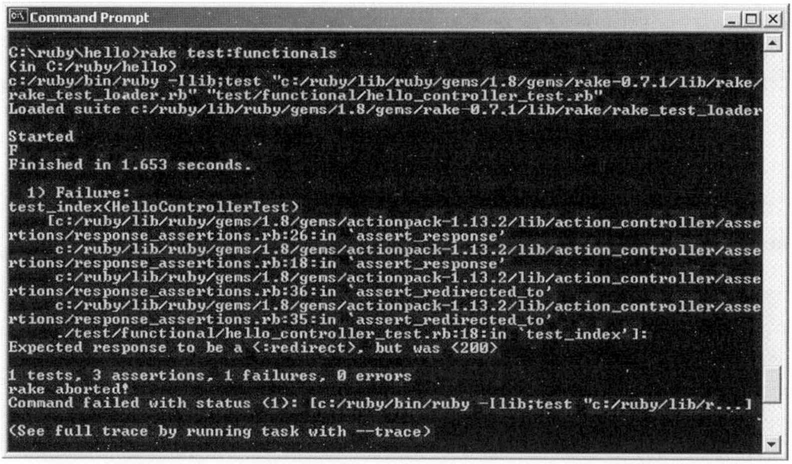

Fig. 11.14 Controller Test with assert_template and assert_redirected_to

After a request has been sent the hash objects listed in Table 11.2 become available in the test method.

Table 11.2 Test Method Hash Objects

Hash Object	Description
assigns	Contains any objects stored in instance variables of controller actions.
cookies	Cookies objects.
flash	Flash objects.
Session	Session variable objects

As an example, modify the hello action to define an instance variable @msg.

```
def hello
    @msg="Hello"
  end
```

Modify the test_index method to send a GET request to hello action. Add assert_equal statement to assert that the @msg instance variable's value is "Hello". Add a assert_not_nil statement to assert that the hello instance variable is not nil, but the hello instance variable is not defined.

```
def test_hello
    get :hello
    assert_response :success
    assert_equal "Hello", assigns["msg"]
    assert_not_nil assigns["hello"]
 end
```

Run the controller test case. The output, shown in Figure 11.15, indicates that 2 assertions passed and one assertion failed.

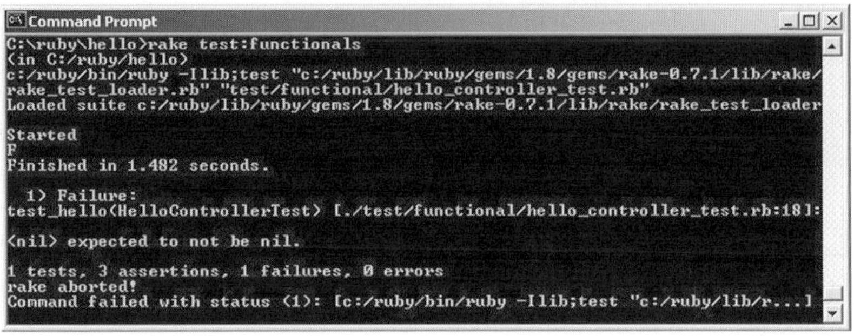

Fig. 11.15 Using the assigns hash object

The Rails controller framework provides some routing assertions to assert the routing of requests. The assert_generates(expected_path, options, defaults={}, extras = {}, message=nil) method asserts that the specified options generate the specified path. Each of the options constitutes an assertion. For example, run the following test in the HelloController test case.

```
def test_index
    assert_generates("/hello",       :controller    =>
"hello", :action => "index")
    end
```

The output, shown in Figure 11.16, indicates that the test with 2 assertions passed.

```
Command Prompt                                                    _ □ ×
C:\ruby\hello>rake test:functionals
(in C:/ruby/hello)
c:/ruby/bin/ruby -Ilib;test "c:/ruby/lib/ruby/gems/1.8/gems/rake-0.7.1/lib/rake/
rake_test_loader.rb" "test/functional/hello_controller_test.rb"
Loaded suite c:/ruby/lib/ruby/gems/1.8/gems/rake-0.7.1/lib/rake/rake_test_loader

Started
.
Finished in 0.671 seconds.

1 tests, 2 assertions, 0 failures, 0 errors

C:\ruby\hello>
```

Fig. 11.16 Using assert_generates

The assert_recognizes(expected_options, path, extras={}, message=nil) method asserts that the routing of the specified path was handled correctly and the path generated from the options match the path. In the example controller, the following assertion passes.

```
def test_index
    assert_recognizes({:controller    =>    'hello',
:action => 'hello'}, 'hello/hello')

    end
```

The second argument to the assert_recognizes method may be hash specifying the request method. The following assertions contains a hash as the second argument. The hash specifies the :path and the :method as get.

```
def test_index
    assert_recognizes({:controller    =>    'hello',
:action => 'hello'}, {:path => 'hello/hello', :method
=> :get})
    end
```

Method   assert_routing(path,   options,   defaults={},   extras={}, message=nil) asserts that the path and options match both ways. The path generated from the options is the same as the path specified and the options obtained from the path are the same as the options specified. The following assertion passes.

```
def test_index
    assert_routing("/hello",   :controller => "hello",
:action => "index")
    end
```

The controller framework provides some tag assertions to assert tag content returned by a controller action. The tags are required to be closed to use tag assertions; a few of the tags such as <br> and <hr> may not be closed. The assert_tag(*opts) method asserts that the response contains the tag that meets all the conditions specified in a conditions hash. The options the may be specified in assert_tag() are discussed in Table 11.3.

Table 11.3 Method assert_tag() Options

Option	Description
:tag	Specifies the node type. For example, :tag=>"table"
:attributes	Specifies a hash of attributes.
:content	Specifies text content.
:parent	A hash specifying the node's preceding tag.
:child	A hash specifying a child tag of the node.
:ancestor	A hash specifying an ancestor tag of the node.
:descendant	A hash specifying a descendent of the node.
:sibling	A hash specifying a sibling of the node.
:after	The node must be after a sibling specified in the hash.
:before	The node must be before a sibling specified by the hash.
:children	A hash for children of the node.

As an example, modify the HelloController class to add a render :text=> statement in the index method.

```
class HelloController < ApplicationController
  def hello
  end
  def index

    render:text =>"<div><div id='div1'></div></div>"
  end
end
```

In the controller test case add a test that includes an assert_tag statement. The assertion asserts that the response contains a <div></div> tag with an attribute id with value "div1".

```
def test_index
    get :index
    assert_tag :tag => "div", :attributes => { :id =>
"div1" }
end
```

Run the controller test. The output indicates that the assertion has passed. The assert_no_tag(*opts) method asserts that the response does not contain a tag specified in the method options.

11.9 Summary

Rails testing consists of unit tests and functional tests. Unit tests are tests run on models and functional tests are tests run on controllers. A test is run by creating a sub class of the Test::Unit::TestCase class and including test methods, which further consist of assertions.

12 Rails in Production

12.1 Introduction

Rails applications may be run in one of the three environments: development, test and production. We used the development environment for all of the chapters except the chapter on testing and fixtures in which we used the test environment. A difference between the development environment and the production environment is that the application code is reloaded on each request in the development environment, which slows down response time, but is suited for development as the web server is not required to be restarted between code changes. Another difference is that in development environment error reporting is enabled and caching is turned off while in production mode error reporting is turned off and caching is turned on. After developing and testing a Rails application may be used in production mode.

12.2 Setting the Production Mode

The Rails environment may be set using the RAILS_ENV variable. To set the environment to production uncomment the following line in config/environment.rb file.

```
ENV['RAILS_ENV'] ||= 'production'
```

A environment file corresponding to each of the environments is created in the config/environments directory when a Rails application is created. The environment file for the production environment is production.rb.

The WEBrick web server may be started in production mode with the following command, which overrides the RAILS_ENV setting.

```
ruby script/server  -e production
```

12.3 Rails Best Practices and Performance

In development mode all localhost requests are run as CGI (Common Gateway Interface). WEBrick web server uses CGI. For small scale Rails applications WEBrick web server may be suitable. Some of the Rails web sites such as instiki.org and wiki.rubyonrails.com use WEBrick web server. For large-scale Rails applications CGI is slow to be used in production environment. For medium to large-scale applications in production environment FastCGI[1] is the recommended and default method. "FastCGI is a language independent, scalable, open extension to CGI that provides high performance without the limitations of server specific APIs." FastCGI is supported by various web servers some of which are Apache web server, Microsoft IIS, SunOne, and Lighttpd If you are using Apache you'll need the mod_fcgi Apache module and the FastCGI development kit. If you are using Apache an alternative to FastCGI is the mod_ruby Apache module. Another alternative to FastCGI is SCGI Rails Runner (SRR), a Ruby script that is as fast as FastCGI and easier to install than FastCGI. SCGI Rails Runner supports Apache, and lighttpd web servers on OSX, Linux, FreeBSD, and Win32 operating systems.

Sending files across a HTTP connection or retrieving data from a database may increase bandwidth usage and database load to effect performance. In production mode caching is turned on to cache models and controllers, which are not expected to change. With caching the cached data is used if the data has not been modified since the previous time the data was requested. With caching models and controllers run faster, thus, increasing performance. Caching is implemented by time stamping the model and checking the HTTP_IF_MODIFIED_SINCE header in the request sent by the browser. To timestamp a model add an updated_at or updated_on field of data type timestamp to the database table. If the client's timestamp, as indicated by the HTTP_IF_MODIFIED_SINCE header, is older than the model timestamp the browser is directed to use the cached copy. The controller sends an HTTP status code to browser indicating that the data has not been modified since the previous request.

```
render_text '', '304 Not Modified'
```

If the status code is '304 Not Modified', the browser uses the cached copy. The controller also sends last modified timestamp to the browser using the LAST_MODIFIED response header. Models may be cached

---

[1] FastCGI- http://www.fastcgi.com/

using the cached_model gem. Memcached[2] is a memory object caching system for increasing the speed of web applications and for reducing database load.

Some of the other best practices include optimizing the SQL queries. Group operations into transactions to avoid multiple transactions. Use filters and helpers only if required. Use logging only for the required information. Using a debug logging level in production may increase load. Use instance variables in controller only if the instance variables are used in the view templates.

Using dynamic finders such as find_by_ does make the code more readable and easier to maintain, but slows down the query and reduces efficiency as the dynamic methods have to be generated by the ActiveRecord and the SQL query has to built from the dynamic finder by the ActiveRecord.

Some of the performance considerations when developing a Rails application are response time and security. Response time is better for code run on the client side and security is better for code run on the server side. Some of the common security problems are SQL injection and cross site scripting (CSS/XSS). SQL Injection is the external modification of SQL statements in a Rails application. SQL Injection becomes a problem if a web application contains strings from form parameters in SQL statements and does not correctly quote any meta characters such as back slashes and single quotes. If you use predefined ActiveRecord methods such as find() and save(), which do not contain any SQL, SQL Injection is not a problem. SQL Injection is prevented by not using strings from form parameters. For example, the following invocation of the find_all method should not be used.

```
Catalog.find_all "catalog_id = 123 AND journal =
'#{@params['journal']}'"
```

Instead the following find_all method invocation should be used.

```
journal = @params['journal']
Catalog.find_all [ "user_id = 123 AND journal = ?",
journal ]
```

To prevent SQL Injection use "?" placeholders and correctly quote any SQL meta characters such as "\" and "'". Another best practice in ActiveRecord models is to use a function for a query that is to be run with similar options in several instances in the model code. For example, if the

---

[2] Memcached- http://www.danga.com/memcached/

web application contains multiple instances of the following query create a method to run the query.

```
catalogs = Catalog.find_all ["journal = ?", journal]
```

Create the following class method for the query.

```
class Catalog < ActiveRecord::Base
  def self.find_with_journal(journal)
    Catalog.find_all ["journal = ?", journal]
  end
end
```

The method is used as follows.

```
catalogs = Catalog.find_with_journal(journal)
```

Cross Site Scripting (CSS/XSS) is the code injection, including HTML code and client –side scripts, into web pages to obtain information, such as login information, about other users of the web page. To prevent CSS convert HTML characters ("<" and ">") to the equivalent HTML entities ("<" and ">"). Use the Rails helper method h() for HTML meta character conversions in views as in the following example.

```
<%=h catalog.journal %>
```

Various tools are available for measuring performance or Ruby on Rails applications. Web Application Testing in Ruby (WATIR) is an open source functional resting tool for automating browser-based tests of web applications. Railsbench is a tool for measuring performance of Rails applications. Ruby Performance Validator is tool for source code performance analysis of Ruby applications. Ruby-prof is a profiler for Ruby. The Ruby testing tools may be used to optimize the Ruby code in the Ruby on Rails applications.

12.4 Deployment on Apache2 and FastCGI

While WEBrick is well suited for development and small-scale production applications, for medium and large-scale production applications an application server such as Apach2 web server that supports FastCGI is recommended. With WEBrick the following invocation path is followed.

1. Request is sent to the Web Server
2. Web Server forwards request to dispatch.rb.
3. routes.rb gets invoked.

4. Controller gets loaded.

With Apache web server using FastCGI the following invocation path gets invoked.

1. Request is sent to web server
2. The .htaccess gets invoked
3. dispatch.fcgi gets invoked
4. routes.rb gets invoked
5. Controller gets loaded

In this section we shall discuss deploying a Ruby on Rails application to Apache2 web server using FastCGI.

First we need to install Apache2[3] web server. Install the Apache 2.0.x version. Apache 2.2.x version does not include the FastCGI module. Double-click on *apache_2.0.59-win32-x86-no_ssl.msi* file. The Installation Wizard gets started. Click on Next as shown in Figure 12.1.

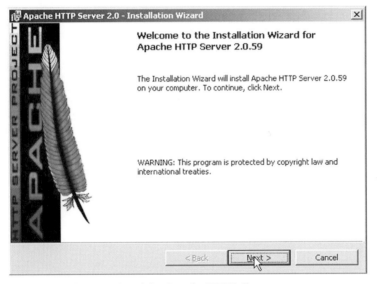

Fig. 12.1 Installation Wizard for Apache HTTP Server

Accept the license agreement and click on Next. In the Read This First click on Next. Select the default server settings and click on Next. Select Setup Type as Typical and click on Next. Select the default destination

---

[3] Apache2- http://httpd.apache.org/

folder,   C:\Program Files\Apache Group, and click on Next. Click on
Install. Apache 2 web server gets installed. Click on Finish.   Install
MySQL 5 database if not already installed. Download RubyForApache[4].
Double-click on the *RubyForApache-1.3.1.exe* application. Select the
default destination folder and click on Next. Select the Apache Web Server
directory and click on Next. Select the Ruby installation directory and
click on Next. In the Installation Options window select the component
mod_fastcgi and click on Install as shown in Figure 12.2.

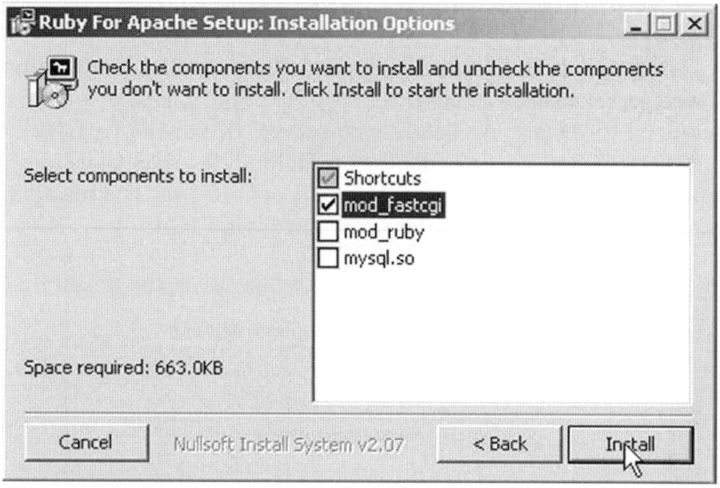

Fig. 12.2 Selecting mod_fastcgi

RubyForApache gets installed as shown in Figure 12.3.

[4] RubyForApache- http://rubyforge.org/projects/rubyforapache/

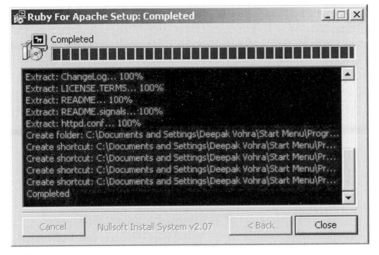

Fig. 12.3 Installing RubyForApache

We need to create a rails application.

```
C:/ruby>rails catalog
```

We need to configure Apache web server. Modify the httpd.conf file in the conf directory. Uncomment the following line.

```
LoadModule rewrite_module modules/mod_rewrite.so
```

To load the FastCGI module, add the following line.

```
LoadModule fastcgi_module modules/mod_fastcgi.so
```

In the httpd.conf configuration file we need to modify the DocumentRoot directive. The DocumentRoot directive is the following before modification.

```
DocumentRoot "C:/Program Files/Apache
Group/Apache2/htdocs"
```

Modify the DocumentRoot directive to the following.

```
DocumentRoot "C:/ruby/catalog/public"
```

We also need to modify the following line.

```
<Directory        "C:/Program        Files/Apache
Group/Apache2/htdocs">
```

Modify the line to the following setting.

```
<Directory "C:/ruby/catalog/public/">
```

We need to add the following VirtualHost element to the bottom of the httpd.conf file.

```
<VirtualHost *:80>
      ServerName rails
      DocumentRoot "C:/ruby/catalog/public"
        <Directory "C:/ruby/catalog/public/">
        Options ExecCGI FollowSymLinks
          AllowOverride all
          Allow from all
         Order allow,deny
          AddHandler cgi-script .cgi
          AddHandler fastcgi-script .fcgi
        </Directory>
   </VirtualHost>
```

After making modifications to the httpd.conf file we need to restart the Apache2 web server.

We also need to modify the Rails application for FastCGI. Replace the cgi dispatcher with the fastcgi dispatcher. In the public/.htaccess file replace the following line.

```
RewriteRule ^(.*)$ dispatch.cgi [QSA,L]
```

The replacement setting is shown below.

```
RewriteRule ^(.*)$ dispatch.fcgi [QSA,L]
```

We also need to comment out the Apache options in the .htaccess file with #.

```
#AddHandler fastcgi-script .fcgi
#AddHandler cgi-script .cgi
#Options +FollowSymLinks +ExecCGI
```

The dispatch.fcgi file should contain the path to the ruby application as the first line.

```
#!c:/ruby/bin/ruby
```

We need to add a new host for the Rails application. To the C:\WINNT\system32\drivers\etc\hosts file add the following line at the beginning of the mappings.

```
127.0.0.1         localhost
```

Invoke the index.html page with the url http://localhost as shown in Figure 12.4.

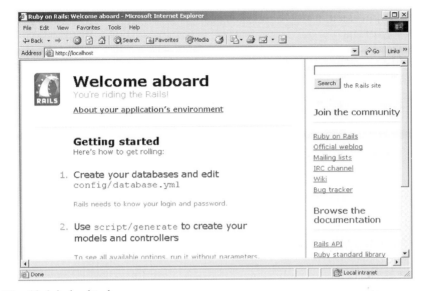

Fig. 12.4 index.html

Next, we shall create scaffolding for a MySQL database table. First, we need to create a database table 'catalogs' with the following SQL script.

```
CREATE TABLE catalogs(id VARCHAR(25)
PRIMARY    KEY,    journal    VARCHAR(25),    publisher
VARCHAR(25),
    edition VARCHAR(25), title Varchar(255), author
Varchar(25));

INSERT INTO catalogs VALUES(1, 'Oracle Magazine',
'Oracle Publishing', 'July-August 2006', 'Evolving
Grid Management', 'David Baum');

INSERT INTO catalogs VALUES(2, 'Oracle Magazine',
'Oracle Publishing', 'July-August 2005','Tuning Undo
Tablespace', 'Kimberly Floss');
```

We need to create scaffolding for the 'catalogs' table with the scaffold generator.

```
C:\ruby\catalog>ruby script/generate scaffold catalog
```

The catalogs list may be displayed with the URL http://localhost/catalogs as shown in Figure 12.5.

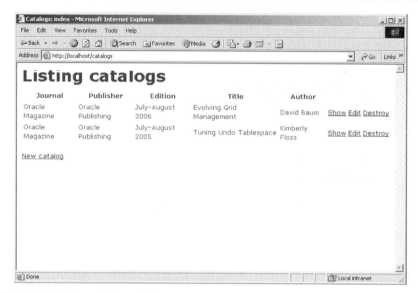

Fig. 12.5 Listing catalog entries

12.5 Rails Web Hosting

In this section we shall create a Rails application and host the application on a web site using a Rails web host. Various Ruby on Rails web hosts[5] are available. Any of the web hosts that support Rails may be used. We shall be using the AVLUX web host. Join a hosting plan provided by AVLUX. Specify a domain name. We shall be using the domain railscrud.com. Select the checkbox Ruby on Rails in "Your custom domain choices." as shown in Figure 12.6.

---

[5] Rails Web Hosts- http://wiki.rubyonrails.org/rails/pages/RailsWebHosts

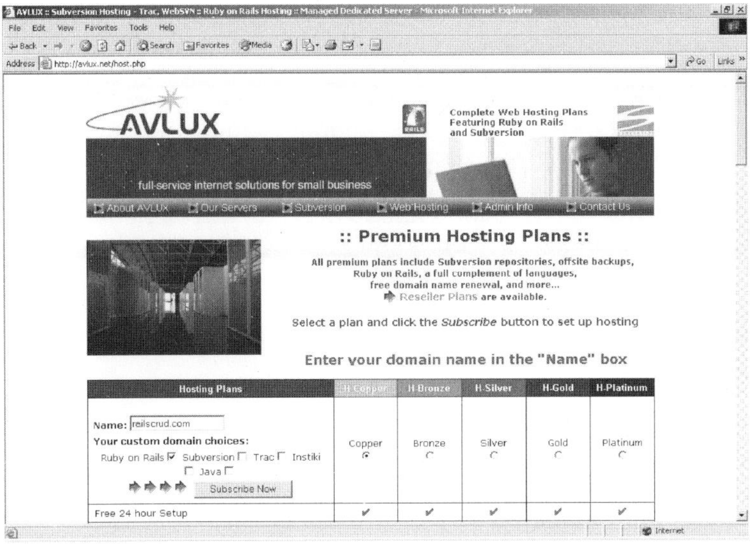

Fig. 12.6 AVLUX Hosting

You shall receive a AVLUX domain setup information kit, which includes the links for the Domain Admin Control Panel and Database Admin Tool. Also the FTP hostname, logon and password are provided.

First, we need to create a Ruby on Rails application that is to be hosted on the Rails web host. We shall be using a CRUD application. Create a rails application, *catalog*.

```
C:/ruby>rails catalog
```

We need to modify the config/database.yml configuration file to specify the database as test.

```
development:
  adapter: mysql
  database: test
  username: root
  password:
  host: localhost
```

We need to create a MySQL database table 'catalogs' with the following SQL Script.

```
CREATE TABLE catalogs(id VARCHAR(25)
  PRIMARY KEY, journal VARCHAR(25), publisher
VARCHAR(25),
```

```
edition VARCHAR(25), title Varchar(255), author
Varchar(25));

INSERT INTO catalogs VALUES(1, 'Oracle Magazine',
'Oracle Publishing', 'July-August 2006', 'Evolving
Grid Management', 'David Baum');

INSERT INTO catalogs VALUES(2, 'Oracle Magazine',
'Oracle Publishing', 'July-August 2005','Tuning Undo
Tablespace', 'Kimberly Floss');
```

We need to create scaffolding for the database table 'catalogs' using the scaffold generator.

```
C:\ruby\catalog>ruby script/generate scaffold catalog
```

Next, we shall deploy the rails application on the AVLUX web host, which uses lighttpd web server and FastCGI. AVLUX provides the MySQL database for Rails applications.

First, create a MySQL database and a database user account. Login to the Domain Admin Control Panel. Login to the Domain Admin Control Panel with the logon and password included in the setup kit.The Domain Admin Control Panel gets displayed. Select the link Home. To create a database user account select the Databases icon as shown in Figure 12.7.

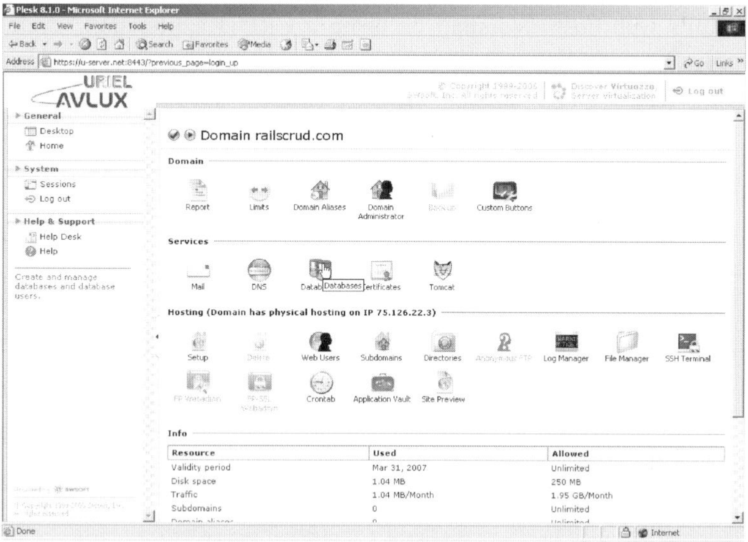

Fig. 12.7 Selecting the Databases

We need to select the Add New Database icon as shown in Figure 12.8.

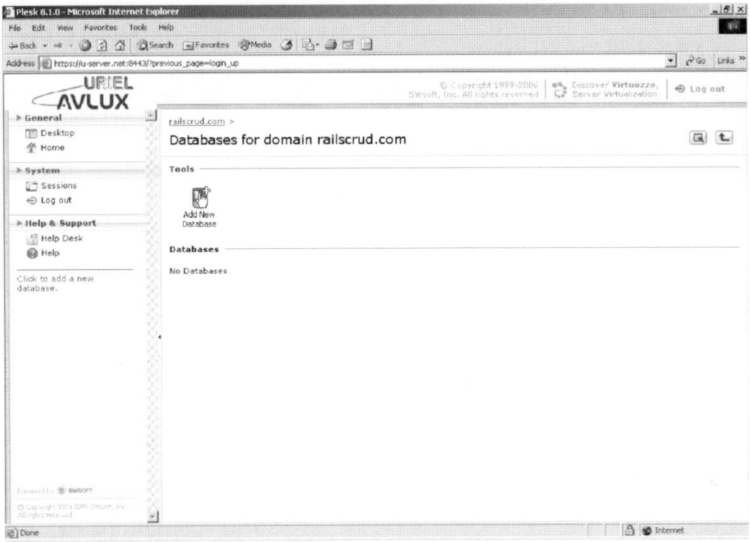

Fig. 12.8 Add New Database

Specify a database name, 'test' for example, and select Type as MySQL. Click on OK as shown in Figure 12.9.

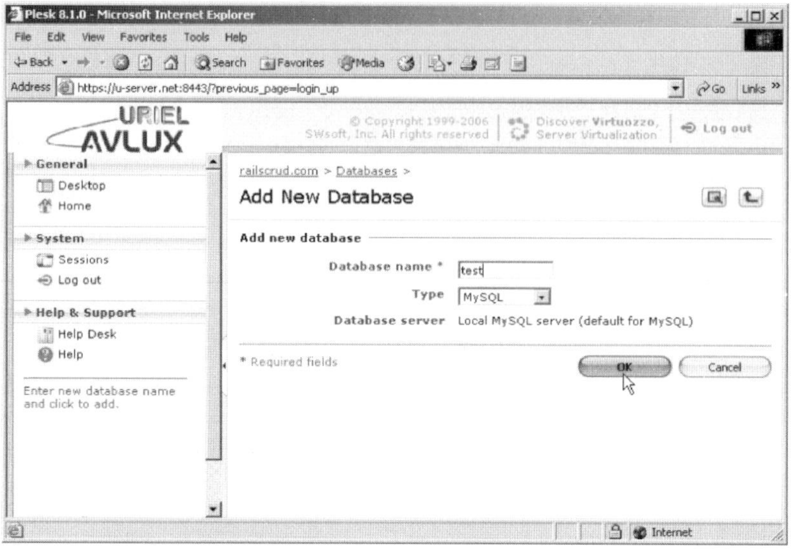

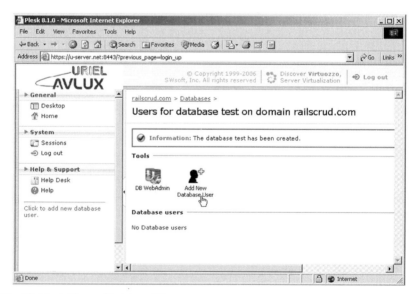

Fig. 12.9 Adding new database

The database test gets created. Next, create a database user. Click on Add New Database User as shown in Figure 12.10.

Fig. 12.10 Add new Database User

Specify a username and password and click on OK as shown in Figure 12.11.

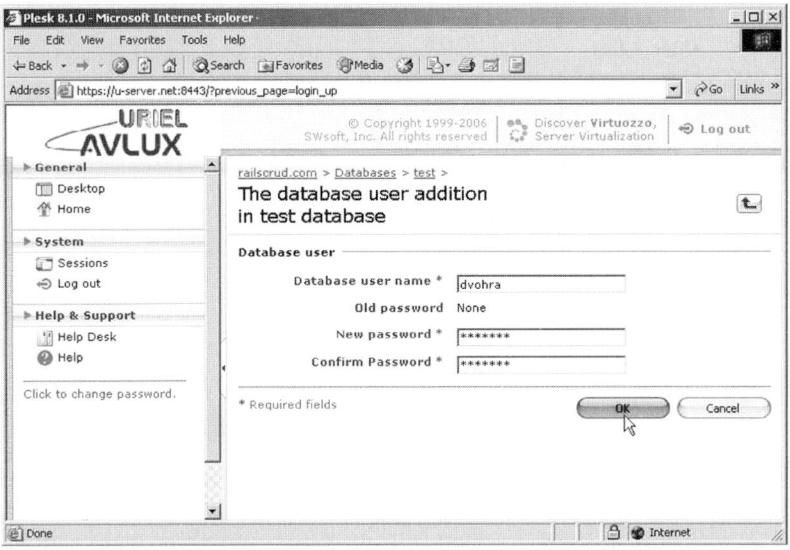

Fig. 12.11 Adding new database user

A new database user gets created as shown in Figure 12.12.

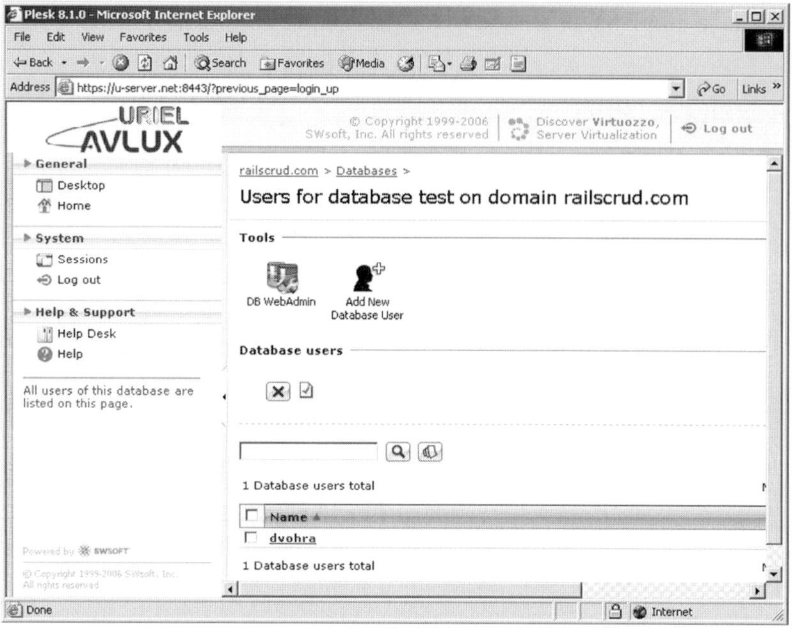

Fig. 12.12 New database user

We shall create a database table, 'catalogs' in the test database. Login to the Database Admin Tool using the username and password created. Select the Databases link in the Database Admin Tool as shown in Figure 12.13.

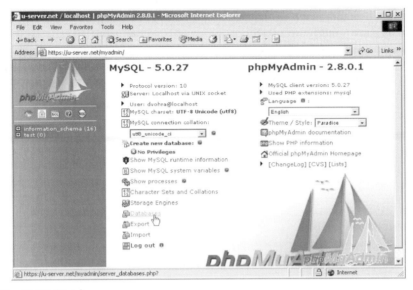

Fig. 12.13 Databases

A list of available databases gets displayed. Select the test database as shown in Figure 12.14.

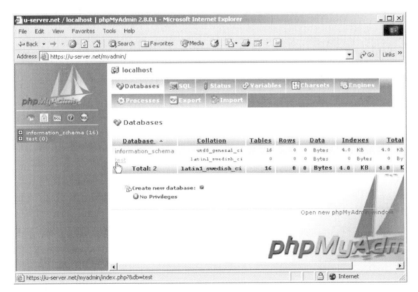

Fig. 12.14 Available Databases

Specify table name as 'catalogs' and number of fields as 6 and click on Go as shown in Figure 12.15.

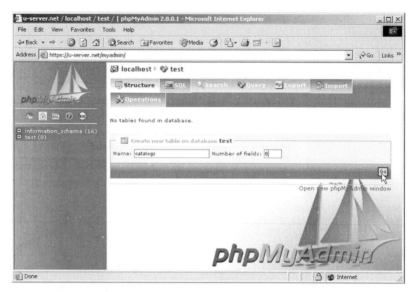

Fig. 12.15 Creating Database Table

Specify the fields as id, Journal, Publisher, Edition, Title, and Author. The field names and types should be the same as those used to create the scaffolding for the 'catalogs' database in development mode. Specify the id field as NOT NULL and a primary key. Click on Save as shown in Figure 12.16.

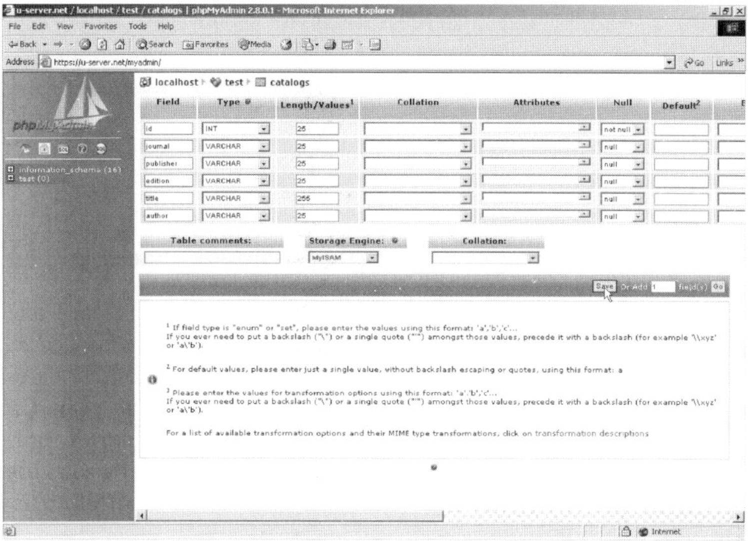

Fig. 12.16 Creating Table Columns

A database table 'catalogs' gets created. Click on Insert to add data to the 'catalogs' table as shown in Figure 12.17.

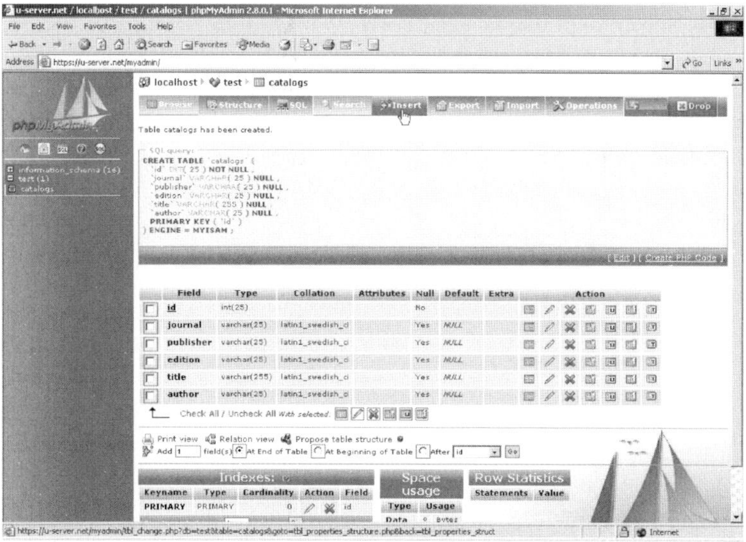

Fig. 12.17 Adding Data

Specify values for the different fields to create two rows in the 'catalogs' table as shown in Figure 12.18. The field values should be the same as created for the test database when creating the Rails CRUD application in development. Click on Go.

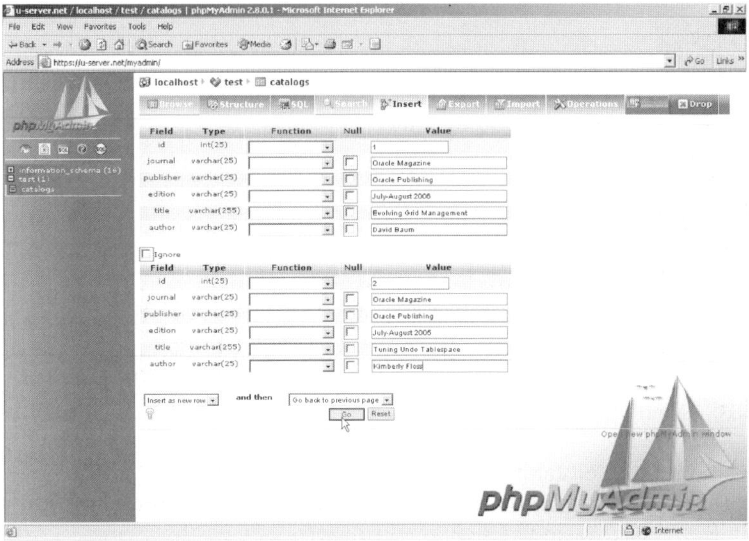

Fig. 12.18 Specifying Column Values

Two rows of data get added as shown in Figure 12.19.

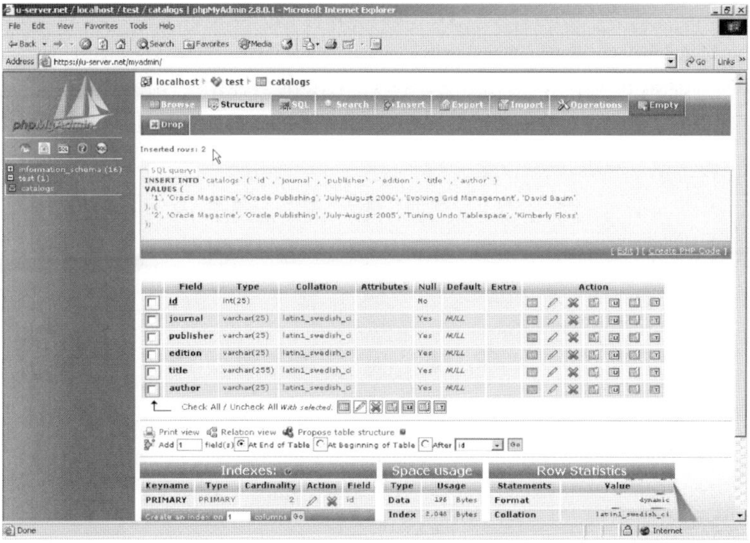

Fig. 12.19 Rows Added

A Rails application structure is pre-installed for the web host. We shall be uploading the scaffolding files created for the catalogs table to the default Rails application. Click on File Manager in the Domain Admin Control Panel as shown in Figure 12.20.

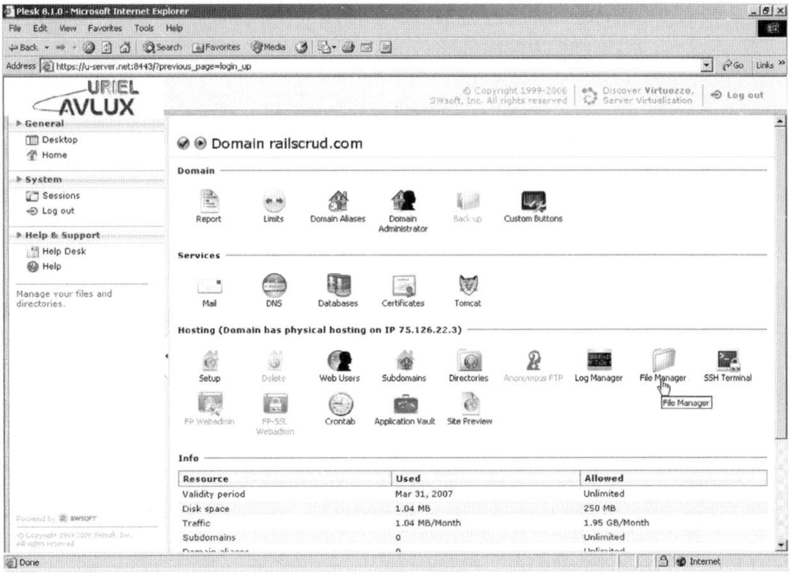

Fig. 12.20 File Manager

The directory structure for a Rails application is installed in the rails directory. We shall be uploading the Rails application we created to the rails folder. Click on the rails folder as shown in Figure 12.21.

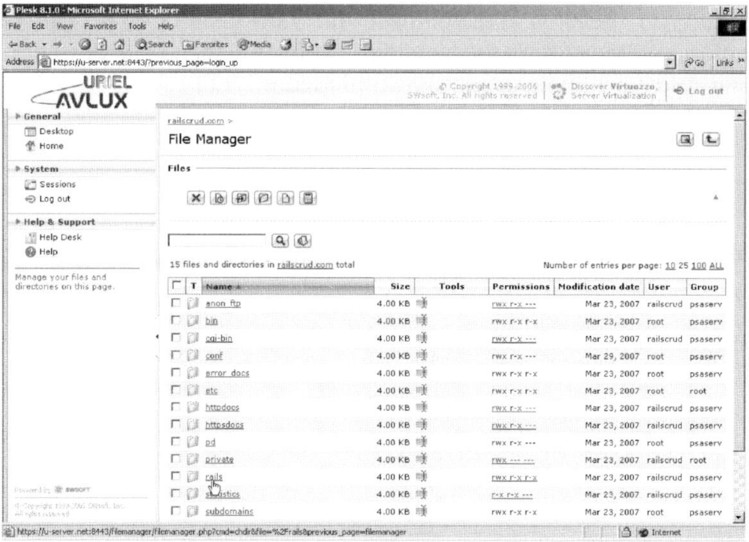

Fig. 12.21 Selecting Rails Application Folder

A Rails application directory structure gets displayed as shown in Figure 12.22. Click on the app folder and subsequently the views folder.

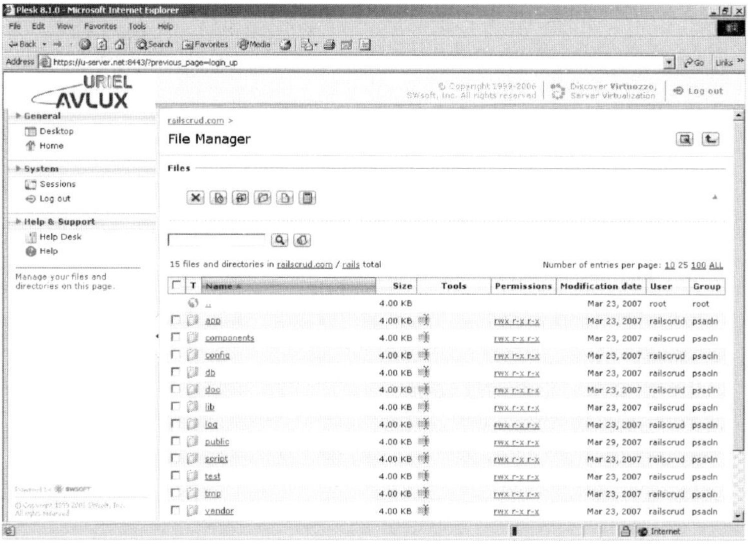

Fig. 12.22 Rails Application Directory Structure

We need to create a directory for the view templates of the Rails application catalog. Create a 'catalogs' folder in the 'views' folder by selecting Add New Directory as shown in Figure 12.23.

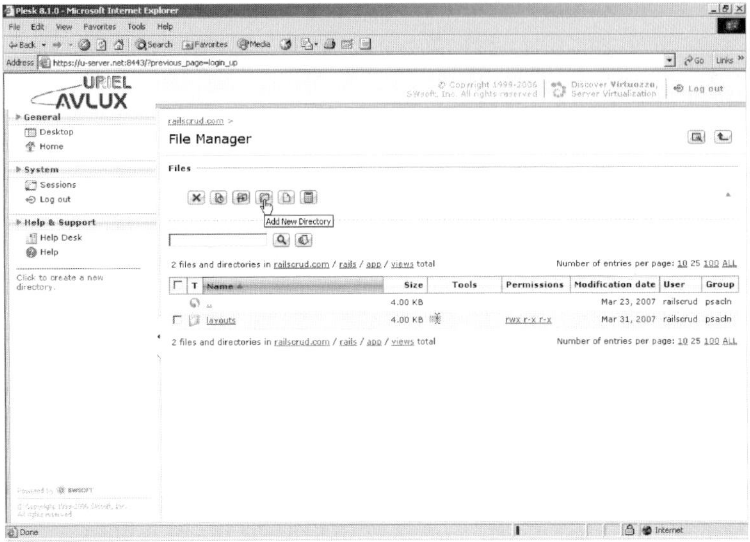

Fig. 12.23 Add New Directory

Specify a directory name and click on OK as shown in Figure 12.24.

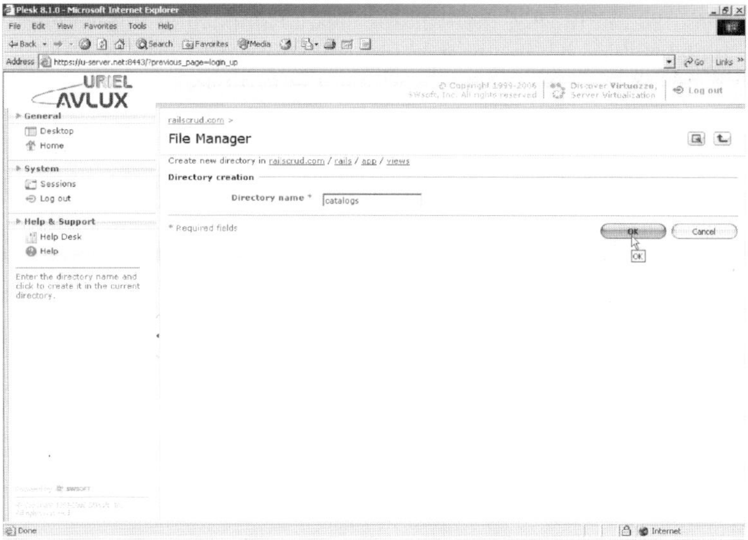

Fig. 12.24 Adding new directory

A 'catalogs' directory gets created in the 'views' directory as shown in Figure 12.25.

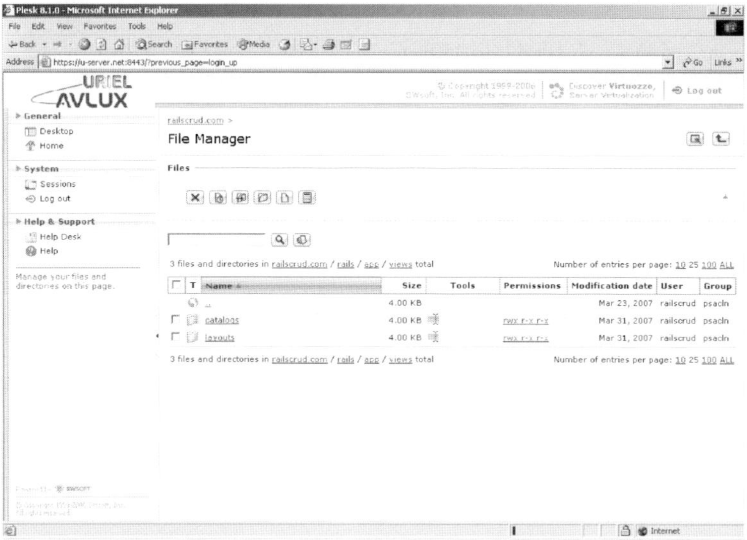

Fig. 12.25 catalogs directory

Next, upload the files of the 'catalog' Rails application that we created to the 'rails' folder on the host using ftp. Specify the command `ftp hostname` to login to the host as shown in Figure 12.26.

Fig. 12.26 FTP Command

Ftp gets connected to the railscrud.com host. Specify username that is provided in the setup information kit, specify the password and select Enter. User gets logged in as shown in Figure 12.27.

Fig. 12.27 User Logged In

List the directories in the host using the dir command as shown in Figure 12.28. The rails directory in which we shall be uploading the Rails application also gets listed. Cd to the rails directory with the `cd rails` command.

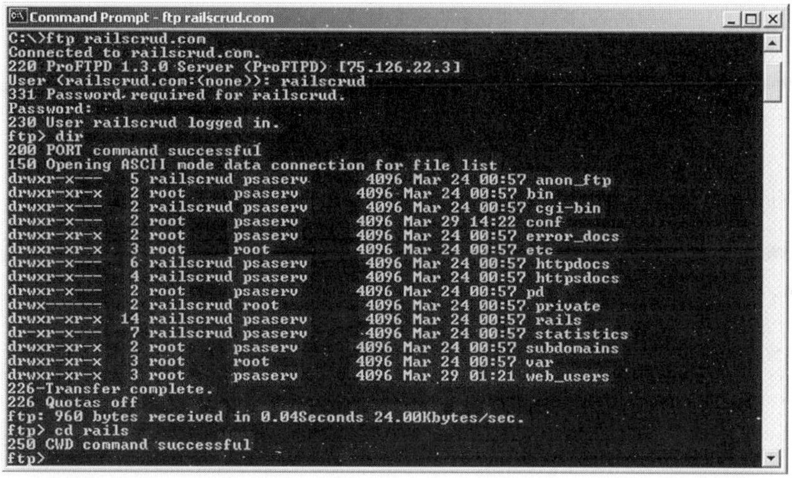

Fig. 12.28 Rails directory on the web host

Cd to the local directory c:/ruby/catalog/app/controllers using the following lcd command.

```
lcd ruby/catalog/app/controllers
```

On the host cd to the controllers directory using the following cd command as shown in Figure 12.29.

```
cd app/controllers
```

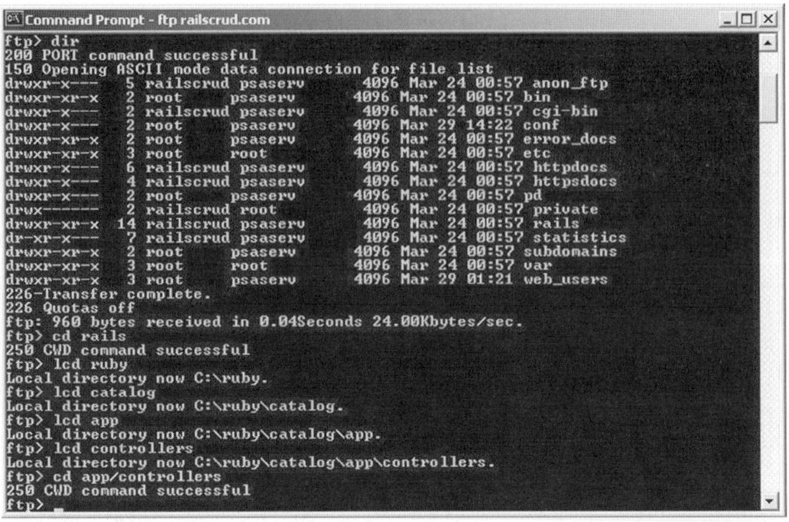

Fig. 12.29 app/controller directory on the web host and local rails application

Upload all the controller ruby scripts from the catalog/app/controllers
directory to the rails/app/controllers directory using the mput command
mput * . rb as shown in Figure 12.30.

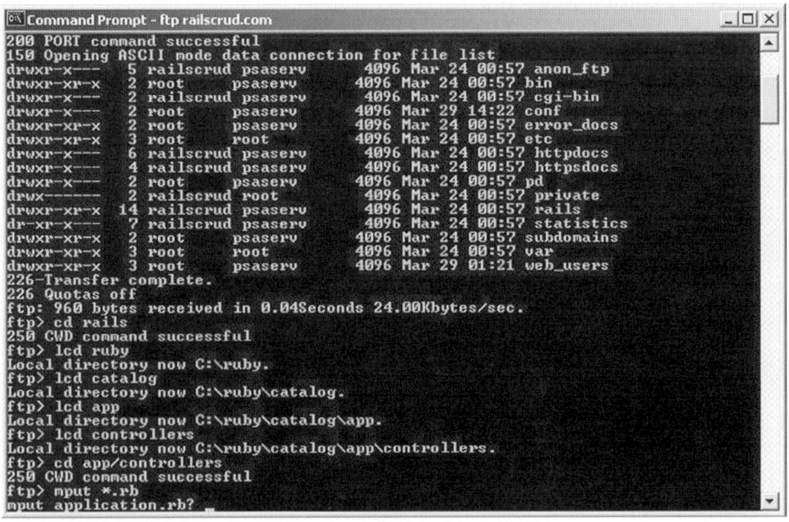

Fig. 12.30 mput command

Select the files to upload when prompted for each file as shown in Figure 12.31.

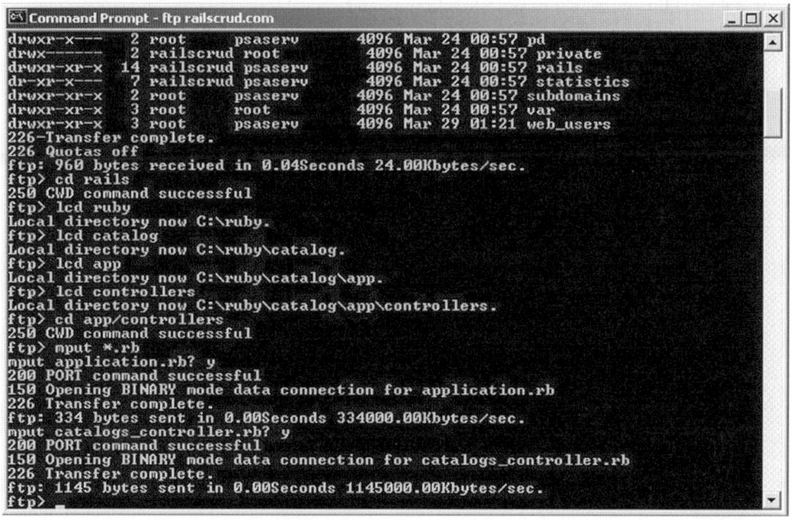

```
Command Prompt - ftp railscrud.com
drwxr-x---    2 root       psaserv       4096 Mar 24 00:57 pd
drwx------    2 railscrud  root          4096 Mar 24 00:57 private
drwxr-xr-x   14 railscrud  psaserv       4096 Mar 24 00:57 rails
dr-xr-x---    7 railscrud  psaserv       4096 Mar 24 00:57 statistics
drwxr-xr-x    2 root       psaserv       4096 Mar 24 00:57 subdomains
drwxr-xr-x    3 root       root          4096 Mar 24 00:57 var
drwxr-xr-x    3 root       psaserv       4096 Mar 29 01:21 web_users
226-Transfer complete.
226 Quotas off
ftp: 960 bytes received in 0.04Seconds 24.00Kbytes/sec.
ftp> cd rails
250 CWD command successful
ftp> lcd ruby
Local directory now C:\ruby.
ftp> lcd catalog
Local directory now C:\ruby\catalog.
ftp> lcd app
Local directory now C:\ruby\catalog\app.
ftp> lcd controllers
Local directory now C:\ruby\catalog\app\controllers.
ftp> cd app/controllers
250 CWD command successful
ftp> mput *.rb
mput application.rb? y
200 PORT command successful
150 Opening BINARY mode data connection for application.rb
226 Transfer complete.
ftp: 334 bytes sent in 0.00Seconds 334000.00Kbytes/sec.
mput catalogs_controller.rb? y
200 PORT command successful
150 Opening BINARY mode data connection for catalogs_controller.rb
226 Transfer complete.
ftp: 1145 bytes sent in 0.00Seconds 1145000.00Kbytes/sec.
ftp> _
```

Fig. 12.31 Selecting Files to upload

Similarly upload the model script catalog/models/catalog.rb, the helpers, the view templates, the layout templates and the public/stylesheet/scaffold.css stylesheet.. We don't need to upload the Rails application files such as database.yml and routes.rb, which are already in the default Rails application on the host. Using the File Manager check that the files have been uploaded to the host as shown in Figure 12.32.

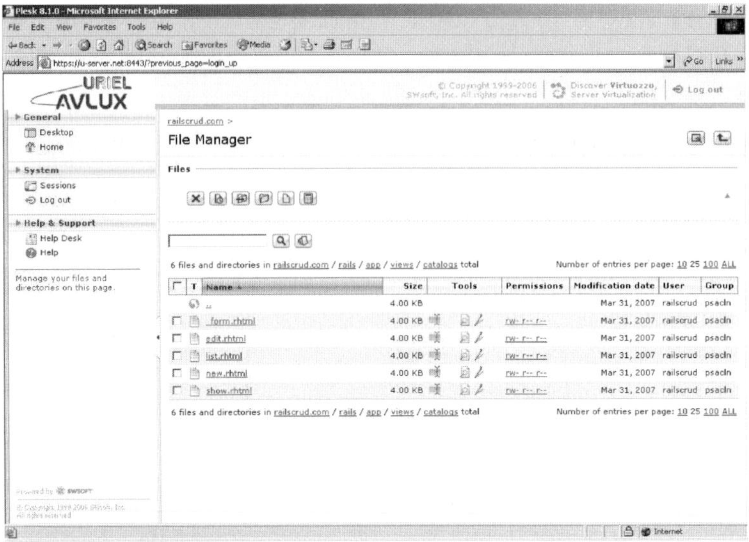

Fig. 12.32 Uploaded Files

We need to modify a few of the files. Select the edit tool for the config/environment.rb file as shown in Figure 12.33.

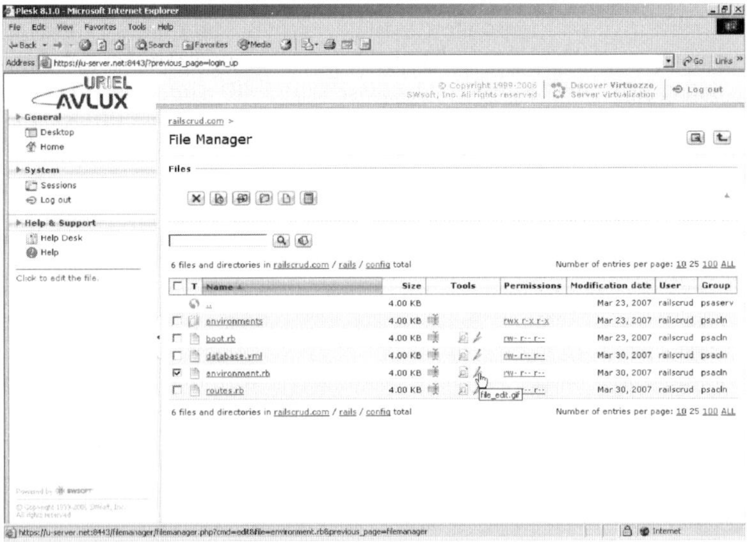

Fig. 12.33 Selecting environment.rb

Uncomment the following line in environment.rb to set the production mode as shown in Figure 12.34.

```
ENV['RAILS_ENV'] ||= 'production'
```

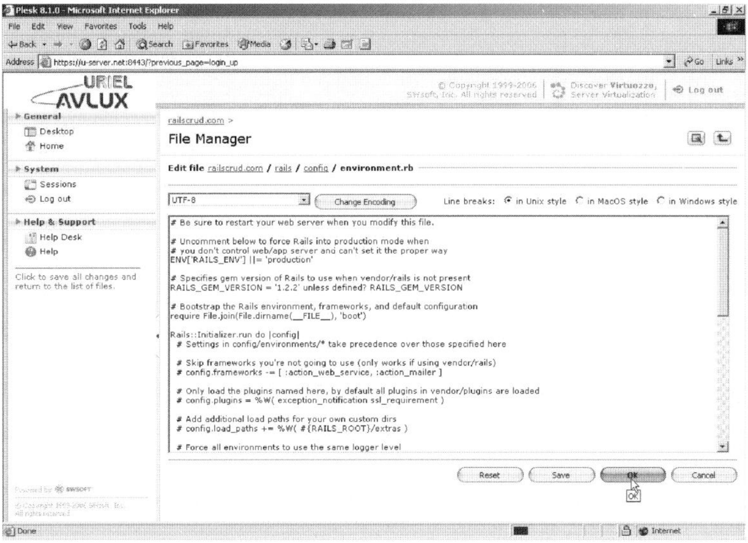

Fig. 12.34 Modifying environment.rb

We also need to edit the config/database.yml file to set the production mode. Select the edit tool for the database.yml file as shown in Figure 12.35.

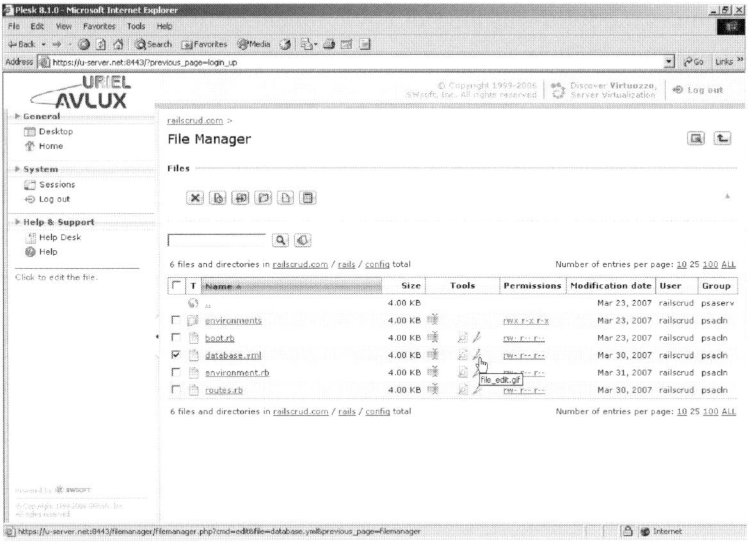

Fig. 12.35 Selecting database.yml

Modify the production database settings as follows.

```
production:
  adapter: mysql
  database: test
  username: username
  password:  password
  host: localhost
```

Click on OK as shown in Figure 12.36.

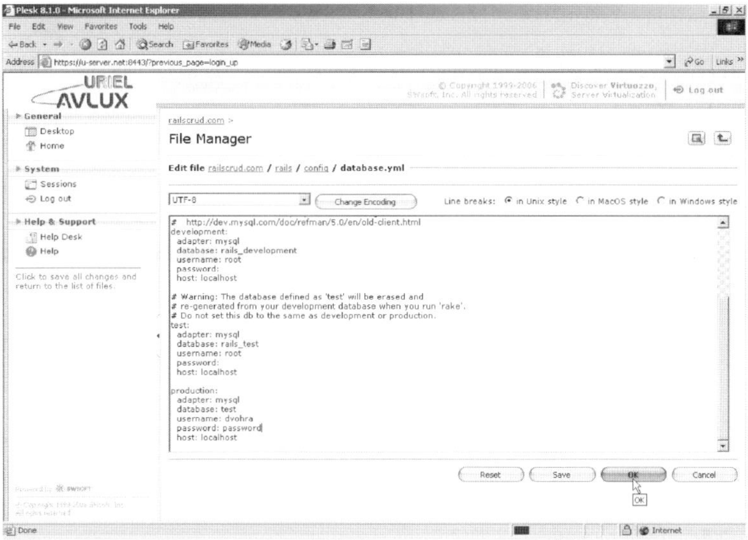

Fig. 12.36 Modifying database.yml

We have uploaded the files for the Rails application 'catalog' and modified the environment.rb and database.yml files. We need to restart the FastCGI processes on the host. Select the SSH Terminal icon in the Domain Admin Control Panel as shown in Figure 12.37.

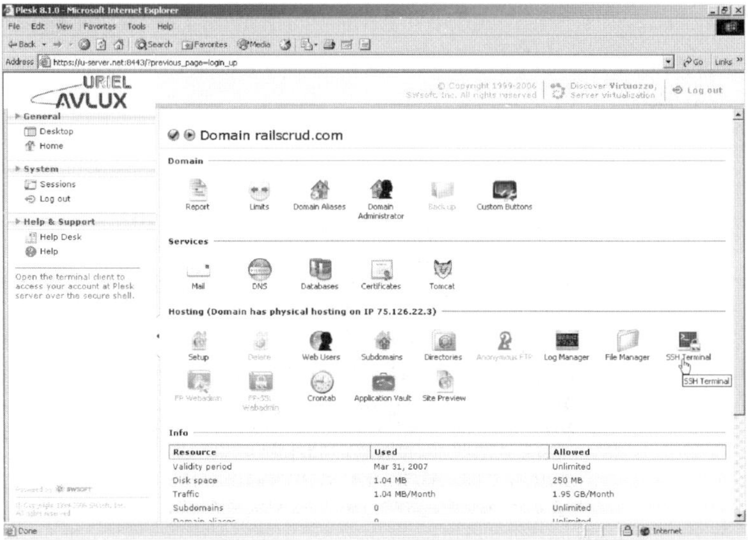

Fig. 12.37 SSH Teminal

Specify username and password, which are the same as for the FTP host and login to the SSH Terminal. Restart fcgi with the following command as shown in Figure 12.38.

```
service fcgi restart
```

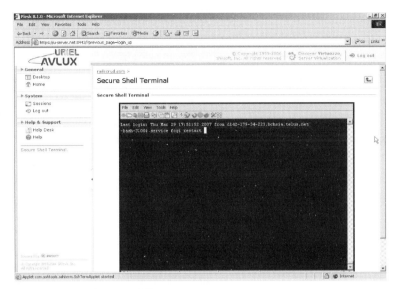

Fig. 12.38 Restarting FastCGI

The FCGI processes get restarted as shown in Figure 12.39.

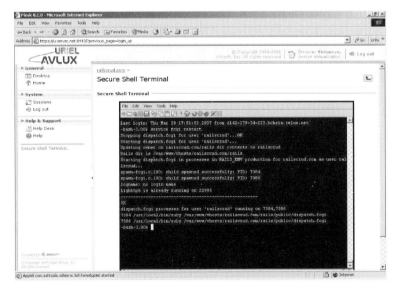

Fig. 12.39 FastCGI Restarted

The Rails application has been deployed to the web host. Specify the URL http://www.railscrud.com in a browser as shown in Figure 12.40.

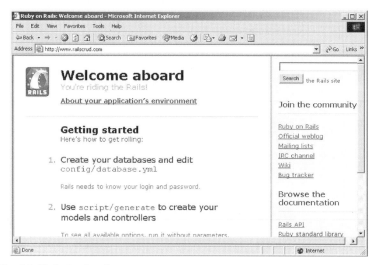

Fig. 12.40 index.html

Invoke the controller for the Rails application with the URL http://www.railscrud.com/catalogs. The listing of catalog entries created in the MySQL database table 'catalogs' gets displayed using the Rails scaffolding for the 'catalogs' table as shown in Figure 12.41. Catalog entries may be added, modified, or deleted.

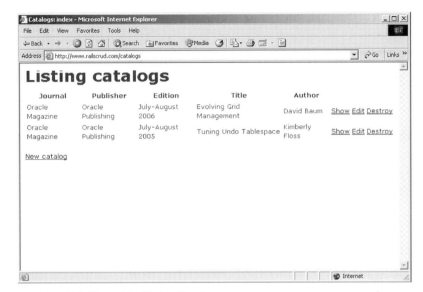

Fig. 12.41 Web Hosted Rails Application

12.6 Summary

In this chapter we discussed Rails best practices and the procedure to deploy a Rails application on Apache2 and FastCGI. Subsequently, we hosted a Rails application on a Rails web host.

Sources of Information

- Ruby on Rails Web Site: http://www.rubyonrails.org/
- Ruby Web Site: http://www.ruby-lang.org/en/
- Rails Framework API: http://api.rubyonrails.org/

Index

Printing: Krips bv, Meppel
Binding: Stürtz, Würzburg